Glad Rags

Sept 25/87
Blanket

GLAD RAGS
Stories and Activities
Featuring Clothes for Children

Jan Irving
and
Robin Currie

Illustrated by
Tom Henrichsen

1987
LIBRARIES UNLIMITED, INC.
Littleton, Colorado

LIBRARIES UNLIMITED, INC.
P.O. Box 263
Littleton, Colorado 80160-0263

Library of Congress Cataloging-in-Publication Data

Irving, Jan, 1942-
    Glad rags.

        Includes index.
        1. Libraries, Children's--Activity programs.
    2. Clothing and dress--Social aspects--Study and
    teaching (Elementary) 3. Clothing and dress in
    literature. 4. Storytelling. 5. Children--Books and
    reading. I. Currie, Robin, 1948-   . II. Title.
    Z718.3.I78   1987   027.62'51   87-16921
    ISBN 0-87287-562-8

Libraries Unlimited books are bound with Type II nonwoven material that meets and exceeds National Association of State Textbook Administrators' Type II nonwoven material specifications Class A through E.

To all of our children:
  Kathleen, Brian, Michael, and Bethany—
  but especially to Bethany for her flair
  and Michael for his reluctance.

Contents

Introduction

Glad Rags is a sourcebook for librarians, teachers, and adults working with young children. It is a sequel to *Mudluscious: Stories and Activities Featuring Food for Preschool Children* (Libraries Unlimited, 1986) in its purpose and structure. Both books introduce quality picture-book literature and extend that literature through a variety of enrichment activities. One apparent difference between the books is the subtitles. *Mudluscious* targeted preschool children for its audience. But numerous elementary school teachers have found the activities in this book to be useful and suggested its subtitle was too limited. While both books consider the interests and attention spans of preschool-aged children, *Glad Rags* covers an even-broader range of materials. We believe the subtitle "Stories and Activities Featuring Clothes for Children" accurately reflects this scope.

Glad Rags uses clothes as the vehicle to appreciation of language just as *Mudluscious* used the theme of food. Children will learn clothes expressions such as "walk in my shoes," "too big for your britches," and "pass the hat" through the various activities and stories. Finery such as Cinderella's ball gown and Red Riding Hood's cape and hood have been featured in traditional folk literature just as clothes continue to be the subject of contemporary picture books. We have identified over 200 picture books that are annotated in the eight chapters of *Glad Rags*. The range spans simple board books on getting dressed to the ever-popular Halloween costume story books.

Children benefit from early language and literature experiences. And, as we stated in *Mudluscious*, "nothing is as crucial in developing a child's reading interest and later success in school as the early storytime experience." Television, even outstanding series such as "Reading Rainbow," is no substitute for a "live" story in which a child can listen and participate actively. Stories we have created for this book include many participatory tales so children will take roles in the stories and remember the characters long after the story has ended.

Through the theme of clothes, children will learn self-awareness and decision making. Clothes identify us: the work we do, the activities we choose, and the roles we play. A special effort has been made to include stories and enrichment activities that encourage children to try on different roles, so that they become liberated from rigid gender associations of clothes and explore choices. Selecting appropriate clothes for different weather and occasions will help children learn basic decision making. Learning to shop and care for clothes will reinforce these skills and teach responsibility as well. Finally, clothes are a natural vehicle for imaginative play. Even the simplest article of apparel allows a child to enter into the world of make-believe.

The scope of the chapters ranges from specific articles of apparel—hats, shoes, pockets and other paraphernalia—to broader concepts—getting dressed, shopping and caring for clothes, fairytale and fantasy clothes, and clothes worn in past times and in other cultures.

Each chapter is structured in parallel form. The chapter introduction presents the overall theme and purpose of each subject. It is followed by an initiating activity to introduce children to the books and activities on the subject. The literature section of each chapter first annotates picture books on a subtheme, then includes related literature activities—fingerplays, action rhymes, poems, songs, flannel-board stories, cut-and-tell and draw-and-tell stories, as well as more unusual presentation methods (for example, tube stories and story wheels). Games follow the quieter literature activities, and crafts provide another change of pace. Each chapter is concluded with display suggestions since the clothes theme especially lends itself to a visual approach. Many of the craft projects children make from this book will also become appealing displays in themselves.

We have also included a two-part skills index to guide you in selecting activities that teach cognitive and social interaction skills. The fifteen skill areas include self-awareness skills, gross motor skills, color recognition skills, size and shape recognition skills, rhythm and rhyming skills, counting skills, following directions skills, group cooperation skills, musical skills, artistic skills, role and dialogue invention skills, sequencing skills, classification skills, word recognition skills, and left-right orientation skills. The index is organized into a "Breakdown of Activities by Skills Area" and an "Alphabetical Index of Activities Showing Associated Skills." A "Literature Index" is also provided.

We would like to thank the many people who have written to us and have enthusiastically responded to *Mudluscious*. Their encouragement has sustained us in writing *Glad Rags*. We also thank the following people for their support: Heather Cameron, Shirley Lambert, Nancy Jennings, Paula Brandt, Carol Elbert, Lorna Caulkins, Ginny Cameron, Pat Franzen, Phyllis Hilston, Donna Solis, Duffy De France, Joyce Denslow, and especially Bruce Currie.

Setting Up the Program

We suggest books and activities so that you might create your own program. Your final selection of the type and length of activities and stories should be based on your own situation. But here are two sample programs the way we might set them up. The programs are derived from chapters 4 and 7.

LONG AGO AND FAR AWAY

Sample Program*

Initiating Activities:	Begin with "Walk in My Shoes" (pp. 114-15) as children arrive. Repeat this several times until all children can participate easily. Then, when all children come, share the poem, "Special Dress, Special Days" (p. 108).
First Story:	Begin with *They Put on Masks* by Byrd Baylor (p. 107) to introduce native American cultures.
Related Activities:	Follow up this story with "Buffalo Clothes" chant (p. 115) so children can actively participate in the drama of this culture. Then continue this thoughtful mood by telling the story "A Feather in His Cap" (pp. 115-16).
Second Story:	Introduce the Masai culture of Africa by reading *Who's in Rabbit's House* by Aardema (p. 107).
Related Activity:	After you've read this picture book in which the story is told with masked players, give children an opportunity to tell a story with masks. "The Pride of the Lion" (pp. 108-12) involves children actively through movement and chant.
Third Story:	Conclude with the Japanese culture by reading *A Pair of Red Clogs* by Matsuno (p. 107).
Related Activities:	Follow up this final story with "Feet 'Round the World" (p. 117) and "Fan Dancing" (p. 112).

---

*Based on chapter 4.

Final Activities: You may not have time to do all these activities, but we have selected games and crafts to represent native American, African, and Japanese cultures.

Game: "Feather Frolic" (p. 118).

Crafts: "African Animal Masks" (p. 121) and "Kimono Doll" (p. 121). (Point out the kimono worn by the girl in *A Pair of Red Clogs* before you make this project.)

Finish the program by repeating the poem "Walk in My Shoes."

SNEAKERS, SOCKS, AND HAPPY FEET

Sample Program*

Initiating Activity: Begin with "Right Shoe, Left Shoe" (pp. 189-90) as the children arrive. Repeat this get acquainted chant until all children have had a chance to introduce themselves.

First Story: Begin with one of the longer picture books while children are the most attentive. Read *New Shoes* by Corey (p. 190).

Related Activities: Follow up this story with three shoe activities. The poem "Shoe Shopping" (p. 192) explores the kind of shoes children might shop for. The story "The Centipede Buys Sneakers" (pp. 196-97) gives children a chance to be actively involved. The song "The Best Shoes" (p. 193) will let children "get the wiggles out" and lead into the next story.

Second Story: Read *The Reason I'm Not Quite Finished Tying My Shoes* by Hickman (p. 190).

Related Activities: Give children a chance to locate lost shoes by telling the participatory story "Lost and Found Shoes" (p. 191). Then all enjoy together the action rhyme "Where's My Shoe?" (p. 196).

Third Story: Read *Shoes* by Winthrop (p. 191).

Related Activities: Since Winthrop concludes your own feet are best of all, follow up with the "Barefeet Song" (p. 208).

Final Activities: Choose from games and crafts such as "Shoe Scramble" (p. 211), "Talky Terry, the Tennis Shoe Puppet" (p. 213), or "Big Foot, Little Foot Mural" (p. 214). Then sing "Shoe Jumble" (pp. 191-92) to conclude the program.

*Based on chapter 7.

1
All by Myself

INTRODUCTION

Learning how to get dressed is a chore for young children; just putting the right articles of clothing on the appropriate parts of the body may not be as easy as it seems. Even children who have mastered the skills of getting dressed may resist, become forgetful, or have difficulty deciding what to wear. Parents and teachers end up nagging or losing patience. On the other hand, some children so love trying on clothes that the situation can get completely out of hand.

The first subtheme of this chapter "Clothes and Closings" identifies basic articles of apparel and clothing fasteners. The books and activities presented are especially simple, with the youngest preschooler in mind. Recent board books such as *Dressing* and *Ernie Gets Dressed* help very young children by simply identifying articles of apparel. Cloth books with buttons, zippers, and snaps provide experiential learning. Expand on these books by singing "Now You're Getting Dressed" and enjoying the action rhyme "Clap for Clothes."

The books and activities in "Struggles and Successes" show the child learning to master getting dressed skills. Numerous picture books, such as *Max's New Suit* and *How Do I Put It On?* show the humorous results of wearing clothes on the wrong parts of the body. Some children may wish their clothes to actually dress them as in "Lazy Lisa and the Crazy Clothes." They'll enjoy telling Agnes when she's finally dressed in "Not Yet, Agnes." They'll identify with Billy's eventual success in "Billy Buttons Up." And when children do become successful in getting dressed, they still have to face decisions about appropriate clothing throughout the day. Children will enjoy helping Samantha Jane decide which outfit is just right in "All by Myself." Stories and activities on dressing for various seasons are included in chapter 3 on weather-related clothes.

"Taking It Off and Tucking In" reverses the dressing process. Sometimes children need a little help or prodding, but once out of togs, they'll beg to stay in the tub or never want to take off a favorite pair of pajamas. Ormerod's *Moonlight* presents a realistic picture of bedtime rituals while Burningham's *Time to Get Out of the Bath, Shirley* takes us on a fanciful adventure beyond the bath itself. In a similar vein, the action rhyme "Do I Have To?" re-enacts a typical pattern many families experience each night while "Baby Llama's Pajamas" is fanciful fun.

The crafts and games in this chapter provide further opportunities for clothing identification, skills development, and making decisions about appropriate clothes for different occasions and times of the day.

INITIATING ACTIVITY

Clap for Clothes
(An Action Rhyme)

This chant helps introduce the items of clothing with lots of action. You may wish to teach it at the beginning of a session and use it several times to "get the wiggles out."

We wear some shoes.
   (Point to shoes.)
They come in twos.
One, two,
   (Point to one shoe, then the other.)
Clap your hands.
   (Clap two times.)

We wear a shirt.
Brush off the dirt.
Brush, brush.
One, two.
Clap your hands.

We wear some pants
To do a dance.
Dance, dance.
Brush, brush.
One, two.
Clap your hands.

We wear some socks
To jump on rocks.
Jump, jump.
Dance, dance.
Brush, brush.
One, two.
Clap your hands.

Now we're all dressed.
We look our best!
Jump, jump.
Dance, dance.
Brush, brush.
One, two.
Clap your hands.

LITERATURE-SHARING EXPERIENCES

Books about Clothes and Closings

Bruna, Dick. **I Can Dress Myself**. Methuen, 1978.

Two children going to a party identify the clothes they wear and can put on by themselves. Easy text and simple illustrations complement each other for the very young preschooler.

The Busy Animal Dress-Up Book. Illustrated by Vivienne DeMuth. Gingerbread House/Elsevier Dutton, 1979.

Cloth book with manipulatives teaches young children how to work a zipper, button, shoelace, snap, and belt, and to tie a ribbon.

Ernie Gets Dressed. Illustrated by Pat Sustendal. Random House, 1985.

This "baby fingers" sturdy board book with tabs to help turn pages will appeal to the very youngest child. Pictures on the tabs identify various articles of clothing Ernie puts on to wear for the day.

Martin, Janet. **Ten Little Babies Dress**. Photographs by Michael Watson. St. Martin's Press, 1986.

This board text simply recalls the familiar "Ten Little Indians" rhyme, but substitutes ten babies getting dressed.

Oxenbury, Helen. **Dressing**. Wanderer Books, 1981.

In this simple board book, the left-hand pages identify articles of apparel—diaper, undershirt, sock, shirt, overalls, hat—and the right-hand pages show a toddler wearing the clothing.

Rubel, Nicole. **I Can Get Dressed**. Macmillan, 1984.

A spiralbound, split-page format book invites young children to choose appropriate attire for different seasons and activities.

Ziefert, Harriet. **Baby Ben Gets Dressed.** Illustrated by Norman Gorbaty. Random House, 1985.

It's time for Baby Ben to get dressed. As he puts on his shirt, socks, sneakers, overalls, jacket, and hat, his Teddy Bear dresses, too—but not as successfully as Baby Ben! Foldouts of the Teddy Bear getting clothes on wrong will amuse young children who have just learned to dress themselves.

Related Activities about Clothes and Closings

You Think You Have Problems ...
(A Poem)

We tried a sweater,
We tried a vest,
But porcupines are
Hard to dress!

Jeffrey McFarland
(A Poem)

Since this poem talks about vests and canes that children may not know firsthand, it will be fun to have a life-size cardboard cutout of a man to dress in paper clothes, like a huge paper doll.

Jeffrey McFarland put on his vest.
He's so well dressed!

Jeffrey McFarland put on his tie.
My, oh, my!
He put on his tie
To go with the vest.
He's so well dressed!

Jeffrey McFarland put on his shoes.
One red and one blue!
He put on his shoes
To go with the tie,
To go with the vest.
He's so well dressed!

Jeffrey McFarland put on his coat.
Silly old goat!
He put on his coat
To go with the shoes,
To go with the tie,
To go with the vest.
He's so well dressed!

Jeffrey McFarland put on his hat.
Fancy that!
He put on his hat
To go with the coat,
To go with the shoes,
To go with the tie,
To go with the vest.
He's so well dressed!

Jeffrey McFarland took his cane off
    the floor
And ran out the door!
He's all dressed!

Dressing the Baby
(To the tune of "Mulberry Bush")

There's a baby at our house,
    (Fold arms to rock baby.)
At our house, at our house.
This new baby at our house
Can't even dress himself.
    (Shake head.)

This is how we put on his bib,
    (Wiggle fingers behind neck.)
Put on his bib, put on his bib.
This new baby at our house
Can't even dress himself.
    (Shake head.)

This is how we put on his diaper,
    (Wiggle fingers by stomach.)
Put on his diaper, put on his diaper.
This new baby at our house
Can't even dress himself.
    (Shake head.)

This is how we put on his booties,
    (Wiggle fingers by ankle.)
Put on his booties, put on his booties.
This new baby at our house
Can't even dress himself.
    (Shake head.)

This is how we put on his blanket,
    Cross hands in front of chest.)
Put on his blanket, put on his blanket.
This new baby at our house
Can't even dress himself.
    (Shake head.)

I'm so glad that I can put on my shoes,
    (Bend over and wiggle fingers by shoes.)
Zip my coat, zip my coat.
    (Imitate zipping.)
With this new baby at our house
    (Fold arms to rock baby.)
My mom sure needs the help!
    (Hands on hips, nod head.)

Now You're Getting Dressed
(To the tune of "Mary Had a Little Lamb")

As you sing these words pretend to put on each item as it is mentioned. On the last verse run or jump in place.

First put on your underwear,
Underwear, underwear.
First put on your underwear.
Now you're getting dressed.

Stick your arms down in your shirt,
In your shirt, in your shirt.
Stick your arms down in your shirt.
Now you're getting dressed.

Pull your pants up to your waist,
To your waist, to your waist.
Pull your pants up to your waist.
Now you're getting dressed.

Wiggle toes down in your socks,
In your socks, in your socks.
Wiggle toes down in your socks.
Now you're getting dressed.

Slip your shoes on, tie them tight,
Tie them tight, tie them tight.
Slip your shoes on, tie them tight.
Now you're getting dressed.

Now you can go out and play,
Out and play, out and play.
Now you can go out and play.
You got yourself all dressed.
YES!

Underwear
(To the tune of "Jingle Bells")

Underwear, underwear,
We wear underwear!
Undershirts and jockey shorts,
T-shirts, fancy pants!

Underwear, underwear!
We wear underwear!
No matter what you wear outside,
Start first with underwear!

Animals Are Lucky!
(An Action Rhyme)

Act out the clothing or point to the part of the body worn for the animals. Shake head on "never, never, never." You could eliminate actions and just enjoy the poem.

Does a turtle need a turtle neck to stay inside his shell?
Does a snake need a zipper for his snakeskin suit?
Does a bunny need a snap for his fluffy cotton tail?
Does a polar bear buckle up his snowshoe boots?

Does a frog strap on his funny floppy flippers?
Does a pig need a red bow to curl his silly tail?
Does a beaver put on mittens with his warm fur coat?
Do the minnows hold umbrellas when they're swimming by a whale?

When I get dressed there are zippers to zip.
There are buttons and hooks and buckles and bows.
I wish I was an animal with fur or scales or feathers,
And I never, never, never had to put on any clothes!

Buttons, Zippers, Snaps, and Bows
(To the tune of "Mulberry Bush")

Older children will enjoy singing the last verse very fast.

Buttons, zippers, snaps, and bows
Snaps and bows, snaps and bows
Buttons, zippers, snaps and bows
That's the way we close our clothes!

Buttons poke in button holes
　　*(Form circle with one hand;
　　point finger through hole.)*
Button holes, button holes
Buttons poke in button holes
That's the way we close our clothes!

Zippers run along a track.
　　(Run thumb from belt to chin.)
'Long a track, 'long a track.
Zippers run along a track.
That's the way we close our clothes!

Snaps together pop and snap.
　　(Snap fingers.)
Pop and snap, pop and snap.
Snaps together pop and snap.
That's the way we close our clothes!

Make two loops to tie a bow.
　　(Wiggle fingers by shoes.)
Tie a bow, tie a bow.
Make two loops to tie a bow.
That's the way we close our clothes!

Buttons, zippers, snaps, and bows.
　　(Do all four actions.)
Snaps and bows, snaps and bows.
Buttons, zippers, snaps and bows.
That's the way we close our clothes!

Alligators All Dressed
(A Fingerplay)

Have fun with these Wild West cow-punching alligators.

Five little alligators get up to dress.
   (Hold up five fingers.)
The first one buttons up his vest.
   (Wiggle fingers by stomach.)
The second one wears tall boots with taps.
   (March in place.)
The third one laces up his chaps.
   (Slap sides of legs.)
The fourth one ties a big bow tie.
   (Touch thumbs under chin, fingers spread.)
The fifth one tips his hat. Good-bye!
   (Touch head and wave.)

Books about Struggles and Successes

Barbato, Juli. **From Bed to Bus**. Illustrated by Brian Schatell. Macmillan, 1985.

   A little girl encounters many familiar difficulties getting ready to go to school, including putting her clothes on inside out, mixing up her shoes, and getting her chin caught in the zipper of her coat.

Blocksma, Mary. **The Best Dressed Bear**. Illustrated by Sandra Cox Kalthoff. Childrens Press, 1984.

   The easy-read text tells the story of a bear who wants to be the best dressed bear at a dance. All the animal clerks in the store help with outfitting him. Each animals supplies an article of clothing that rhymes — for example, fox provides socks; kangaroo, shoe; goat, coat; and cat, hat. He almost forgets an essential article, but everyone chimes in, "There's one more thing you need for the dance. Bear, you need a pair of ... pants!" Everyone agrees he is the most wonderful, best dressed bear!

Brandenberg, Franz. "Early in the Morning" from **Leo and Emily.** Illustrated by Aliki. Greenwillow, 1981.

   As Leo and Emily meet outside early in the morning, they take care not to wake their parents. But their funny appearances (trousers inside out, dress backwards, shoes on the wrong feet), because they've dressed in the dark, results in so much laughter that their parents do wake up.

Carlstrom, Nancy White. **Jesse Bear, What Will You Wear?** Illustrated by Bruce Degen. Macmillan, 1986.

   A joyful rhyme asks the question — "Jesse Bear, what will you wear?" — then proceeds to answer by showing daily activities and appropriate attire. Not only does Jesse Bear wear "pants that dance," but he "wears" such unlikely objects as "rice in his hair" and his chair, because "he's stuck in there." The illustrations and text combine perfectly to recapture the pleasures of getting dressed and undressed from a young child's perspective.

Kuskin, Karla. **The Dallas Titans Get Ready for Bed**. Illustrated by Marc Simont. Harper & Row, 1986.

   This sequel to The Philharmonic Gets Dressed *will answer every kid's questions about the equipment, clothing, and behind the scenes dressing and undressing of the football team. Such fascinating details include the number of socks a football team wears — 198!*

Kuskin, Karla. **The Philharmonic Gets Dressed**. Illustrated by Marc Simont. Harper & Row, 1982.

   One hundred and five people (92 men and 13 women) get dressed to go to work — taking baths or showers, putting on underclothing, trousers, shirts, suspenders, skirts, bow ties, jackets, etc. They have to be ready to walk on stage at Philharmonic Hall at 8:25 for their evening concert. A true inside story.

Peek, Merle. **Mary Wore a Red Dress and Henry Wore His Green Sneakers**. Clarion, 1983.

Each animals wears a different color of clothing to a birthday party in this book, based on the traditional folk song. Children can add their own articles of clothing in the manner of the song after you read this book.

Watanabe, Shiego. **How Do I Put It On?** Illustrated by Yashuo Ohtomo. Collins, 1977.

Young children will identify with a bear's problems in getting dressed and will happily respond to the right places to wear shirt, pants, cap, and shoes.

Weiss, Ellen. **Millicent Maybe**. Franklin Watts, 1979.

Millicent can't make up her mind, so she wears "a little of this and a little of that." Clad in dresses, hats, coat, carrying an umbrella and several purses, she goes on indecisively until she learns the hard way to make up her mind.

Wells, Rosemary. **Max's New Suit.** Dial, 1979.

Max's sister Ruby dresses him for the party, but Max wants to dress himself. He does, but in a rather unorthodox fashion. Young children will delight in Max's obvious mistakes—putting his legs in his shirt, his arms in his pants, and buttoning his jacket over his ears.

Related Activities about Struggles and Successes

Lazy Lisa and the Crazy Clothes

Teach the various sounds and actions to the children before telling this story so they can participate fully. For the pants, march stiff-legged; for the shirts, wave arms; for the shoes, jump. If you think the children may not be familiar with socks rolled in balls, bring one pair to show them.

Lisa was a lazy kid. She was too lazy to pick up her toys. Lisa was even too lazy to chew the crusts on her bread, so she just left them. But the one thing she was laziest of all about was getting herself dressed in the morning.

"Gee," said Lisa. "I wish I didn't have to dress myself. I wish my clothes would help."

Well, one morning, before Lisa was even out of bed, the closet door swung open and out marched her pants. (*All march stiff-legged.*)

> We are pants.
> We are jeans.
> Some are dirty.
> Some are clean.
> Coveralls
> And dungarees,
> We have patches on our knees!

When the closet was empty, Lisa had on four pairs of pants. And before Lisa could move, her shirts flew off their hangers. (*All wave arms in air.*)

We are shirts,
Striped or plaid.
Some are good,
Some are bad.
Sweatshirts,
T-shirts,
Just brand new.
Some with elbows poking through!

And when the hangers were empty, Lisa had on six shirts. She had not even put her feet on the floor when little balls of socks rolled out of the drawers. *(Roll one hand over the other.)*

We are socks.
We come in twos.
Red and white,
Green and blue.
Tube socks,
Knee socks,
Socks with bows.
Some will show your wiggly toes!

When the drawers were empty, Lisa had on eight pairs of socks. Before Lisa could stand up, her shoes jumped out of their boxes.

We are shoes,
Left and right.
Some are loose,
Some are tight.
Cowboy boots
And tennis shoes.
One of us you always lose.

When the boxes were empty, Lisa had on ten pairs of shoes!

Lisa tried to roll out of bed and stand up, but she now had on four pairs of pants, six shirts, eight pairs of socks, and ten pairs of shoes. So when Lisa rolled out of bed, she landed in a heap on the floor.

Flop.
Plop.
POP! Her eyes came open.

Lisa woke up. She looked around her room. All her pants were in the closet. All her shirts were on the hangers. All her socks were rolled in little balls in her drawers. And all her shoes were in their boxes.

Then Lisa knew she had just had a crazy dream.

Lisa is still lazy about picking up her toys and chewing her crusts. But there is one thing she is never lazy about now—getting herself dressed in the morning!

Bend, Stretch, Shake, Wiggle, and Twist
(To the tune of "The Hokey-Pokey")

It will be even more fun if you struggle with a slightly too small sweater as you teach it. Then enjoy it all together matching actions to the words.

You bend your right arm up.
You stretch your right arm out.
You shake your arm all over
And wiggle all about.
You twist and you turn
And you push it through.
Sweaters are so much fun!

You bend your left arm up.
You stretch your left arm out.
You shake your arm all over
And wiggle all about.
You twist and you turn
And you push it through.
Sweaters are so much fun!

You bend both arms up.
You stretch both arms out.
You shake your arms all over
And wiggle all about.
You twist and you turn
And you push them through.
Sweaters are so much fun!

You bend your head over.
You stretch your head out.
You shake your head all over
And wiggle all about.
You twist and you turn
And you push it through.
Sweaters are so much fun!

I'M DONE!

Pop! On Your Clothes

(To the tune of "Pop! Goes the Weasel")

All around the family room,
The mommy chased the children.
The children thought it so much fun.
Whoop! 'Til she caught one.

Now get dressed you pokey poke.
All good children know-o,
P.J.'s can't be worn outside.
Pop! On your clothes!

Danny the Dawdler

Once there was a little boy who was called Danny the Dawdler. Danny the Dawdler poked around or fooled around just about all day long. When his mother called to him, "Danny, come in for dinner," Danny fooled around. By the time he came in, his dinner was always cold.

When his father called him, "Danny, time for bed," Danny poked around until he sometimes got in trouble.

Now, one day when the alarm clock went off in the morning, Danny's mother and father came into his room and said, "Danny, time to get up!" And then they left his room to get dressed themselves.

Danny crawled under his covers. He pretended he was lost in a blizzard of white sheets. After a while, he looked out from his covers and saw his parents go down to breakfast.

Danny thought it must be getting late, but he rolled over in bed and looked out his window. Outside, in a nearby tree, he watched a mother robin feed a juicy fat worm to her baby robin. Then he remembered—breakfast! So Danny ran downstairs. His mother and father were just finishing the last pancake.

"Didn't you save one for me?" asked Danny.

"The early bird gets the worm!" said his father.

"But I don't want a worm!" said Danny. "I want a pancake!"

"Sorry," said his mother. And she put the dishes in the dishwasher.

"See you tonight," said his father. And then he said, "Unusual clothes you're wearing to school today!"

Danny's father left before Danny could tell him he still had on his Space Ace pajamas with the antigravity feet.

"Is it too late to get dressed?" asked Danny.

"I'm afraid so, astronaut!" Mother answered. "The school bus will be here before you know it!"

And it was, too. Danny had just enough time to stick his antigravity feet into his boots and grab his raincoat. It wasn't raining outside that day, but Danny decided he couldn't ride the bus in his pajamas.

That night Danny came right in for dinner and got ready for bed with no poking or fooling around. And the next morning when his mother and father came into his room, he was already dressed.

"Danny, it's Saturday," they said. "There's no school today. It's O.K. to dawdle on Saturday!"

After that, on most days of the week Danny is an early bird. He gets dressed right away, except on Saturdays. Because on Saturday, it's O.K. to be a dawdler.

Overnight Sensation
(A Poem with Visual Aid)

For this poem use a pair of shoes, sweater, hat, scarf, and mittens. The funnier and bigger they are, the better. Take them out of a bag or box and place them on the floor in front of you as indicated in the poem.

I always forgot to wear my shoes
    (Show shoes.)
As I was going out the door,
And so my mother said to me,
"Lay them out the night before!"

So I laid my shoes
Upon the floor.
    (Place shoes on floor.)

I always forgot to wear my sweater
    (Show sweater.)
As I was going out the door,
And so my mother said to me,
"Lay it out the night before!"

So I laid my sweater
Next to my shoes
Upon the floor.
    (Place sweater on floor.)

I always forgot to wear my hat
    (Show hat.)
As I was going out the door,
And so my mother said to me,
"Lay it out the night before!"

So I laid my hat
Next to my sweater
Next to my shoes
Upon the floor.
    (Place hat on floor.)

I always forgot to wear my scarf
    (Show scarf.)
And so my mother said to me,
"Lay it out the night before!"

So I laid my scarf
Next to my hat
Next to my sweater
Next to my shoes
Upon the floor.
    (Place scarf on floor.)

I always forgot to wear my mittens
    (Show mittens.)
As I was going out the door,
And so my mother said to me,
"Lay them out the night before!"

So I laid my mittens
Next to my scarf
Next to my hat
Next to my sweater
Next to my shoes
Upon the floor.
    (Place mittens on floor.)

Now here are my mittens, my scarf, and my hat.
>   *(Lift articles when mentioned; make messy pile with them.)*
Here are my sweater and shoes on the floor.
My room's such a mess of "clothes for tomorrow"
I can't get out of the bedroom door!

Dressed in Time
(To the tune of "Mary Had a Little Lamb")

Put your clothes beside your bed,
>   'Side your bed,
>   'Side your bed,
Put your clothes beside your bed
Before you go to sleep.

Undershirt and underpants,
Top and jeans,
Belt and socks,
Hat and scarf and coat and gloves,
And don't forget your shoes!

Next day let's jump up and see,
>   Up and see,
>   Up and see,
Next day let's jump up and see
Everything's just right.
Right!

Not Yet, Agnes
(A Flannel-board Story)

For this story you will need a figure of a girl dressed in underwear and cutout pieces of clothing, including white socks, brown shoes, red coveralls, yellow shirt, and a funny green hat. You may adjust the color of the cutouts and the story as desired. This story can be told on a flannel board, or you can bring a large doll to dress. Teach the children to say the words "Not yet, Agnes" with you during the story.

Agnes was three and three-quarters years old, and she could get dressed all by herself. Sometimes she had trouble remembering everything, and sometimes she got it just right.

One morning Agnes got up. *(Place the figure of the girl on the board.)* It was a beautiful day, and Agnes wanted to go out and play on her trike right after breakfast. So Agnes had on her funny green hat. *(Place hat on girl's head.)* Is Agnes ready to go out? *(Help children reply "Not yet, Agnes.")*

"Oh, of course," said Agnes. She went back to her room and this time she had on her funny green hat and her clean white socks. *(Place socks on girl's feet.)* Is Agnes ready to go out? *("Not yet, Agnes.")*

"Oh, of course," said Agnes. She went back to her room. *(Point to each item as you mention it.)* This time she had on her funny green hat and clean white socks and yellow shirt. *(Place shirt on girl.)* Is Agnes ready to go out? *("Not yet, Agnes.")*

"Oh, of course," said Agnes. She went back to her room. This time she had on her funny green hat and her clean white socks and her yellow shirt and her brown shoes. *(Place shoes on girl.)* Is Agnes ready to go out? *("Not yet, Agnes.")*

"Oh, of course," said Agnes. She went back to her room and this time she had on her funny green hat and her clean white socks and her yellow shirt and her brown shoes and her red coveralls. *(Place coveralls on girl.)* Is Agnes ready to go out? Yes! Now Agnes has all her clothes on just right.

Just a Little Help

(A Flannel-board Story)

You can use a flannel board to tell this story. You'll need a boy in pajamas, shoes, hat, and mittens, and a boy fully clothed.

Franklin Jason was four years old and he was learning lots and lots of things at preschool. He could color wonderful pictures of dogs. He could count to ten. He could spell his name. But best of all, Franklin Jason had learned to put on his own sneakers and hat and mittens.

One morning Franklin Jason decided to get dressed just like he did at preschool and surprise his daddy. He put on his sneakers—just like he did at preschool. He put on his hat—just like he did at preschool. He put on his mittens—just like he did at preschool. Then he went into the kitchen where Daddy was making breakfast.

"Surprise!" said Franklin Jason. "I put on my sneakers and my hat and my mittens just like I do at preschool."

"I certainly am surprised," said Daddy. "Good for you! But are you sure you are all ready for preschool this morning?"

"Yep!" said Franklin Jason. "I have on my sneakers and my hat and my mittens."

"Yes, you do," agreed Daddy. "You have on your sneakers and your hat and your mittens—and your PAJAMAS!"

So Daddy helped Franklin Jason put on his shirt and coveralls and socks and coat. Then Franklin Jason finished getting ready by putting on his sneakers and hat and mittens—just like he did at preschool.

Lickety-Split

(A Story)

Once there was a little boy named Larry. Larry liked to play in the sand and romp with his dog and eat spaghetti. What Larry did not like to do was to get dressed. Oh, he liked to wear clothes. He liked his cowboy shirt and his old blue sneakers and his red jacket.

But the buttons on his cowboy shirt never matched up. The laces on his old blue sneakers always got themselves tangled. And the zipper on his red jacket always got stuck halfway up. Larry did not like to stand still while his mother buttoned the buttons and tied the laces and zipped the zipper. So each time his mother said, "Larry, time to get dressed!" he would run and hide. Larry did not like to get dressed.

One day Larry's mother said, "Larry, time to get dressed." Larry ran and hid under the bed. "Oh, dear," said Larry's mother. "I have some new clothes for Larry. I think he will really like them, but I can't find him anywhere. I'll just leave them on the bed. If he doesn't get them on soon, he'll miss story time at the library."

Now, Larry loved story time at the library, so he thought and thought and thought and finally decided to try to put on the new clothes.

The first thing he tried to put on was his shirt. "Buttons," muttered Larry. "I wonder how many buttons it has." But when he started to count the buttons, he saw it had none! His mother had bought him a football T-shirt that just slipped over his head and on. "I can do that," said Larry, and he pulled the shirt over his head and on. Lickety-split.

Then Larry looked at his new shoes. "Ties and laces and tangles, I bet," said Larry. But there were no ties on his new green sneakers, only little straps that went RRRRRip when you open them, but close without a sound. "I can do that," said Larry, and he opened and shut them a couple of more times. Lickety-split.

Then Larry saw his new jacket. It was the color of chocolate, and he liked it right away. "Oh, no," he thought. "The zipper will stick." But when he looked closely at the jacket, he saw it was a warmup jacket with a hood and one-two-three big snaps that went snap-snap-snap shut. "I can do that," said Larry, and snap-snap-snap, the jacket was closed with Larry inside. Lickety-split.

So Larry was dressed in no time at all, and they made it just in time for the story at the library. Then Larry played in the sand and romped with his dog. He had spaghetti for dinner.

And at bedtime, Larry got undressed lickety-split, too.

Billy Buttons Up
(A Story)

Billy hated to button up his coat. Every morning his mother had to remind him, "Billy, button up your coat. You'll catch cold."

Billy struggled and struggled. He stuck his bottom button in the bottom button hole, the next button in the next button hole, the next button in the next button hole, and finally the top button in the top button hole. It was a lot of work. It took so much time. He was always the last kid in his neighborhood to go outside to play.

Sometimes Billy got the buttons buttoned up wrong. He stuck a button in a button hole. The next button in the next button hole. And the next button in the next button hole. And the top button in the .... Uh, oh! One more button, but no more button holes. The extra button hole was on the bottom. Billy had to unbutton his buttons and start all over again. By the time Billy got his buttons in the right holes, all the kids had gone back home.

One day Billy played at his friend's house. When it was time to go home, Billy didn't button up his coat. His mother wasn't there to remind him. But when Billy's mother saw him with his coat open, she said, "Billy, you forgot to button up."

"No, I didn't," he said. "I didn't forget. I hate to button my coat. Buttons take too long. Buttons are hard work."

"Yes," said his mother. "But buttons keep clothes on. You just need a little more practice."

So Mother took one of Billy's old coats he had worn when he was little. She put the coat on his teddy bear, and she said, "Maybe your bear needs a little help learning to button his coat. Do you think you could help?"

Billy put the bottom button in the bottom hole, the next button in the next hole, the next button in the next hole, and the top button in the top hole. It was fun buttoning up bear's coat. Billy buttoned and unbuttoned it over and over again until one day Billy buttoned up his own coat without his mother having to remind him. He had practiced so much that this time he was the first kid in the neighborhood outside to play. Now Billy always remembers to button up!

Zip 'Em Up
(To the tune of "Good-Night, Ladies")

As you sing these words, do the actions indicated. Older children will enjoy trying this as a round or dividing into groups with each taking a different verse, but all singing at once. Then sing the last verse as fast as possible.

Zip, zip, zip, zip
   (Run thumb from belt to chin.)
Zip, zip, zip, zip
Zip, zip, zip, zip
Zip, zip, zip, zip 'em up!

Snap, snap, snap, snap
   *(Tap fingertips of each hand together
   or snap fingers.)*
Snap, snap, snap, snap
Snap, snap, snap, snap
Snap, snap, snap, snap 'em up!

Tie, tie, tie, tie
   *(Bend over to wiggle fingers
   over shoes.)*
Tie, tie, tie, tie
Tie, tie, tie, tie
Tie, tie, tie, tie 'em up!

Zip, zip, zip, zip
   (Same motions as above.)
Snap, snap, snap, snap
Tie, tie, tie, tie
We'll zip, snap, tie 'em up! Yup!

Getting Dressed All Day
(A Flannel-board Story)

To prepare for this story, make felt cutouts of Barbara Ann and her clothes: red shirt, red pants, two red socks, purple striped top, purple and green polka-dot skirt, green tights, pink jumper, white blouse, necklace, yellow T-shirt, blue jeans, one orange sock, one yellow sock, and red pajamas. Place the clothes on Barbara Ann when the story mentions the various articles.

Barbara Ann loved to get dressed. Now some kids' parents have to remind them to put on a clean shirt or to find matching socks. But not Barbara Ann's parents.

One morning Barbara Ann got up, went to her chest of drawers, and pulled out a clean red shirt, a pair of corduroy pants, and two matching red socks. Then she went to her closet and found her favorite sneakers. She got dressed all by herself, and she even tied her sneakers.

But, before breakfast Barbara Ann got undressed. (She liked getting undressed, too.) Then she went back to her chest of drawers and found a purple striped top, a purple and green polka-dot skirt, and a pair of green tights. Then she went to her closet and got out a pair of sandals. And she got dressed all over again.

Just before lunch, Barbara Ann wanted to look really spiffy, so she went back to her room. She opened her chest of drawers. This time she found a pink jumper, a white blouse, and a fancy pearl necklace. She put these on with her green tights and her sandals.

But, at lunch, Barbara Ann got mustard on her blouse, so she said happily, "Guess I'll just have to change."

So Barbara Ann went back to her room. She opened her chest. But her clothes seemed to be disappearing. The only things she could find were a yellow T-shirt, an old pair of blue jeans, and one orange sock and one yellow sock. They didn't match, but she put on everything anyway.

After playing in her sandpile, Barbara Ann needed to change her clothes again. But this time when she went up to her room and looked, she could only find a pair of red pajamas. She put them on.

Her father had just come home from work and saw Barbara Ann in her pajamas.

"Didn't you get dressed all day?" asked her father.

"Yes! I got dressed. I got dressed all day," said Barbara Ann.

Barbara Ann's mother looked at her in the red pajamas, and then she went up to Barbara Ann's room. There on the floor was a big pile of clothes.

"O.K.," said her mother, "let's put everything back!"

Can you help Barbara Ann find everything she had on?

First—the red shirt and red corduroy pants and two red matching socks. Don't forget the sneakers! Then—the purple striped top, the purple and green polka-dot skirt, the green tights, and the sandals. Next—the pink jumper, the white blouse, and the necklace. Then—the yellow T-shirt, the blue jeans, one orange sock, and one yellow sock.

Good for you!

After all that work Barbara Ann was so tired that she fell asleep in her red pajamas. (It was a good thing she was already ready for bed!)

The next day Barbara Ann decided to wear the same thing all day long. But she had to wear her red pajamas until her mother did the laundry!

All by Myself

Tell this story using a poster with doors. Cut a piece of posterboard in half. On one half make four doors attached at the top or side so they can be closed. You may wish to label these 1, 2, 3, 4. Tape the board with the doors over the second board. Behind door 1 put a picture of a girl in coveralls. Behind door 2 show the girl in a swimsuit. Behind door 3, the girl should be in a party dress. Behind door 4, she is wearing a nightgown. As you tell the story, open the doors as indicated. The children will enjoy and learn from Samantha Jane's mistakes during the day.

Samantha Jane was old enough to get dressed all by herself. She could zip zippers and buckle buckles and button buttons. And she liked to do it all by herself.

One morning her mother said, "Samantha Jane, time to get dressed. We are going to the park. Do you want me to help?"

"I can do it, Mommy," said Samantha Jane. "I can get dressed all by myself."

So she put on her swimsuit and sandals. *(Open door 2.)* Was that right for going to the park? *(No.)* Samantha Jane's mommy didn't think so either, so she helped Samantha Jane put on her coveralls and sneakers. *(Open door 1.)* And Samantha Jane went to the park.

When Samantha Jane came home, her mother said, "Samantha Jane, time to get dressed. We are going to the beach. Do you want me to help?"

"I can do it, Mommy," said Samantha Jane. "I can get dressed all by myself."

So she put on her party dress and shiny black shoes. *(Open door 3.)* Was that right for going to the beach? *(No.)* Samantha Jane's mommy didn't think so either, so she helped Samantha Jane put on her swimsuit and sandals. *(Open door 2.)* And Samantha Jane went to the beach.

When Samantha Jane came home, her mother said, "Samantha Jane, time to get dressed. We are going to a birthday party for Grandma. Do you want me to help?"

"I can do it, Mommy," said Samantha Jane. "I can get dressed all my myself."

So she put on her nightgown and fuzzy slippers. *(Open door 4.)* Was that right for going to the birthday party? *(No.)* Samantha Jane's mommy didn't think so either, so she helped Samantha Jane put on her party dress and shiny black shoes. *(Open door 3.)* And Samantha Jane went to the birthday party for Grandma.

It was late when Samantha Jane came home, and her mother said, "Samantha Jane, time to get dressed for bed. Do you want me to help?"

"I can do it, Mommy," said Samantha Jane. "I can get dressed all by myself."

So she put on her coveralls and sneakers. *(Open door 1.)* Was that right for going to bed? *(No.)* Samantha Jane's mommy didn't think so either, so she helped Samantha Jane put on her nightgown and fuzzy slippers. *(Open door 4.)* Then Mother tucked Samantha Jane into bed.

"Samantha Jane, you have had a busy day," said Mommy. "You have been to the park and the beach and a party and now to bed."

"Yes," said Samantha Jane in a sleepy voice. "And the best part is that I got dressed all by myself."

What Will You Wear?
(To the tune of "Mulberry Bush")

This song is the perfect followup for *Jessie Bear, What Will You Wear?*

What would you like to wear today?
Wear today, wear today?
What would you like to wear today?
On your pretty head?
　　(Point to head.)

I'll wear the sunshine on my hair.
　　(Touch fingertips over head.)
On my hair, on my hair.
I'll wear the sunshine on my hair,
High upon my head.

What would you like to wear today?
Wear today, wear today?
What would you like to wear today?
On your busy feet?
　　(Point to feet.)

I'll wear the sand between my toes.
　　(Wiggle toes.)
'Tween my toes, 'tween my toes.
I'll wear the sand between my toes,
On my busy feet.

(Song continues on page 18.)

What would you like to wear today?
Wear today, wear today?
What would you like to wear today?
'Round about your neck?
  (Point to neck.)

I'd like to wear a daisy chain.
  (Wiggle fingers around neck.)
A daisy chain, a daisy chain.
I'd like to wear a daisy chain,
'Round about my neck.

What would you like to wear tonight?
Wear tonight, wear tonight?
What would you like to wear tonight?
When you go to bed?
  (March in place.)

I'd like to wear a sleepy dream.
  (Rest head on hands.)
A sleepy dream, a sleepy dream.
I'd like to wear a sleepy dream,
When I go up to bed.

Books about Taking It Off and Tucking In

Artis, Vicki Kimmel. **Pajama Walking.** Illustrated by Emily Arnold McCully. Houghton Mifflin, 1981.

   Four short stories about two girls spending the night together include such fun as Clara's invention of "pajama walking." Both girls get inside Dad's giant pajamas and walk and play around until they finally giggle themselves asleep.

Barrett, Judi. **I Hate to Go to Bed.** Illustrated by Ray Cruz. Four Winds, 1977.

   A child lists all the reasons he hates to go to bed, including having to get out of clothes, but if has to go, he's happy to wear his "number 25 football pajamas."

Burningham, John. **Time to Get Out of the Bath, Shirley.** Thomas Y. Crowell, 1978.

   A sparse text telling the story of a mother trying to get her daughter to bed is punctuated with constant reminders of "I wish you would learn to fold up your clothes nicely" and "Look at your clothes all over the floor." The illustrations on the opposite pages tell another story—the girl's fantastical journey down the bathtub drain and into a world of kings and queens riding on rubber ducks.

Chittum, Ida. **The Cat's Pajamas.** Illustrated by Art Cumings. Parents, 1980.

   Fred goes to a lot of trouble making the cat's pajamas, but the cat won't wear them. Fred ends up making them into a stuffed cat pillow for the sofa.

Gackenbach, Dick. **Poppy the Panda.** Houghton Mifflin, 1984.

   Katie's panda, Poppy, doesn't want to go to bed because he doesn't have something nice to wear. Katie tries her doll's dress on him, two unmatching shoes, bath towels, and even toilet tissue. Finally Katie's mother gives him her ribbon for a bow around his neck so Poppy and Katie go to sleep.

Hurd, Edith Thacher. **I Dance in My Red Pajamas.** Illustrated by Emily Arnold McCully. Harper & Row, 1982.

   A young child enjoys many noisy pleasures and activities when she visits her grandparents—dancing in her red pajamas.

Ormerod, Jan. **Moonlight.** Lothrop, Lee and Shepard, 1982.

   A wordless story sequence of bedtime ritual includes leaving clothes all over the bathroom and dressing for bed.

Related Activities about Taking It Off and Tucking In

Properly Undressed
(To the tune of "Paw-Paw Patch")

Look! I can untie my shoe strings.
   (Wiggle fingers by feet.)
Look! I can untie my shoe strings.
Look! I can untie my shoe strings.
Getting undressed is a lot of fun.

Look! I can unzip my zipper.
   (Run thumb from chin to waist.)
Look! I can unzip my zipper.
Look! I can unzip my zipper.
Getting undressed is a lot of fun.

Look! I can pull off my sweat socks.
   (Pull on toes.)
Look! I can pull off my sweat socks.
Look! I can pull off my sweat socks.
Getting undressed is a lot of fun.

Look! I can take off my blue jeans.
   (Rub hands from hips to knees.)
Look! I can take off my blue jeans.
Look! I can take off my blue jeans.
Getting undressed is a lot of fun.

Mommy says it makes her happy.
   (Clap.)
Mommy says it makes her happy.
Mommy says it makes her happy.
But don't take clothes off when you
   play outside!
   (Shake finger.)

Help!
(A Story)

To use masks with this story, invite five children to stand up front. Give each one an animal mask as the character is mentioned in the story. All the children can help "pull and pull and pull," and the mouse can run over and whisper to the moose as indicated. You will need a mask of a moose (with large antlers), cow, pig, dog, and mouse.

ADD
PAPER
ANTLERS

Moose had a new blue sweater. His Grandma Moose knit it for him, and he could put in on all by himself. He put on one arm and the other arm. *(You may wish to bend elbows and reach out as if putting arms in sleeves.)* Then he buttoned the five shiny buttons: 1-2-3-4-5. And Moose went out to play.

Today he decided to play ball with Cow. "That's a fine blue sweater you have," said Cow.

"Yes," said Moose, "and I can put it on all by myself."

Pretty soon Pig came to play ball with them. "That's a fine blue sweater you have," said Pig.

Next, Dog joined the game. "That's a fine blue sweater you have," said Dog.

"Yes," said Moose, "and I can put it on all by myself."

Last of all Mouse came to play ball with the others. "That's a fine blue sweater you have," said Mouse.

"Yes," said Moose, "and I can put it on all by myself."

Before too long, the sun rose higher and higher in the sky and Moose started to get warm. Then he got very warm. Then he got HOT! Moose wanted to take off his new blue sweater. So he took out one arm and he took out the other arm, but when he tried to pull it over his head, it would not come off over his antlers. Moose's antlers were stuck in his sweater.

"Help!" called Moose. And all his friends came running.

"I'll help," said Cow. He took hold of the new blue sweater and pulled and pulled and pulled, but it was no use. Moose's antlers were stuck in his sweater.

"I'll help," said Pig. He took hold of Cow, who took hold of the new blue sweater. They pulled and pulled and pulled, but it was no use. Moose's antlers were stuck in his sweater.

"I'll help," said Dog. He took hold of Pig, who took hold of Cow. Cow took hold of the new blue sweater and pulled and pulled and pulled, but it was no use. Moose's antlers were stuck in his sweater.

"I'll help," said Mouse. But Dog and Pig and Cow laughed and laughed. "We are big and strong. We pulled and pulled and pulled," they said. "And we can't get Moose's sweater off over his antlers. You are little and weak. How can you help?"

Mouse smiled. "I can help by whispering," he said. Mouse walked over to Moose and whispered, "Unbutton the buttons."

So Moose put one arm back in and the other arm back in. Then he unbuttoned the five shiny buttons: 5-4-3-2-1. And his sweater came right off. He folded it neatly and took it home to his mother so that it wouldn't get lost.

Mother Moose said, "Moose, I am glad you did not lose your sweater. It is a fine blue sweater."

"Yes," said Moose, "and I took it off *almost* all by myself!"

Do I Have To?

I've played hard all day
In my jeans and my shirt.
I'm covered all over
With smudges of dirt.

[Yawn] I'm ready for bed.
Mom says, "Into the tub!
Get out of THOSE THINGS,
And, let's see you scrub!"

"Do I have to use soap?
Isn't water enough?
Hey, don't wash my neck,
You're rubbing too rough!"

"Do I have to get out?
I was just having fun!
I don't need a towel—
I'll dry when I run!"

"Put on pajamas?
Gee, I want to stay up!
O.K., I'm tucked in now—
Can I sleep with the pup?"

Tub Time

(To the tune of "Good-Night, Ladies")

Now it's bath time.
Now it's bath time.
Now it's bath time.
Time to get undressed.
        (March in place.)
La la la la la la la
La la la
La la la
La la la la la la la la
La la la la la!

Take off both shoes.
        (Point to shoes.)
Take off both shoes.
Take off both shoes.
Time to get undressed.
La la la la la la la
        (Wiggle fingers by feet.)
La la la
La la la
La la la la la la la la
La la la la la!

Take off sweater.
        (Point to shoulder.)
Take off sweater.
Take off sweater.
Time to get undressed.
La la la la la la la
        (Bend and straighten elbows.)
La la la
La la la
La la la la la la la la
La la la la la!

Take off blue jeans.
        (Point to knees.)
Take off blue jeans.
Take off blue jeans.
Time to get undressed.
La la la la la la la
        (Rub hands from hips to knees.)
La la la
La la la
La la la la la la la la
La la la la la!

Take off both socks.
        (Point to ankles.)
Take off both socks.
Take off both socks.
Time to get undressed.
La la la la la la la
        (Pull toes.)
La la la
La la la
La la la la la la la la
La la la la la!

Take off underwear.
        (Point to chest.)
Take off underwear.
Take off underwear.
Time to get undressed.
La la la la la la la
        (Pretend to pull undershirt over head.)
La la la
La la la
La la la la la la la la
La la la la la!

Now we're ready.
        (Spread arms wide.)
Now we're ready.
Now we're ready
To jump into the tub—
        (Jump.)
SCRUB!

The Cat's Pajamas
(A Cut-and-Tell Story)

Charles was a curious cat. He always got into things. And sometimes he got in trouble. Whenever Mr. and Mrs. White, his owners, left the house in the morning, Charles would run up the stairs. *(Fold paper in half; make first cut, as shown.)*

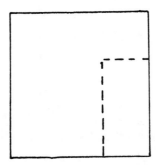

And he would sneak about in the attic. *(Make second cut, as shown.)*

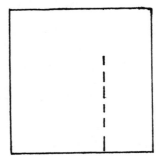

He got into trunks and boxes and closets. *(Make third cut, as shown.)*

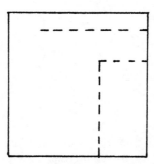

He tried on hats and coats and shoes. He found old nightshirts. *(Make fourth cut, as shown.)*

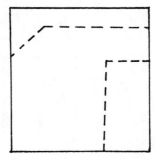

(Open shape to show nightshirt.)
Charles loved to dress up and "put on the dog"—even if he was a cat!
(Close shape, put cardboard behind it so you can draw the next lines.)

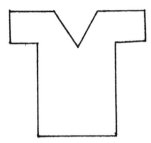

One day just after Mr. and Mrs. White left the house, Charles ran upstairs. *(Draw zig-zag line from bottom to top of shape, as shown.)*

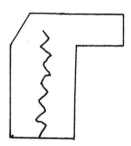

But outside he heard a racket. So he jumped out the window *(make zig-zag line across to edge of sleeve, as shown)*

and ran out on the roof. That racket he heard was thunder. Well, Charles was so scared, he just sat on the edge of the roof. Thunder roared and lightning flashed just like this. *(Draw a second zig-zag line up and across, as shown.)*

After a while Mr. and Mrs. White came home. They heard Charles cry, so Mrs. White ran upstairs *(turn shape over and draw another zig-zag line, as shown)*

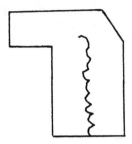

and she went out on the roof.

Mr. White ran upstairs *(draw another zig-zag line, as shown)*

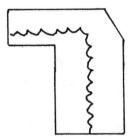

and he went out on the roof. But they couldn't reach Charles. He was way out on the edge of the roof. They called and called, but Charles wouldn't come.

Luckily, Mr. Black heard them. He went straight to the phone and called the fire department. *(Make next cut, then lay down big piece and make small cuts in smaller piece, as shown.)*

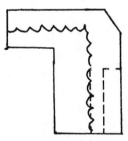

The firemen came in their truck. They got out rescue nets and said, "Jump, Mrs. White!" But she wouldn't jump. "Jump, Mr. White!" But he wouldn't jump. "Jump, Charles!" But, of course, Charles wouldn't jump. Charles was a scaredy cat.

So the firemen got out their ladders. *(Hold up ladder shape.)*

FOLD →
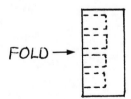

They climbed up and carried down Mr. and Mrs. White and Charles, who was shivering all over by this time.

Mr. and Mrs. White scolded Charles for causing so much trouble. *(Put down ladder, pick up big piece.)* But then they dried him off and gave him a pair of pajamas, so he could get warm. *(Open big piece to show pajama shape.)*

And do you know, those pajamas fit him to a *T. (Trace T shape with your finger.)*

After that Charles never went up in the attic to dress up again. In his new clothes, everyone said he was "the cat's pajamas!"

Baby Llama's Pajamas
(A Story in Rhyme for Sock Puppets)

Tan-colored socks pulled over the arm with the heel worn on top resemble heads of llamas, especially if you make little ears from the extra part of the sock. Just add two small buttons for eyes or embroider on eyes, with *long* eyelashes. When Mama makes the red pajamas for Baby Llama, just pull on a "cuff" from a red sock for the pajamas.

"Mama, Mama,"
Said Baby Llama.
"Make me a pair
Of red pajamas!
Red pajamas
To wear at night,
To keep me cozy
And tucked in tight."

"Pajamas?" said Mama.
"Where did you hear
Of *red* pajamas,
My silly dear?
Llamas wear hair—
Hair brown or black.
Llamas wear coats—
Coats on their backs!"

"But Mama, Mama
I want pajamas!
Pajamas red.
Pajamas for bed.
Pajamas instead
Of a coat brown or black.
Red pajamas to wear
On my back!"

"But a llama's coat is warm.
A llama's coat grows.
It keeps you snug,
Right down to your toes!"

"But *pajamas* are soft!
Pajamas are snuggily!
The hair on my back
Is scraggily and ugly!"

So Mama Llama
Got out her scraps,
Her needle and thread
She'd tucked in her lap.
She sewed all day.
And because she was wise,
She made red pajamas
Baby Llama's own size!

So there's no more complaining—
Baby Llama's snug in his bed.
Now he's wearing pajamas,
Pajamas bright red!

Bunny Sleepers

(An Action Rhyme)

Max's wolf suit sleepers in *Where the Wild Things Are* have always been an enviable night-time outfit for young children. In this action rhyme, invite children to pull on "bunny suit" sleepers and romp through the actions of this rhyme.

My fuzzy bunny sleepers
Have two long and floppy ears.
(Arms up like two ears.)

It's fun to put them on
(Put on pajamas.)
And see myself back in the mirror.
(Point to self, then imaginary mirror.)

Wiggle goes my nose-y.
(Wiggle nose.)
Bunny wiggles back at me.
(Point to mirror, wiggle nose.)

Hop, hop go my footsies.
(Hop twice.)
Bunny hop hops back at me.
(Point to mirror, hop twice.)

Ready for Bed

(A Story)

You can use a doll to undress and dress as you tell the story, or make a flannel-board set of Ted and his clothes. In either case, it would be fun to have a dog puppet to play Fred. The children will enjoy helping him bark "No."

Ted and his mother and father had been at the band concert in the park all evening. It was very late when they got in the car to come home, and Ted was so sleepy that he closed his eyes and went fast asleep. Ted was so sleepy he didn't wake up when they pulled into the driveway. He didn't wake up when his father carried him up to the house. He didn't even wake up when his dog Fred met them at the door.

Daddy said, "Look, Fred, your boy Ted is sound asleep. We will have to get him out of his shirt and jacket and socks and pants and hat and mittens and into his pajamas."

They all went up to Ted's room. Mother took off Ted's shoes and mittens and put them in the closet. Is Ted ready for bed?

"No," barked Fred.

So Father took off Ted's shirt and jacket and hung them up. Is Ted ready for bed?

"No," barked Fred.

So Mother took off Ted's socks—1, 2—and put them in the laundry hamper. Is Ted ready for bed?

"No," barked Fred.

Then Father took off Ted's pants and put them in the dresser drawer. Is Ted ready for bed?

"No," barked Fred.

So Mother put on Ted's sleeper pajamas. Father pulled up the blankets and called Fred.

"Here, Fred," called Father. "Come lay down in your usual place. Ted is all ready for bed."

Is Ted ready for bed?

"No," barked Fred.

"What is wrong, Fred?" asked Mother. The dog crawled up to the top of the bed and took off Ted's hat. Then Fred turned in a circle three times and lay down in his usual place. Now is Ted ready for bed?

Yes.

Good night!

GAMES FOR ALL BY MYSELF

Put It On

This traditional relay can be adapted for any age group. If the children are very young (three to four years), you may wish to have them run to a spot and simply put a hat on, take it off, and run back to tag the next person. As the children get older, more complex articles, involving zipper and ties, can be added.

Dress Your Favorite Space Creature

Ever since E.T. was dressed up, children have loved to imagine dressing up space creatures in their own clothes. Draw a space creature on a posterboard and give each child a different kind of clothing cut from paper to attach to the creature, like an outer space "Pin the Tail on the Donkey." You can have several creatures if there are many children, or play a couple of times through, so each child has a chance to add several pieces of clothing.

Where Does It Go?

Collect various items of children's clothing. Show them one at a time and put them on the wrong places indicated. Then invite a child to come demonstrate how to put it on right.

Here is my mitten.
Who knows where it goes?
Does it keep my knee warm?
Does it hang on my nose?
Does it fit on my left foot?
Does anyone know?
Who can show me
Where my mitten should go?

Back to Front

Bring several adult-size jackets or sweaters for the children to try on backwards. Older children will enjoy a relay race where they must put on the item and zip or button it before passing it to the next in line. Trying to button or zip up the back will convince them it is worth the effort to put things on right.

Teddy Bears Button Up

Play this variation of "Simon Says" by directing children to pretend to put on various articles of clothing. Begin directions with "Teddy Bears." Here is a sample game.

Teddy Bears, pull on your shirts.
Teddy Bears, take off one shoe.
Take off the other shoe.
   *(No penalty for doing it at the
   wrong time.)*
Teddy Bears, take off the other shoe.

Teddy Bears, button up.
Teddy Bears, zip your jacket.
Teddy Bears, all sit down.
Teddy Bears, pull up the sheets.
Teddy Bears, go to sleep.

Packing for a Trip—Several Ways

The traditional "Packing Grandmother's Trunk" game can be adapted as a "packing for a trip" game in a couple of ways.

One way is to simply let the children name things that go in the suitcase, not repeating them all backwards or worrying about repetitions.

For slightly older children, bring a collection of clothing to put in a suitcase. Each child in turn takes a piece out of the case and adds it to the list. Repeating the list backwards is easier, since the articles of clothing are in sight.

Another trick is to think up an action for each article of clothing mentioned, such as tapping head for hat or holding up fists for mittens. This gives an additional challenge and nonverbal clues for older children.

CRAFTS FOR ALL BY MYSELF

My Very Own Paper Doll

Children love paper dolls and will love this craft. The paper doll's face is the child's own! Have children bring photographs of themselves or take instant photos of each child. Then provide each child with a simple outline of a paper doll child to decorate and glue on the photos. Supply a few simple outlines of outfits to color (or decorate with fabric scraps). Pieces of plastic tack stuck to the back of the clothes may work better than paper tabs to dress the paper dolls.

Mix and Match

Draw a simple figure on each paper. Out of magazines and catalogs cut various articles of clothing, such as boots, pants, sweater, and hat. The children may paste these on the proper location on the figure. They do not need to match or fit the figure. In fact, the funnier the completed ensemble looks, the more the children will like it.

Fashion Plate Craft

Supply each child with a paper plate and catalogs of clothes. The children may simply cut out the clothes they like best and glue them on the plates, or you may divide the plate into sections and suggest they find pictures of shirts or tops for one section, pants for another section, shoes for another section, and hats for another section.

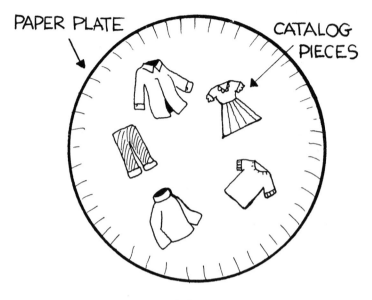

Overnight Bag

A center-cut file folder can become a small suitcase or overnight bag if you draw around the tab to make it look like a handle. Write the child's name on the front ("Jenny's Suitcase"). Then give children pictures of clothes cut from catalogs so they can plan what kind of clothes to take on an imaginary trip. Will they need dress-up clothes to visit Grandma? Or will they be going on a camping trip and need hiking boots? After children decide what kind of clothes they want to take, they can glue the appropriate pictures on the inside of the file folder.

DISPLAYS FOR ALL BY MYSELF

Dress Me Doll or Pet

Stuffed animals and dolls with zippers, buttons, and snaps are made commercially and will be popular with young children if you have several of these around the room to give young hands an opportunity to try the different closings. You can convert old stuffed animals by adding buttons, zippers, and snaps so that more children will be able to join in the fun of learning how to dress and undress the doll or pet.

Child-Size Dress Me Doll

For this display you will need a bedsheet, some stuffing from an old pillow or fiberfill, felt-tipped markers, and old children's clothes.

Draw around a child and cut out the two body pieces from an old sheet. Draw on features with felt-tipped markers. Place right sides together and stitch, leaving a long enough opening to turn right side out. Stuff the sheet child with pillow stuffing (or newspapers crumpled up) and sew opening shut. Now, the fun begins! Dress the child or let children help you. This display can be played with and enjoyed again and again.

Dressing Teddy Bear

Make a simple felt teddy bear and a few pieces of clothing for him. Place on a low flannelboard where the children can learn by dressing and undressing him.

Scarecrow Clothes

Have fun learning the names of clothes by decorating a bulletin board with a scarecrow figure in hat, shirt, pants, gloves, and boots. Write each word in large letters on paper that contrasts to the background and run string or yarn between the word and the clothing on the scarecrow.

How We Close Our Clothes Display

Children will enjoy this display after you've taught them the song "Buttons, Zippers, Snaps, and Bows." Simply glue an assortment of large buttons, zippers, snaps, bows, hooks and eyes, and belts to a large piece of fabric or posterboard. This display is not meant to be a manipulative, but you could make smaller fabric squares with the different devices for children to use, too.

2
Shopping Bags and Laundry Tags

INTRODUCTION

Shopping and the various ways we acquire clothes—from the age-old method of making them to the more recent experiences of catalog shopping and garage sales—can be valuable learning experiences and fun times for young children. Early decision-making skills are taught when children are included in shopping trips and looking for bargains. Although children may become tired of trying on clothes, they usually love to get a new shirt or pair of favorite jeans in the end.

The scope of this chapter includes the various ways of acquiring clothes and taking care of them. The first subtheme "Shopping, Swapping, and Growing without Stopping" includes shopping for clothes, outgrowing clothes, and receiving hand-me-downs. The next subtheme "Make and Mend" includes stories and activities about sewing, as well as stories about the cloth-making process. Finally, the subtheme "It Will All Come Out in the Wash" covers laundry day activities and the lost-and-found box.

Picture books cover the shopping and swapping experience for the youngest child. Oxenbury's *Shopping Trip* captures typical childlike behavior on a shopping trip, from playing in racks of clothes to trying on big shoes. Patrick in *Patrick Buys a Coat* is a reluctant shopper until he finds just the right coat all by himself. The not-always-popular hand-me-down clothes may appeal to children when they have heard the rollicking verse of Hoberman's *I Like Old Clothes* or identify with Titch in *You'll Soon Grow into Them, Titch*. We have extended these themes with a story about an enthusiastic shopper, the "Clothes Horse," a song about garage sale shopping, and a fantastic tale about a pair of pants for kids who grow like weeds.

Although most clothes are purchased as ready-to-wear items today, children will be fascinated by the process of making clothes, from the sheep shearing to the weaving and sewing of a cloak or coat. *Charlie Needs a Cloak* clearly explains this process for young children. Our activities provide opportunities to try a hand at weaving and sewing, too. Mothers probably make fewer clothes (or have less time to mend them!) for children today, but the idea of "fixing up" and recycling the old makes good sense if we are trying to teach children to make wise use of the world's resources. "A Party Dress—Yes!" shows that you can turn a plain dress into a party frock, and children will ask you to mend rips after they have learned the song "Fix It."

Washing clothes is just as much fun as getting them dirty in the first place as many picture books illustrate. No one could resist washing in *The Marvelous Mud Washing Machine* or walking through the tar in new socks with the little pigs in *Amanda and April*. Generations of children have sung "This is the way we wash our clothes" and will continue to enjoy the experience with songs about modern conveniences they know: the automatic washer and dryer. Songs, stories, and activities in this chapter will involve children in laundry day fun as well as teach the responsibility of caring for their own clothes.

INITIATING ACTIVITY

Let's Go Shopping

Shirts in red
Jeans in blue
Let's go shopping
You come, too!

(Point to a child and ask that child's name. Then incorporate it into the next verse of the poem.)

Shirts in red
Jeans in blue
Carol goes shopping
You come, too!

(Point to another child, use his name in the poem, and continue in this manner until all children have had a turn to be part of the poem. Then finish with this verse.)

Shirts in red
Jeans in blue
We all went shopping
Now we're through!
Whew!

LITERATURE-SHARING EXPERIENCES

Books about Shopping, Swapping, and Growing without Stopping

Christian, Mary Blount. "Penrod's Pants" from **Penrod's Pants**. Illustrated by Jane Dyer. Macmillan, 1986.

In the first story, "Penrod's Pants" on pages 4-13, Penrod goes shopping for pants just like the ones Grandmother Quill sent him, but he can't find anything that suits him. The pants Grandmother sent him had a five-dollar bill in the pocket.

Edwards, Linda Strauss. **The Downtown Day**. Pantheon, 1983.

Linda's Aunts Sophie and Dadie take her downtown to shop for school clothes, but all Linda wants is a red sweater. Linda gets bored and tired of shopping, so she hides from them until she decides it's best to come out after all.

Gibbons, Gail. **Department Store**. Thomas Y. Crowell, 1984.

The activities in a department store will show children a children's wear department, shoes, hats, women's wear, men's wear, and a fashion show.

Green, Mary McBurney. **Whose Little Red Jacket?** Illustrated by Tony DeLuna. Franklin Watts, 1965.

Jimmy's mother makes him a little wool jacket, and he loves it so much he sometimes wears it to bed on top of his pajamas. He wears it all year until he outgrows it and gives it to his friend Andy. Andy also loves the jacket and wears it constantly until he outgrows it and hands it down to Molly. Molly's mother alters the sleeves and she wears it nearly all the time. Finally the jacket wears out, so it becomes a smaller red jacket for yet another little girl's doll. And then it is given back to Jimmy for his new pet monkey.

Hayes, Geoffrey. **Patrick Buys a Coat**. Knopf, 1985.

Patrick Bear reluctantly goes shopping with his mother to buy a new coat, but ends up finding just the right one all by himself.

Hirsch, Marilyn. **The Pink Suit**. Crown, 1970.

Eugene's mother comes home with a bargain: a pink suit. Eugene doesn't like it, so he tries to get lost in the crowd and finds places where he feels at home—the pink suit begins to blend with a display of pink kites and stalls of flowers. When he arrives home late and is punished, he begins to plot ways to get rid of the suit. Finally he trades suits with a boy in the neighborhood.

Hoberman, Mary Ann. **I Like Old Clothes**. Illustrated by Jacqueline Chwast. Knopf, 1976.

Rollicking rhyme announces the fun of getting hand-me-down clothes, not-my-own clothes. For this child old clothes have "a history ... a mystery"—sweaters and shirts are "brother-and-sistery." Part of the fun, of course, is wondering what the clothes have done and all the places they've been and where they will be going next!

Hutchins, Pat. **You'll Soon Grow into Them, Titch**. Greenwillow, 1983.

Titch has outgrown his pants, so his brother Pete gives him his outgrown pants. Although they are a bit big, Pete says, "You'll soon grow into them." And when Titch needs a new sweater, his sister Mary gives him her old sweater, saying, "You'll soon grow into it." He gets socks, too—too big. Dad and Titch go shopping to buy new clothes that will fit. And, when Mother brings home the new baby, Titch gives him his hand-me-downs.

Krauss, Ruth. **The Growing Story**. Illustrated by Phyllis Rowand. Harper & Row, 1947.

When spring comes a little boy helps his mother put away his winter clothes. He sees animals and plants growing and wonders if he is, too. But when fall comes and he helps take out his winter clothes again, he happily discovers that he has outgrown them.

Lobel, Arnold. **On Market Street**. Illustrated by Anita Lobel. Greenwillow, 1981.

The shops along Market Street hold such clothing treasures as gloves, hats, jewels, ribbons, shoes, umbrellas, wigs, and zippers!

Numeroff, Laura. **The Ugliest Sweater**. Franklin Watts, 1980.

Peter's grandmother gives him a sweater for his birthday, but Peter thinks it's the ugliest sweater he has ever seen. Peter begins thinking how he can get rid of the sweater, but his mother insists he wear it to school. Then Peter is selected to perform a special task at school—all because he is wearing his sweater.

Oxenbury, Helen. **Shopping Trip**. Dial, 1982.

In his wordless board book for the very young, a child tries on grown-up shoes, plays with mother's purse while she's trying on clothes, and whirls around in racks of clothes. This is all too familiar in capturing the young child's behavior on a shopping trip.

Rockwell, Anne. **Our Garage Sale**. Illustrated by Harlow Rockwell. Greenwillow, 1984.

A child describes the many items sold in the family's garage sale, including his sister's outgrown ballet shoes and his old snowsuits.

Wells, Rosemary. **Martha's Birthday**. Bradbury, 1970.

Martha receives a pair of argyle socks for her birthday from Aunt Elizabeth, so her mother insists she wear them as she takes a pie to her aunt. Martha hates the socks and tries to cover them up on the bus with the pie and her coat. On the way she meets a German shepherd, lets him lick the pie, and ends up leaving it. When she finally arrives at Aunt Elizabeth's, she is told the socks are for her father, and she gets a present that makes her happy after all—a pet skunk.

Related Activities about Shopping, Swapping, and Growing without Stopping

A-Shopping We Will Go
(To the tune of "A-Hunting We Will Go")

Be sure to teach the children, when you ask "Is it time to go?" to say, "No."

A-shopping we will go,
A-shopping we will go,
We'll try on boots and swimming suits,
Now is it time to go?
    (No.)

A-shopping we will go,
A-shopping we will go,
We'll try on shirts and pleated skirts,
Now is it time to go?
    (No.)

A-shopping we will go,
A-shopping we will go,
We'll try on coats and petticoats,
Now is it time to go?
    (No.)

(Much slower.)
A-SHOPPING WE WILL GO,
A-SHOPPING WE WILL GO,
WE'LL TRY ONE HAT—
AND THAT IS THAT!
LET'S BUY IT QUICK AND GO!

The Clothes Horse

Harrison was not an ordinary horse. He didn't run horse races or give children rides. He didn't live on a farm and frisk about in the pasture. And he certainly didn't wear the kind of heavy iron shoes that most horses wear. Harrison was a city horse who loved shopping for fancy clothes.

Sometimes Harrison went to garage sales for his clothes. He always went early so he could get the best selection. Sometimes Harrison went to sidewalk sales with racks and racks of clothes standing out on the streets and sidewalks. But most of all, Harrison loved to go to big department stores to shop for his clothes.

Harrison loved department stores with at least six floors and an elevator with buttons to push. Harrison always went early to the department store so he could avoid the rush. Besides, he took up so much room in the elevator that he liked to have the elevator all to himself.

Harrison was very polite so the sales manager didn't mind at all that a horse shopped at his department store. Besides, Harrison was such a stylish horse and the clothes he bought looked so good on him that men and women always wanted to know where Harrison shopped, so they could go to the store and buy the same fashions!

One day Harrison read in the morning newspaper that his favorite department store was going out of business. The ad said "Clearance Sale! Everything Must Go!"

Well, Harrison simply could not resist trotting right down to the store early that morning and waiting outside for the doors to open.

He started at the first floor. That's where they sold anklets and argyles. Harrison tried on every pair of anklets and argyles and he bought every single pair!

Next, he got on the elevator and read the sign that said "Second Floor—Body Suits and Business Suits." Harrison punched the button and got off on the second floor. He went into the dressing rooms (he took up all six stalls) and tried on pin-striped business suits and double-breasted ones. And he bought every suit on the second floor.

Then Harrison got back on the elevator and saw the sign that read "Third Floor—Cardigans, Crew Necks, and Cashmere Sweaters," so he punched the button for the third floor. He went into the dressing rooms and tried on sweater after sweater, and Harrison bought every one the store had left.

The store was starting to get crowded by the time Harrison got back on the elevator to go to the fourth floor, where underwear was sold, but he waited patiently for an empty elevator. He was just in time to buy twenty-five pairs of denim drawers on the fourth floor.

By lunchtime Harrison's shopping bags were full, but he still hadn't gone to the fifth floor. He got on the elevator and read the sign "Mackintoshes and Galoshes." Harrison was so excited because he didn't own even one mackintosh, so he went right up to the fifth floor and bought two dozen—the last two dozen on the rack. And then he bought three dozen pairs of galoshes. After all, he had four feet to fit!

Finally, Harrison got to the top floor of the store and there weren't many clothes left to buy. Shoppers were going crazy because nobody else could try on clothes. Harrison was in the dressing rooms—all six of them—and he was trying on tuxedos, top hats, and fancy cravats. He was dressed fit to kill! But the shoppers were so angry they were ready to kill him!

"What could you possibly want with all those clothes?" asked the sales manager. "You've bought everything in the store!"

"This is a clearance sale, isn't it?" said Harrison. "And if everything must go, I'm the horse who knows just what to do with it!"

And he did, too. Harrison opened up his own store the very next week so everyone could shop for the best bargains in town. Harrison called his store "The Clothes Horse," of course.

Shopping, Shopping

(To the tune of "Bluebird, Bluebird")

Shopping, shopping, let's go downtown, *(March in place.)*
Shopping, shopping, let's go downtown,
Shopping, shopping, let's go downtown.
Oh, Mommy, I'm excited! *(Jump up and down.)*

Try a little shirt and put it on your shoulders, *(Pat shoulders.)*
Try a sweater vest and put in on your shoulders,
Try a big coat and put it on your shoulders.
Oh, Mommy, I am tired.

Try a pair of socks and put 'em on your footsies, *(Touch feet.)*
Try a pair of shoes and put 'em on your footsies,
Try a pair of boots and put 'em on your footsies.
Oh, Mommy, I am tired.

Try some underpants and put 'em on your bottom, *(Pat bottom.)*
Try a pair of shorts and put 'em on your bottom,
Try a pair of jeans and put 'em on your bottom.
Oh, Mommy, I'm exhausted! *(Plop down on bottom in the end.)*

J-E-A-N-S

(To the tune of "B-I-N-G-O")

Of all the clothes I like to wear,
My favorite are my blue jeans.
J-E-A-N-S
J-E-A-N-S
J-E-A-N-S
Don't you like them, too?

Of all the clothes I like to wear,
My favorite are my blue jeans.
(Clap.) E-A-N-S
(Clap.) E-A-N-S
(Clap.) E-A-N-S
Don't you like them, too?

(Continue singing and clapping, eliminating one letter of the word "Jeans" until you are clapping and not saying letters by the last stanza.)

T-Shirt Tops

(To the tune of "Jingle Bells")

T-shirt tops,
T-shirt tops,
Printed with your name.
Superheroes, cuddly bears,
Rockets, aeroplanes!

T-shirt tops,
T-shirt tops,
Striped or shimmery.
We love T-shirts anyway,
They suit us to a T!

My Old T-Shirt

(To the tune of "On Top of Old Smoky")

Most kids do not like to wear dress shirts and will go to any length to wear their favorite T-shirt instead. This silly song should appeal to the child who dreams of a preposterous way of getting to wear a favorite shirt.

My mom buys me dress shirts
To cover my chest.
But I do not like them,
They're really not best.

She starches the collar.
It scratches my throat.
I'll give my best dress shirt
Away to a goat.

The goat eats my dress shirt
In one great big slurp.
The only thing left now
Is one belly burp.

I'm not at all sorry
That I've lost my shirt,
'Cause I've got another—
It's my old T-shirt!

The Bargain Jacket

(An Object Story)

If you don't have a green jacket, use green felt or a paper cutout.

For his birthday Danny got a battery-operated robot, two picture books, and a fancy green velvet jacket. He loved the robot and he loved the picture books. But he did not love the fancy green velvet jacket. In fact, he hated the fancy green velvet jacket. He thought it made him look silly. (Danny liked the way he looked in blue jeans and old plaid jackets.)

Danny's Aunt Priscilla had sent him the fancy green velvet jacket. Aunt Priscilla liked fancy dress-up clothes and she thought Danny would look like a little gentleman in the jacket. Danny didn't like to look like a little gentleman. Danny liked to look like a real kid.

Danny hid the jacket in the back of his closet. Maybe his mother would forget about it, and he would never have to wear the jacket.

But the next night Danny's mother said, "Danny, we're going out to dinner at a fancy restaurant tonight. Please wear your new green velvet jacket that Aunt Priscilla gave you."

"I don't think I can find it," said Danny.

"Look in your closet," said Mother.

Danny went to his closet. "I don't see it there," said Danny.

"Look in the back of your closet," said Mother. "I'll find it for you." And she did.

So Mother helped Danny find his green velvet jacket, and she buttoned it up for Danny. "There, don't you look good?" said Mother.

Danny didn't think he looked good. And he certainly didn't feel good. He felt uncomfortable all evening in the fancy green velvet jacket. So when he got home from the fancy restaurant, Danny hid his jacket in the cedar chest, at the bottom of the cedar chest where his mother kept the out-of-season clothes. Maybe he would outgrow the jacket by the time Mother found it again.

But the next week Mother opened the cedar chest to look for clothes to sell in a garage sale.

"Danny," she cried, "what's your fancy green velvet jacket doing in the trunk? I almost put it in the garage sale by mistake! Go hang it up in your closet immediately!"

So Danny hung up the fancy green velvet jacket in his closet. But then he waited until Mother got out piles and piles of old coats and pants and snowsuits and boots for the garage sale. Danny waited until Mother was busy putting little price tags on all the clothes for the garage sale. Then he slipped the fancy green velvet jacket under a pile of clothes in the garage.

Mother was so busy when people came to the sale that she didn't see the jacket.

A tall woman with three little boys came to the sale and bought all of Danny's old jeans. Another woman with two boys bought Danny's old winter ski jacket and his snowsuit. And a man with one little boy bought Danny's old boots.

Then an older woman picked up Danny's fancy green velvet jacket.

"What a beautiful jacket for my grandson," she said. "It looks just like new, but there isn't any price tag on it. Perhaps it's a mistake."

"No," said Danny, "it's just a real bargain. Only twenty-five cents."

"That is a bargain jacket," agreed the woman. "I'll take it."

"Let me put it in a bag for you," said Danny. And he quickly put the green velvet jacket in a bag before his mother could see what was happening.

"My, my," said the older woman. "You are such a little gentleman. My grandson will be so happy with such a beautiful new jacket."

But no one was happier than Danny. He waved good-bye to the woman—and to his fancy green velvet jacket—and he ran out to play in his blue jeans and old plaid jacket.

Garage Sale Shopping

(A Poem)

Isn't it fun to shop for clothes
At the neighborhood garage sale?
Shirts and pants and socks and shoes—
All outgrown and a little bit used.

I don't care 'cause I like things
Nice and soft—all broken in.
Lots of bargains—just bring your cash.
Garage sale shopping is such a bash!

Never Looked Better

(A Hand-Me-Down Rhyme)

Big sister Barbara bought a new shirt.
It matched her favorite lavender skirt.
She wore it to dances, she wore it to school.
She even wore it to the swimming pool.

But one day the shirt didn't quite fit,
So she told sister Beth, "You can have it."
The shirt fit Beth, and it was so soft,
She didn't want to take it off!

But one day the shirt got too small,
Or maybe Beth grew too tall.
So she handed it down to Emily.
Now Emily was only three.

The shirt covered Emily, feet to her head,
So she called it a nightshirt and wore it to bed.
When Emily grew older, about four and a half,
Mom took one look and started to laugh.

Just how long can a shirt be worn?
It's old and it's tattered and look how it's torn.
But Emily cried, "It's still got some wear.
Let's hand it down to my teddy bear!"

So Mom got her needle and sewed it together,
And on teddy bear's tummy—it never looked better!

Anna, Anna, Second Hander
(A Flannel-board Story)

To tell this story as a flannel board, prepare cutouts of the clothes mentioned (jeans, shirt, and raincoat).

Anna was a little girl about this tall. And Anna had an older sister about this tall.

Anna was jealous of Sue, because Sue always got the new clothes. After she wore the new clothes, they were not so new anymore. Then, when Sue outgrew the clothes, she handed them down to Anna. Anna wore the not-so-new clothes secondhand.

Sue had a new pair of jeans for school. She wore holes in the knees. One day her ankles showed out of the legs. Sue got a new pair of jeans, and she handed down the old jeans to Anna.

Mother sewed patches on the old jeans, gave them to Anna, and said, "They're almost like new."

But Anna said,
"Sue, Sue, always new—
Anna, Anna, second hander."

Sue had a red shirt. She grew so much, all the buttons popped off. Sue got a new red shirt, and she handed down the old shirt to Anna.

Mother sewed new buttons on the old shirt, gave it to Anna, and said, "It's almost like new."

But Anna said,
"Sue, Sue, always new—
Anna, Anna, second hander."

Sue had a shiny yellow raincoat with big pockets. She loved the raincoat—especially the pockets. She put so much stuff in the pockets that they fell off. When her arms grew out of the sleeves, Sue got a new raincoat. And Mother taped new pockets on the old coat and gave it to Anna. "Well," said Mother, "I'm afraid it's not quite new, but it will keep off the raindrops!"

Anna wore the not-so-shiny and not-so-new yellow raincoat and she sang her little song,
"Sue, Sue, always new—
Anna, Anna, second hander."

One day Anna's legs grew out of the blue jeans. She popped the buttons off the red shirt, and her arms stuck out of the sleeves of the yellow raincoat. (Sue was still wearing her jeans and shirt and coat.)

"We must do something," said Mother. "We must go shopping."

So Mother bought a new pair of blue jeans, a green sweater, and a shiny purple raincoat. But, this time, they were not for Sue. They were for Anna. And she changed her name from "Anna, Anna, Second Hander" to "Anna, Anna, Top Banana!"

Catalog Song

(To the tune of "My Bonnie Lies Over the Ocean")

We live way far out in the country.
We drive fifty miles to the store.
So we look inside the big cat'log
To order all we need and more.
Get me, get me,
Oh, get me the stuff on page eighty-three.
Get me, get me,
Oh, get me the stuff from the book!

My mom works all day in the office.
She can't go to shop in the store.
We order stuff from the big cat'log
Delivered right to our front door.
Get me, get me,
Oh, get me the stuff on page eighty-three.
Get me, get me,
Oh, get me the stuff from the book!

If you need a dress or a tractor,
A parachute, snow boots, or frog,
You don't need to jump in your auto.
Just look in the big catalog!
Get me, get me,
Oh, get me the stuff on page eighty-three.
Get me, get me,
Oh, get me the stuff from the book!

Growing Like a Weed

(A Story with Props)

To tell this story with a prop, cut out a pair of pants from paper (see illustration). Make the legs extra long. Fold the legs accordion-fashion, so you will be able to make the legs grow as the story unfolds. During the telling, tape the pants to a board. Unfold legs as pants grow. Then pull the pants down with a quick jerk when the dog pulls off the pants!

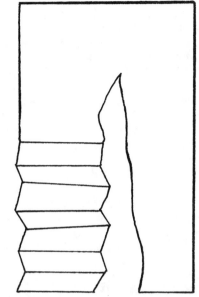

FOLD LEGS OF PANTS ACCORDION FASHION SO LEGS GROW AS STORY UNFOLDS

Walter was growing like a weed. His mother bought him pants one day. But the next day Walter's legs grew right out of the pants.

"You are growing like a weed," said Mother. "I wish I could find you pants that fit, or pants that grew as fast as you do."

The next day Walter's mother went to a big store and bought him a bigger pair of pants. The pants fit. But the next day Walter's legs grew right out of the pants.

"You are growing like a weed," said Mother. "I wish I could find you pants that fit. Or pants that grew as fast as you do."

The next day Walter's mother was too tired to walk around to find pants. She decided to shop by catalog.

Luckily, a new catalog came in the mail that day. It was called "The Whole Earth Catalog of Clothes for Kids Who Grow Like Weeds." There was a special offer inside on pants.

So Mother sent in the money for the pants. And just three days later a big package arrived.

Mother unwrapped the package and took out the pants. She read the label inside: "Prewash in bath *with pants on.* Warning: Garment may tickle at first until it has grown to full size."

"At last," said Mother. "Pants to fit. Walter, come try them on."

So Walter put on the pants and got in the bathtub to prewash the pants.

The pants tickled.

"Let me out," laughed Walter.

"Not 'til the pants fit," said Mother.

The pants tickled.

"Let me out," laughed Walter.

"Do the pants fit?" asked Mother.

"They're growing like a weed," laughed Walter.

"Then the pants fit," said Mother.

So Walter got out of the tub. The pants kept tickling and the pants kept growing.

"Quick," said Mother, "pull the legs. They're growing faster than a weed."

So Walter pulled the right leg. And Walter pulled the left leg. But the pants kept growing.

So Mother pulled the right leg and she pulled the left leg, but the pants kept growing. The pants were tickling Walter so much that he started rolling around on the floor.

Father heard the noise and he came running. Father took hold of Mother, and Mother took hold of the legs of the pants. They pulled and they pulled, but the pants kept growing and Walter kept laughing.

Finally, the dog heard all the noise and he came running. Well, the dog knew just what to do! He took hold of Walter by the seat of his pants. And he pulled those pants right off.

Which is what Mother and Father should have done in the first place. After all, you should never pull someone's leg—especially if they're wearing pants that grow like a weed.

But you all know better than that, don't you? You know I was just pulling your leg. After all, pants don't grow like a weed, do they? Just boys and girls like you!

Books about Make and Mend

Azaad, Meyer. **Half for You**. Illustrated by Naheed Hakeeget. Carolrhoda, 1971.

In the spring as the world is reborn, creatures produce their young and educate them to the ways of the world. In this story a young bird learns about the cloth-making process, seeing how a cotton ball is made into a brightly colored scarf.

Beskow, Elsa. **Pelle's New Suit**. Translated by Marion Letcher Woodburn. Harper & Row, 1929.

Once upon a time in Sweden lived a boy named Pelle, who had a lamb. As the lamb's wool grows longer, Pelle's coat grows shorter, so Pelle shears the sheep, takes it to one of his grandmothers to card, and to his other grandmother to spin into yarn. Pelle performs chores to get dye for the wool and then his mother weaves the cloth and the tailor make sit into a new suit for Pelle.

Blood, Charles L., and Martin Link. **The Goat in the Rug**. Illustrated by Nancy Winslow Parker. Parents, 1976.

Geraldine the Goat tells the story of Glenmae, her Navajo friend, who weaves a rug. The entire weaving process is described from clipping Geraldine's hair (mohair) to cleaning it with yucca root to carding, spinning, dying, warping the loom, and weaving the mohair into a beautiful rug. Parker's whimsical illustrations are a perfect accompaniment.

Christian, Mary Blount. "Just Perfect" from **Penrod's Pant's**. Illustrated by Jane Dyer. Macmillan, 1986.

In the story "Just Perfect" Penrod tries to fix his friend Griswold's pants that are too long. After several attempts to snip off each leg so they will match, Penrod ends up wearing the pants himself because they are too short for his friend.

De Paola, Tomie. **Charlie Needs a Cloak**. Prentice-Hall, 1973.

Charlie needs a new cloak, so in the spring he shears his sheep, washes the wool, cards it, spins it, dyes it with pokeweed berries, then puts the strands on the loom, and weaves it into cloth. Then he cuts the cloth and sews it, so when winter comes he has a beautiful red cloak. A simple glossary appends the story of the cloth-making process.

Doganis, Sally. **Three Bags Full**. Photos by John Claxton. Hamish Hamilton, 1976.

Andrew and Eve visit a farm on sheep shearing day and learn all about the process of preparing wool to take to a mill to be carded and woven into woolen clothing.

Hall, Adelaide. **Mrs. McGarrity's Peppermint Sweater**. Illustrated by Abner Graboff. Lothrop, Lee and Shepard, 1966.

Mrs. McGarrity enjoys knitting a peppermint striped sweater, but in her enthusiasm it grows too big for her cat. She continues her knitting only to realize the sweater's gotten too big for her dog. As she continues, it gets too big for her horse, even too big for an elephant. But it makes the grandest peppermint striped circus tent! Mrs. McGarrity then begins a new sweater for her cat—black and white like a licorice stick "and it will be a perfect fit," she declares.

Hest, Amy. **The Purple Coat**. Illustrated by Amy Schwartz. Four Winds, 1986.

Mama insists Gabrielle should get a navy coat as she always does, but she begs her tailor "grampa" for a purple one. Grampa satisfies them both by making a navy and purple reversible coat.

Schimmel, Nancy. "The Tailor" from **Just Enough to Make a Story**. Sisters' Choice Press, 1978.

Schimmel's story was inspired by a Yiddish folk song about a tailor who makes himself an overcoat then remakes it into a jacket, a vest, a cap, a button, and finally into a story. This one is perfect for telling and for teaching a sequence of events.

Walker, Barbara K., and Ahmet E. Uysal. **New Patches for Old**. Illustrated by Harold Berson. Parents, 1974.

For the upcoming holidays, Hasan the shoemaker buys new clothes for everyone in his family and new trousers for himself, since his old ones are "patches on patches." The new trousers are too long, but no one has time to shorten them, so Hasan carefully does it himself. In the morning they are too short because everyone else decided to shorten them, too!

Ziefert, Harriet. **A New Coat for Anna**. Illustrated by Anita Lobel. Knopf, 1986.

Anna's mother has no money to buy a new coat for Anna, so they trade possessions with a farmer for the wool, a spinner to spin the wool into yarn, a weaver to weave the wool into cloth, and a tailor to make the cloth into a coat. For Christmas they invite everyone to a celebration.

Related Activities about Make and Mend

Fix It
(To the tune of "Old MacDonald Had a Farm")

Jumping, climbing, falling down.
   (Jump and squat.)
Oops! My pants are ripped!
   (Slap seat of pants.)
Not to worry, not to pout,
   (Shake head.)
You can get it fixed!
   (Point to children.)
With a rip, rip here,
   (Slap one side of seat.)
And a rip, rip there,
   (Slap other side of seat.)

Here a rip,
   (Slap one knee.)
There a rip,
   (Slap other knee.)
Everywhere a rip, rip.
   (Both hands out, palms up.)
Not to worry, not to pout,
   (Shake head.)
You can get it fixed!
   (Point to children.)

(Song continues on page 44.)

Take the needle, take the thread,
  (*Touch thumb to forefinger of one hand and thumb to forefinger of other hand.*)
Stitch and stitch and stitch.
  (*Wiggle thumb and forefinger vertically as if pulling imaginary thread.*)
In and out and up and down,
  (*Horizontal wavy motion, as if stitching.*)
You can get it fixed!
  (*Point to children.*)
With a stitch, stitch here,
  (*Point to one side of seat.*)

And a stitch, stitch there,
  (*Point to other side of seat.*)
Here a stitch,
  (*Point to knee.*)
There a stitch,
  (*Point to other knee.*)
Everywhere a stitch, stitch.
  (*Hands out, palm up.*)
In and out and up and down,
  (*Horizontal wavy motion.*)
You can get it fixed!
  (*Point to children.*)

Worn-Out Rags
(To the tune of "This Old Man")

This old shirt has a tear. (*Point to chest.*)
I can't wear it anywhere. (*Shake head.*)
So I'll roll it up and put it in a bag. (*Roll hand over hand.*)
That's the place for worn-out rags.

These old pants have no seat. (*Point to seat of pants.*)
I can't wear them on the street. (*Shake head.*)
So I'll roll 'em up and put 'em in a bag. (*Roll hand over hand.*)
That's the place for worn-out rags.

This old sock has no toe. (*Point to foot.*)
It got threadbare long ago. (*Throw hands over shoulders to indicate past time.*)
So I'll roll it up and put it in a bag. (*Roll hand over hand.*)
That's the place for worn-out rags.

This old coat lost a collar. (*Point to neck.*)
It's not worth a single dollar. (*One finger up, shake head.*)
So I'll roll it up and put it in a bag. (*Roll hand over hand.*)
That's the place for worn-out rags.

Worn out clothes in a bag, (*Sling hands over shoulder.*)
Looking like a bag of rags, (*Thrust hands down in disgust.*)
But I'll patch 'em up and mend the tears. (*Clap hands over head.*)
Now I've got glad rags to wear! (*Hands out, palms up.*)

The Sewing Basket Song
(To the tune of "Good-Night Ladies")

Sew on patches,
Sew on patches,
Sew on patches,
Cover up your knees!

Sew on buttons,
Sew on buttons,
Sew on buttons,
Fasten up your sleeves!

Darn that stocking,
Darn that stocking,
Darn that stocking,
So your toes won't freeze. Please!

A Party Dress—YES!

(A Sew-and-Tell Story)

For this story cut out a brown felt dress shape and have ready a needle and thread, a bit of lace, a bow, and a red felt heart shape to sew on the dress as you tell the story.

Mrs. Mouse was an excellent seamstress. She made fancy evening gowns for all the ladies of the town and elegant coats for the gentlemen in town. And she sewed the clothes so well with such fine stitches that everyone wanted more and more of Mrs. Mouse's clothes.

But Mrs. Mouse got so busy making gowns and coats for all the people in town that her own little mouse, Mona, only had one dress to wear. It was a plain brown dress, just the color of Mona's mouse brown hair. *(Hold up brown dress.)*

One day Mona's best friend Mitzi invited Mona to her fifth birthday party.

"Wear your best dress," said Mitzi. "This will be the fanciest party in town."

But I only have one dress, one plain brown dress, said Mona to herself. I guess I won't go.

That night when Mona went to bed, she tried not to think about the party, but before she knew it, little mouse-sized tears dripped down her whiskers.

Mrs. Mouse put down her needle and thread and the fancy party dress she was making. She asked Mona what was wrong, so Mona told her all about the party. It was the very next day.

"Tsk! Tsk!" said Mrs. Mouse sadly as she rubbed her whiskers. "No party dress. No time to make a new one for you. But—yes, yes! I know just what to do!"

And she did, too. Mrs. Mouse took out a bit of lace left from one of the evening gowns she was making. *(Start sewing lace on the bottom of the dress.)* And she sewed that lace all around the bottom of Mona's plain brown dress.

"Who would guess—

This was just a plain dress!" said Mrs. Mouse.

And she held up the almost-ready-to-wear party dress.

"Yes, yes!" squeaked Mona.

Then Mrs. Mouse got out a bit of ribbon left from one of the coats she was making and she sewed a big bow on the top of Mona's dress. *(Start sewing bow to the top of the dress.)*

"Who would guess—

This was just a plain dress!" said Mrs. Mouse.

And she held up the almost-ready-to-wear party dress.

"Yes! Yes!" squeaked Mona.

And then Mrs. Mouse took out her best red velvet and she sewed a big heart right on the front of Mona's dress—just to show her little mouse how much she loved her. *(Start sewing heart shape in the middle of the dress.)*

"Now," she said, "no one will *ever* guess this was once a plain brown dress!"

"It's a party dress. Yes! Yes! Yes!" squeaked Mona. And she gave her mother a great, big hug.

The next day Mona went to Mitzi's birthday party after all. There was cheesecake and there were games like Pin the Tail on the Cat, and everyone was dressed up in their best party clothes. But everyone thought Mona's dress was the best—Yes!

Old Blue Jeans

(To the tune of "The Old Gray Mare")

Old blue jeans,
They ain't what they used to be,
Ain't what they used to be,
Ain't what they used to be.
Old blue jeans,
They ain't what they used to be,
Many months ago.

A patch on the seat,
And holes in the knees,
Legs too short—
Aw, fiddle-de-dee!
Old blue jeans,
They ain't what they used to be,
Many months ago.

Don't throw 'em out,
Just get Mom's shears—
Snip, snip here!
Snip, snip here!
Old blue jeans,
They ain't what they used to be:
Now you've got cutoffs!

Tailor, Tailor Make Me a Coat

(To the tune of "Skip to My Lou")

Tailor, tailor make me a coat.
Tailor, tailor make me a coat.
Tailor, tailor make me a coat.
Have you got a billy goat?

Trim that billy goat's long hair.
Trim that billy goat's long hair.
Trim that billy goat's long hair.
Wash and spin it up with care.

Weave it into a piece of cloth.
Weave it into a piece of cloth.
Weave it into a pice of cloth.
Shoo away that flying moth!

Cut the cloth and sew it here.
Cut the cloth and sew it there.
Sew it here and everywhere.
Now I've got me a coat to wear.

The Crazy Mixed PJs

(A Flannel-board Story)

For this story, make a simple pair of red pajamas. Cut the arms and legs apart from the shirt and pants. Trace another set of arms and legs onto a variety of colors. (Here we used blue, green, yellow, and purple.) When Ma Bear gets the red PJs put together wrong, show it on the flannel board, then fix them as she does in the story.

It was quarter to winter, and Pa Bear was grouchy as an old bear can be when it is close to bedtime. The only reason Pa Bear was still up at all was that Ma Bear was sewing him some new PJs, and they were not finished yet. Now Ma Bear was close to bedtime, too, and none too pleased to be sewing so late in the year, but Pa Bear would not decide what color PJs he wanted. So Ma Bear finally made them red.

Pa Bear grumbled and groused and growled his way into the sewing room where Ma Bear was hard at work.

Ma Bear merely sniffed when Pa Bear came in, and went on sewing. She made a red top and red pants. *(Place the red top and pants on the board.)* But because Pa Bear was grumbling and growling and grousing around the sewing room, Ma Bear could not concentrate. *(Place the arms and legs in the wrong places as described.)* So she sewed the left arm where the right leg should be. And the right arm where the left arm should be. And the left leg where the right arm should be. And the right leg where the left leg should be.

And when she showed the new PJs to Pa Bear, they were all wrong!

Pa Bear grumbled and groused and growled. And Ma Bear said, "OUT! Go pick some berries while I get finished!"

So Pa Bear left and Ma Bear took off the wrong arms and legs. *(Remove red arms and legs, replace with other colors as indicated.)* "Now what am I going to do?" she asked. "I don't have any more red material to make more arms and legs!" So she started to look around the sewing room. She found a scrap of blue material. So she made a left arm out of blue—and sewed it where the left arm should be. Then she found some green material, made a right leg out of green, and sewed it where the right leg should be. Then she found some yellow material to make the left leg, and sewed it where the left leg should be. Finally she found some purple material and made the right arm, and sewed it where the right arm should be.

All that sewing was finished just as Pa Bear came back from his walk. When Ma Bear showed him the PJs, Pa Bear was so surprised he dropped his bucket of berries! "Why, they are perfect," he said. "And just the right color!"

Books about It Will All Come Out in the Wash

Ahlberg, Allan. **Mrs. Lather's Laundry.** Illustrated by Andre Amstutz. Golden Press, 1981.

Mrs. Lather grows tired of washing clothes in her laundry, so she turns to washing other things—babies, dogs, and even elephants.

Galdone, Paul. **Three Little Kittens.** Clarion, 1986.

The familiar Mother Goose rhyme about the kittens who lose and soil their mittens is given a new slant through Galdone's lively illustrations.

Hare, Lorraine. **Who Needs Her?** Atheneum, 1983.

Cynthia's clothes grow tired of being thrown around, so the cast-around socks, shirts, jeans, and skirts rise up in revolt and leave. The next morning she has to wear a garbage bag and sandwich bags to school. This starts a new clothes fad. The old clothes find new owners. Cynthia winds up getting clothes from her friends and changes her slovenly habits.

Munsch, Robert. **Mud Puddle.** Illustrated by Sami Suomalainen. Annick Press, 1979.

Every time Jule Ann goes outside in her clean clothes, a mud puddle jumps on her and gets her dirty all over. Her mother washes her in the tub, but Jule Ann finally solves the problem by throwing a bar of soap at the pesky mud puddle.

Paterson, Diane. **Soap and Suds**. Knopf, 1984.

A woman scrubs her laundry clean with soap and suds and hangs it up to dry, but along comes a trail of a cat, birds, dog, goat, pig, horse, and boy to undo her work. Then—it rains. When she takes the laundry in, the animals and boy bring her a meal to repay her for the trouble.

Potter, Beatrix. **The Tale of Mrs. Tiggy-Winkle**. Warne, 1905.

When Little Lucy loses her pocket-handkin, she discovers it is being laundered by the fastidious Mrs. Tiggy-Winkle, a hedgehog washerwoman.

Potter, Beatrix. **The Tale of Peter Rabbit**. Warne, 1903.

This classic tale of the Flopsy Bunnies focuses on Peter, who loses his new jacket in Mr. McGregor's garden because he disobeyed his mother.

Pryor, Bonnie. **Amanda and April**. Illustrated by Diane deGroat. Morrow, 1986.

Amanda and April, little pigs, dressed up in their party clothes, are warned not to walk in mud puddles in their new shoes. But no one told them what to do about the newly tarred streets. The little pigs remember to take off their shoes, but ruin their new socks and nearly miss the party.

Rounds, Glen. **Washday on Noah's Ark**. Holiday House, 1985.

When the rain finally stops, Mrs. Noah does an enormous laundry, but finds Noah forgot to bring along the clothesline. She comes up with a resourceful idea that solves the problem, even if it is "the strangest clothesline the world had seen up to that time."

Schwartz, Alvin. "Mr. Brown Washes His Underwear" from **There Is a Carrot in My Ear and Other Noodle Tales**. Illustrated by Karen Ann Weinhaus. Harper & Row, 1982.

Mr. Brown washes his underwear and hangs it in the apple tree to dry. When the wind blows, it looks like a dancing ghost. Mrs. Brown tells him there's a man in the apple tree, so Mr. Brown goes out to scare him away. The man doesn't answer Mr. Brown when he calls, so Mr. Brown throws tomatoes at him. In the morning when Mr. Brown sees the tomato stains on his underwear, he declares he's lucky he wasn't wearing it.

Thurman, Judith. **Lost and Found**. Illustrated by Reina Rubie. Atheneum, 1978.

This fanciful verse explores the adventures of lost-and-found items, including clothing such as boots, mittens, hats, and buttons. The story suggests the playful idea of scarecrows wearing "scare-clothes."

Wolcott, Patty. **The Marvelous Mud Washing Machine**. Illustrated by Richard Brown. Addison-Wesley, 1974.

A young boy who plays joyfully in the mud climbs into an unusual washing machine that resembles a car wash, so he will be clean from head to toes.

Zion, Gene. **No Roses for Harry!** Illustrated by Margaret Bloy Graham. Harper & Row, 1958.

Harry, the white dog, receives a sweater with roses for his birthday from Grandma, but he doesn't like the roses. He decides to lose the sweater in various departments of a department store. When he finds a loose thread, he pulls it and a little bird flies away with the loose string until the entire sweater becomes a long, long piece of wool flying to the sky. Harry is overjoyed. But when Grandma writes she is coming to visit, everyone looks for the lost sweater. In the end they discover a bird has made a nest with Harry's sweater. For Christmas Harry gets a new sweater from Grandma—one that he likes, white with black spots.

Related Activities about It Will All Come Out in the Wash

Closets, Trunks, and Chests of Drawers
(To the tune of "Mulberry Bush")

Closets, trunks, and chests of drawers,
Chests of drawers, chests of drawers,
Closets, trunks, and chests of drawers,
That's where clothes are often stored.

Keep 'em neat and put 'em there,
Put 'em there, put 'em there,
Keep 'em neat and put 'em there,
So you'll find some clothes to wear!

The Magic Clothes Hamper
(A Flannel-board Story)

Tell this story with a flannel board and articles of clothing, a shape of a clothes hamper, a chest of drawers, a laundry basket, a washer, and a dryer. Move the clothes to the various places as the story indicates.

Billy and Bobby Jones always had a lot of dirty clothes. They played baseball and slid in the dirt. That got their clothes dirty. They made peanut butter and jelly sandwiches, and they often got jelly down the front of their shirts or peanut butter on the seat of their pants. They finger-painted on rainy days, and some of the paint always ended up on their clothes.

Mother told them to put their dirty clothes in the clothes hamper in the hall. And, because Billy and Bobby tried to be helpful boys, they put their clothes in the hamper. But, when Mrs. Jones asked them to take the dirty clothes out of the hamper and carry them to the laundry room, they usually had excuses.

"I can't reach way down in the hamper," said Billy. "I'm too short."

"I got my head stuck in the hamper last time I helped," said Bobby.

So Billy and Bobby did not take their dirty clothes out of the hamper. But the hamper always got empty. Billy and Bobby's drawers were soon full of clean clothes.

"You boys must think we have a magic clothes hamper," said Mrs. Jones one day.

That morning Billy got grape jelly on his dragon T-shirt. And that night Bobby got peanut butter on his dinosaur T-shirt. The next day Billy and Bobby both got dirty playing baseball. Their clothes were filthy. They remembered to put everything in the clothes hamper, but they did not remember to take out the clothes and carry them to the laundry room that night.

The next day Mrs. Jones got on a plane to visit her sister. She reminded Billy and Bobby to help Mr. Jones with the chores while she was gone.

Billy and Bobby made their beds and fixed their own breakfast. But when they went to find clean clothes in their drawers, the drawers were empty. The magic must have gone out of the magic clothes hamper! What were they going to do?

"Do you suppose we could call a clothes hamper repair person?" asked Billy.

"Maybe Dad knows what to do," suggested Bobby.

Well, Dad did know what to do. He sent Billy and Bobby upstairs and gave them a laundry basket and a chair to reach down in the clothes hamper. It was stuffed full! Then he marched the boys downstairs to the laundry room with the dirty clothes and helped them put the dirty clothes in the washing machine. When all the clothes were clean, Billy and Bobby helped Mr. Jones load the clothes in the dryer. Then, when the clothes were dry, Billy folded all the shirts, and Bobby folded all the jeans. And Mr. Jones matched up all the socks. And then everyone put the clothes away in the drawers.

When Mrs. Jones got home, she asked how everything had gone. Billy winked at Bobby, and Bobby winked at Billy.

"Are you boys playing a trick on me?" she asked.

"Just go upstairs," said Mr. Jones. "We did a little magic of our own while you were gone."

So Mrs. Jones went right upstairs to the clothes hamper because she had a good idea what had happened.

"Well, well!" she said, after seeing the empty hamper and the clean clothes in the bedroom drawers. "I guess that hamper must be magic after all."

"You just have to know the trick!" said Billy and Bobby.

And after that Billy and Bobby remembered the trick so the clothes hamper didn't have to do the magic all by itself.

The Very Old, Very Greedy Washing Machine

Everyone who has ever lost some clothing in the wash will identify with the plight of the lost clothes in this story. Prepare cardboard clothes for children to put in the washing machine as the washing machine gobbles up the various articles of clothing. Use a box with a cutout flap for the washing machine (attach a lunch bag to the inside of the box for the clothes to be gobbled up). Children who do not put clothes in the machine can do the actions of the other characters—fist shaking, foot stomping, etc.

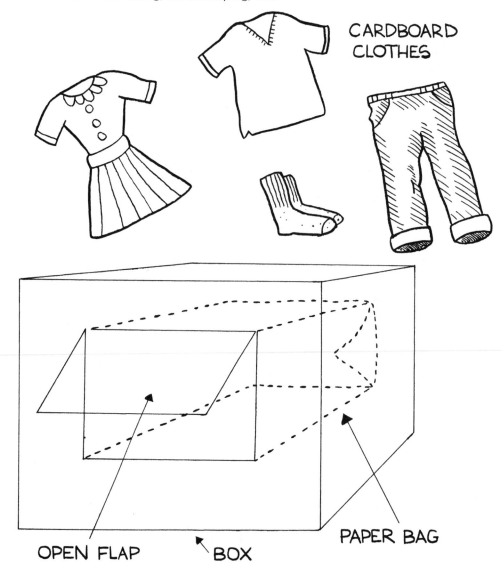

CARDBOARD CLOTHES

OPEN FLAP   BOX   PAPER BAG

Once there was a very old washing machine stuck in the back corner of a laundromat. People never put their clothes in the very old washing machine because there were so many bright, shiny washing machines in the front.

But one day Gertie Green came into the laundromat. She put her green dress in the very old washing machine. *(Child puts dress in machine.)* Now the washing machine was very hungry because it hadn't been used for such a long time. The very old, very greedy washing machine spun around and around. It gobbled up Gertie's green dress.

Gertie shook her fist at the machine. "Give me back my dress," she shouted. But the very old, very greedy washing machine just spun around and around.

The next day Rosy Redfield came into the laundromat. She put her favorite red T-shirt in the very old washing machine. *(Child puts shirt in machine.)* Oh, the washing machine was so happy to get the T-shirt that it spun around and around and it gobbled it up!

Rosy stomped her foot at the very old, very greedy washing machine. "Give me back my shirt," cried Rosy. But the washing machine just spun around and around.

The next day Bobby Brown came into the laundromat and put two brown socks in the very old washing machine. *(Child puts socks in machine.)* Now the machine was overjoyed to get two whole socks. It spun around and around and it gobbled them both up.

Bobby shook his fist and stomped his foot. "Give me back my socks!" he yelled. But the very old, very greedy washing machine just spun around and around.

The next day Ben Blue came into the laundromat and put his blue jeans into the very old washing machine. *(Child puts blue jeans in machine.)* Well, the washing machine was getting stuffed after swallowing up Gertie's dress and Rosy's T-shirt and Bobby's socks, but it spun around and around and it gobbled up Ben's blue jeans, too!

Ben was so mad that he shook his fist and stomped his foot and hopped up and down. "Give me back my jeans, you old washing machine!" he shouted. But the very old, very greedy washing machine just spun around and around.

Just then a little dog ran into the laundromat. *(Give dog cutout to child and guide him or her around machine.)* The little dog ran around and around the very old, very greedy washing machine. It ran around and around so fast that it got caught in the cord. And the plug came out—POP! The washing machine stopped—CHUNK-A! The washing machine burped—BURRRP!

And out came Ben's blue jeans. *(Hand jeans to child.)*
And out came Bobby's brown socks. *(Hand socks to child.)*
And out came Rosy's red T-shirt. *(Hand shirt to child.)*
And out came Gertie's green dress. *(Hand dress to child.)*

Everyone was glad to get their clothes back, but they were still so angry that they all put a big sign on the very old, very greedy washing machine. *(Put sign on machine.)* And that sign read "Out of Order."

So if you see a sign like this *(point to sign)* on a washing machine, don't ever put your clothes inside because they just might be gobbled up by the very old, very greedy washing machine.

Soap and Suds

(To the tune of "Mulberry Bush")

Soap and suds to wash our jeans.
That's the way to get 'em clean.
Drop 'em in a laundry tub.
Rub-a-dub-a-dub-a-dub!

Oops! Some soap got on the floor.
Scoop it up and out the door.
Doing wash can be so fun—
But I'll be glad when we're all done.

Hang them on the old clothes line,
When the sun comes out to shine.
They'll get dry unless it rains.
Take 'em in and try again.

Wring 'em out, don't let 'em drip
On the floor or you will slip.
Now they're dry so fold 'em flat.
Next time try the laundromat!

The Washing Machine

(To the tune of "I'm a Little Tea Pot")

I'm a little washer
  (Point to self.)
For your clothes.
  (Point to someone else.)
Punch my button,
  (Punch belly button.)
Here it goes.
  (Move upper body from side to side.)

I can agitate
  (Continue moving side to side like an agitator throughout last four lines.)
Around and 'round.
I'm a washday
Merry-go-round.

The Dryer

(To the tune of "I'm a Little Tea Pot")

I'm a little dryer.
  (Point to self.)
'Round and 'round
  (Roll hand over hand these three lines.)
Go your clothes
Without a sound.

Open up the door
  (Open imaginary door with one hand.)
And you will see
  (Peek in.)
All your nice dry
  (Spread arms wide.)
Laundry!

Clothesline Action Rhyme

I am fine.
I'm a clothesline.
  (Point to self.)
I like to be dressed
  (Arms out at sides like a clothesline.)
With shirts and with vests,
With socks and blue jeans,
Just after they're clean.
When the wind comes,
  (Blow.)

Then I have fun!
I swing and I sway—
  (Swing arms back and forth.)
That's my kind of play!
But don't load me down
  (Let arms sag.)
Or I'll fall to the ground!
  (Collapse arms and whole body to floor.)

Monkey Business

(A Story with Props)

To tell this story, prepare color-coded boxes for the various animals and their clothing: a red box with a picture of Ms. Hippo and a red dress to tuck inside; green for Ms. Ostrich; purple for Ms. Goat; and orange for Ms. Mouse. When Monkey mixes up the clothes, remove the correct dresses and mix as the story directs.

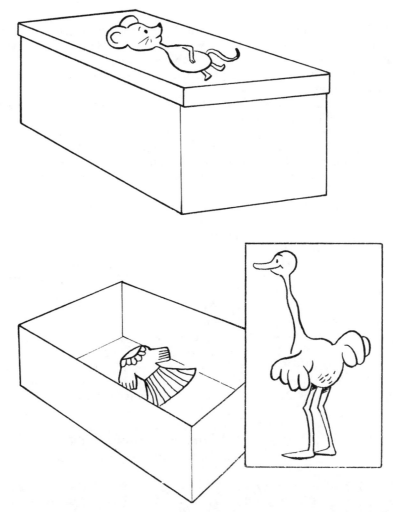

Mr. Walrus had a dry cleaning store that was doing very well. It was doing so well, in fact, that Mr. Walrus was busy day and night with the cleaning and pressing and delivering. So he decided to hire Monkey to deliver the clean clothes.

One reason Mr. Walrus was so busy was that everyone was invited to the Lion's Party. All the ladies wanted their best dresses cleaned and delivered.

When Ms. Hippo brought her red dress in, she said to Mr. Walrus, "Now be sure to get this very, very clean and deliver it on time."

When Ms. Ostrich brought her green dress in, she said to Mr. Walrus, "Now be sure to get this very, very clean and deliver it on time."

When Ms. Goat brought her purple dress in, she said to Mr. Walrus, "Now be sure to get this very, very clean and deliver it on time."

When Ms. Mouse brought her orange dress in, she said to Mr. Walrus, "Now be sure to get this very, very clean and deliver it on time."

Now Monkey knew all these women wanted to look their best, but he still thought it would be fun to do a little monkey business.

So the day of the party, Mr. Walrus finished cleaning all the dresses. He wrapped them all carefully and gave them to Monkey to deliver.

"Now, remember," said Mr. Walrus. "Red dress to Ms. Hippo, green dress to Ms. Ostrich, purple dress to Ms. Goat, and orange dress to Ms. Mouse. You can't go to the party until they are all delivered."

So Monkey delivered the red dress to Ms. Ostrich, the green dress to Ms. Goat, the purple dress to Ms. Mouse, and the orange dress to Ms. Hippo. He just returned to the dry cleaning store when he heard Mr. Walrus on the phone.

"Oh, I am so sorry, Ms. Hippo. Yes, it sounds like monkey business to me. I'll take care of it right away."

Mr. Walrus hung up and said to Monkey, "Deliver those dresses again! You can't go to the party until they are all delivered."

So this time Monkey delivered the red dress to Ms. Goat, the green dress to Ms. Mouse, the purple dress to Ms. Hippo, and the orange dress to Ms. Ostrich. He just returned to the dry cleaning store, when he heard Mr. Walrus on the phone.

"Oh, I am so sorry, Ms. Ostrich. Yes, it sounds like monkey business to me. I'll take care of it right away."

Mr. Walrus hung up and said to Monkey, "Deliver those dresses again! You can't go to the party until they are all delivered."

So this time Monkey delivered the red dress to Ms. Mouse, the green dress to Ms. Hippo, the purple dress to Ms. Ostrich, and the orange dress to Ms. Goat. He just returned to the dry cleaning store when he heard Mr. Walrus on the phone.

"Oh, I am so sorry, Ms. Goat. Yes, it sounds like monkey business to me. I'll take care of it right away."

Mr. Walrus hung up and said to Monkey, "Deliver those dresses again! You can't go to the party until they are all delivered."

So this time delivered the red dress to Ms. Hippo, the green dress to Ms. Ostrich, the purple dress to Ms. Goat, and the orange dress to Ms. Mouse. All the women put on their dresses and left for the party. When Monkey got back to the dry cleaners, he found a note from Mr. Walrus. It read, "See you at the party!" But Monkey was so tired that he lay down and went to sleep. After all, monkey business is hard work!

Lost and Found Song

(To the tune of "Skip to My Lou")

Lost my mittens, what'll I do,
Lost my mittens, what'll I do,
Lost my mittens, what'll I do?
Check the lost-and-found box.

Lost my heavy winter coat,
Lost my heavy winter coat,
Lost my heavy winter coat.
Check the lost-and-found box.

Lost my boots and bumbershoot,
Lost my boots and bumbershoot,
Lost my boots and bumbershoot.
Check the lost-and-found box.

Found my mittens, found my coat,
Found my boots and bumbershoot.
Daddy will be very glad—
I came home with all I had!

Lost and Found

(A Story with Props)

To tell this story, cut head and arm holes in a box. (You will wear the box when the lost-and-found box goes walking.) Tape a paper bag to the outside of the box to hold the articles of clothing—paper cutouts of sunglasses, sweater, mittens, snowpants, and boots. Give these clothes to children as the lost-and-found box does in the story.

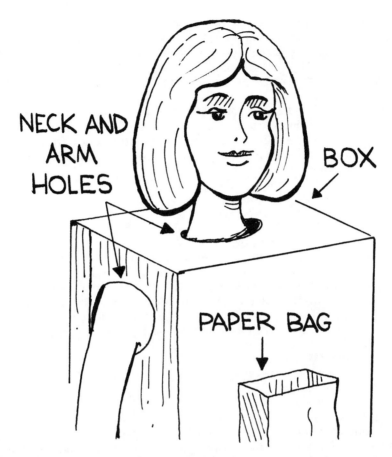

NECK AND ARM HOLES

BOX

PAPER BAG

There was once a lost-and-found box in the corner of a public library. For many months the box was empty. Nobody lost anything, so none of the librarians who worked in the library put anything in the box. Then one day a little girl took off her sunglasses in the library, and she left them on the table in the picture book section. That night the librarian found the sunglasses and put them in the lost-and-found box. But the little girl didn't come back to find her sunglasses.

Many days later when it was cool, a little boy wore a sweater to the library. He got warm in the library when he was listening to records, so he took off his sweater. And he left it draped over a chair. That night the librarian found the sweater and put it in the lost-and-found box. But the little boy didn't come back to the library to find his sweater.

The next day a little girl came into the library with bright red mittens on her hands because it was very cold outside. She thought she had tucked the mittens in the pockets of her coat, but somehow they fell out on the floor near a big pile of puppets and got lost. That night the librarian picked up the puppets and found the mittens. She put them in the lost-and-found box. And even though it was much colder the next day, the little girl didn't come back for the mittens.

One day it snowed and the boys and girls who came into the library were all bundled up in scarves and mittens and coats and snowpants. A big group of preschool children came with their teacher to hear stories. They took off their scarves and mittens and coats and snowpants. And the teacher told them to hang everything up on the hooks in the hall. But when the class left, somebody forgot a pair of snowpants. When the librarian straightened up the library at the end of the day, she found the snowpants on the hook. She took the snowpants and put them in the lost-and-found box. And even though it snowed for days and days, nobody came back to find the snowpants.

Finally one day the days got warmer and the snow began to melt. The ground was wet with slushy snow so children wore boots into the library. A little girl left her boots in the outside hall along with her umbrella. But she hated her boots so much that she just wore her sneakers home. The boots stood in the hall of the library so the librarian put them in the lost-and-found box that night. And, of course, the little girl who hated her boots didn't come back to get them.

That night the lost-and-found box was tired of having all those lost clothes left in him. He was tired of being a lost box, so he decided to leave the library and find the children who belonged to the lost clothes. The lost-and-found box got all dressed up in the sunglasses, sweater, mittens, snowpants, and boots and went walking up the stairs.

Children, children!
Where, oh where,
Where are the children
These clothes
Wear?

called the lost-and-found box.

The box walked out of the library and down the street looking for boys and girls to wear the clothes. But it was nighttime and all the boys and girls were home in bed.

The lost-and-found box walked up a hill and down a street 'til it came to the house of a little girl who was fast asleep in her bed. The box looked in on her and decided she needed a pair of sunglasses, so it left the sunglasses on her window sill.

But it still had a lot of other clothes to give away. The box went to the next house.

Children, children!
Where, oh where,
Where are the children
These clothes
Wear?

called the lost-and-found box.

Nobody answered the box because it was still night, so the box put the sweater in the mailbox at that house. I'm feeling so much better, said the box, that it hopped down the street to another house, and dropped the bright red mittens in another mailbox.

Where am I going to put these snowpants, thought the lost-and-found box. They're much too big to stuff in a mailbox. Then the box saw a clothesline in someone's backyard. So it took off the snowpants and tossed them over the line.

Now the lost-and-found box was feeling ever so much better. The only lost clothes left were the boots.

And do you know what? The lost-and-found box marched down the street in the boots until it came to the house of the little girl who had left the boots in the library in the first place. The box knew her house all right, because outside on the doorstep were two very dirty sneakers. Those sneakers were dirty because they had not been covered up with boots. So the lost-and-found box left the boots on the doorstep next to the dirty sneakers.

By this time it was morning and it was time for the library to open. So the lost-and-found box hopped back to the library (it was hard to walk since it didn't have boots anymore). But the box hopped happily back to the library because it was so glad to be empty again. But it was especially happy to find children for all the lost clothes to wear again.

GAMES FOR SHOPPING BAGS AND LAUNDRY TAGS

Department Store

Play department store in your classroom or library and make murals that can be displayed. Tape large sheets of white paper to different walls of the room and write the names of articles of clothing on them. Children cut out and paste pictures from catalogs in the appropriate "department."

The Needle Needs a Thread

This game will teach cooperation. As each child is added to the growing thread, children must work together so the thread won't break. The first child (or the leader) holds out arms in front of him with palms touching to form the eye of the needle. As he reaches another child, he separates his palms and encircles the waist of that child with his arms. The second child then becomes the needle, taking the first one behind him to another child. The line of children becomes a long piece of thread with each new child, in turn, becoming the needle.

Sing these words to the tune of "The Farmer in the Dell":
        The needle needs a thread.
        The needle needs a thread.
        This is how we sew our clothes:
        With needle and a thread.

When the last child becomes the needle, change to these words:
        The needle's got the thread.
        The needle's got the thread.
        Watch the way we sew our clothes
        With needle and a thread.

Now the needle and thread weave in and out and around the room trying to move together. If anyone falls down, the children must help the broken thread pick up so the full length of thread can move along successfully together.

Pick Up the Clothes

This pick-up game is a kind of treasure hunt with children working in teams. Give each team a laundry basket to gather clothes. Ahead of time hide various articles of clothing around the room, socks, T-shirts, mittens, etc. At a given signal, children scramble around to find the strewn clothes. On the word "Stop," children are seated and asked to then count the articles of clothing in the baskets. Little prizes may be tucked in socks for all children to share.

Dirty Shirt Game

You may wish to have this messy fun outside! Draw a shirt on a large piece of paper or hang an old shirt on a waterproof surface. Using ketchup and mustard in squirt bottles, let kids come up relay-fashion and squirt the shirt one at a time. You can also provide several shirts for team competition. Dirtiest shirt wins!

Laundry Relay Race

This game may get a little messy, so you may want to do it outside or on a floor that can be wiped up. Divide children into two teams in lines. Give each team a laundry basket of doll clothes, a bucket of water, and a clothesline with clothes pins.

At the signal "Wash those clothes!" the first child in each line washes the first article of clothing, squeezes out the water, and passes it down the line. The last child in each line runs up to the clothesline and hangs up the clothing. Then the second child washes the next article of clothing, passes it back to the last child, who hangs it up on the line. Play continues until all the laundry is done.

How Many Bubbles in the Laundry Tub?

This little laundry day frolic will get the wiggles out and give children practice in counting.

Begin with children seated in a circle. (The circle is the laundry.) Tell children that you are making bubbles. As they are tapped, they may "bubble up" by jumping to their feet. Use this little chant for making bubbles:

Rub a dub dub,
Scrub a dub dub—
Count the bubbles
In my laundry tub!
1-2-3-4-5
    (and so on until all children have
    "bubbled up" and are standing)

Bubbles,
Bubbles,
Hop, hop, hop.
    (Children all hop.)
Bubbles,
Bubbles,
Pop! Pop! Pop!
    (Clap three times and all sit down.)

Sock Match

Bring a laundry basket and as many pairs of clean unmatched socks as there are children in your group. Give each child one sock. Then pull socks from the basket and let the children figure out who has the mate. For younger children choose socks of greatly different color and size. Older children will like the challenge of more similar socks and perhaps a relay race to the basket to match the sock they have.

Hand-Me-Down Game

Fill a box with old clothes—shirts, big pants, coats, sweaters, capes—that children can slip on easily over their own clothes. Seat the children in a circle and sing the following song (to the tune of "Mary Had a Little Lamb") as you pass around the various articles of clothing. When each verse ends, the child holding that article of clothing says his or her name and puts the clothing on.

    Here's a shirt—
    Let's hand it down,
    Hand it down,
    Hand it down.
    Here's a shirt—
    Let's hand it down.
    Tell me, what's your name?

Proceed with other clothes, such as:
    Here's a coat ...
    Here's a cape ...
    Here's a sweater ...
    Here are pants ...

CRAFTS FOR SHOPPING BAGS AND LAUNDRY TAGS

Scrap Bag for Glad Rags

Children are always fascinated by fabric scraps and can find dozens of uses for odd bits of material. Encourage children's creativity by supplying them with an assortment of scraps and having them make a decorated bag to keep their treasures. Simply give each child a large brown bag and an assortment of scraps to glue on the outside. Write the words "Scrap Bag for Glad Rags" on the front of the bag. A yarn handle may be added if you wish.

Simple Loom

After you have read *Pelle's New Suit, Charlie Needs a Cloak,* or *The Goat in the Rug,* children will want to try a little weaving of their own. It's not necessary to have a ready-made loom. You can make simple looms for each child by making notches in a shoebox lid. Help children wind fat yarn around the length of the lid and tie off the end of yarn. The lengthwise yard is the warp. Weave another long piece of yarn (called the weft) in and out of the warp. The weft yarn may be wound around a little cardboard shuttle if you wish. When children complete their weaving, simply baste the last and first rows of weaving to secure them. Carefully cut the weaving off the lid-cut, leaving the unwoven warp as fringe, and use the woven strip for a doll-sized scarf.

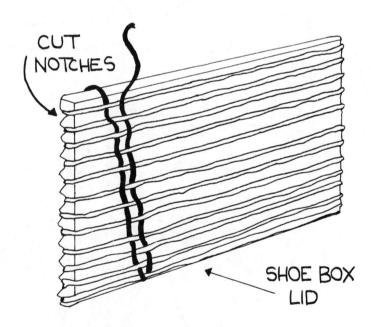

Sew Simple!

Sewing projects help young children practice small motor skills, but sharp needles and thin thread may be frustrating for very young children. Before you try needlecraft projects of this kind, supply children with cardboard sewing projects. You can draw a design on the cardboard and punch holes in the cardboard. Provide children with bright-colored yarn or shoestrings to sew the cardboard. The design may be geometric shapes, or an outline of a shirt or jacket. You might also provide large buttons or cardboard buttons to add to the picture.

Make a Jacket for Peter Rabbit

In the famous tale by Beatrix Potter, Peter Rabbit loses his jacket in Mr. McGregor's garden. Take care of Peter by making him a new jacket with this craft. Give children a drawing of a jacket for them to color and decorate for Peter, or give them a drawing of a jacket with outlines of carrots to color. (See illustration.) You could also supply children with a drawing of Peter so the jacket could be a paper doll craft, too.

Safe Needles

To make "safe needles" for any sewing activity, use wrapped wire from a florist. Bend a piece of the wire and twist the ends together. To use, pass the yarn or string through the loop in the wire and push it through macaroni, beads, or in and out of posterboard with holes punched in it.

Spool Sheep

Use a thread spool as the base for a sheep figure covered with cotton balls. Place three pipe cleaners through the hole in the spool. Bend the ends of two pipe cleaners down for the feet, and the ends of the third up to form the head and tail. Children can glue cotton balls on the spool for wool and put a cotton ball on the head and tail. Bend the ends of the feet so the sheep can stand up.

Garbage Bag Coverups

Use a large kitchen trash bag. Cut a strip off the open end. Cut a *V* in the closed end to slip over the head. Slip the bag on and tie at the waist with the cutoff strip. This coverup is especially good for painting and water play.

Something New under the Sun Shirt

Recycle old cotton T-shirts with a colorful sunburst design. Have on hand three different colors of powdered dye, mixed according to package instructions. Dye entire shirt in the lightest color. Now tie a string around a section of the shirt and dip this section into the medium-colored dye for a few minutes. Tie string around last section of shirt and dip into the darkest-color dye for a few minutes. Rinse with cold water between each dye bath. Untie strings and open your sunburst.

Clothespin Charlie

On one side of the top of a push clothespin, draw two dots for eyes. Help children glue on a pom pom for a hat. Attach yarn below the head and children can wrap the yarn around the figure to form clothes. Younger children will be able to wind as far as the opening. Older children will enjoy changing colors at the opening to make fancy pants on Charlie. Tie a contrasting piece of yarn on the neck for a scarf, fraying the ends.

COTTON BALL

COLORED YARN

Beautiful Bubble Painting

Add a few drops of food coloring to a bowl of liquid soap and water. Provide children with drinking straws to blow a bowlful of bubbles. (Caution children not to suck in. Use your own judgment as to the use of this activity with very young children, as they may drink the soapy water.) As bubbles begin to spill over the top of the bowl, place an absorbent paper towel on top of the bowl to pop the bubbles. The popping bubbles create designs on the towels.

DISPLAYS FOR SHOPPING BAGS AND LAUNDRY TAGS

From Sheep to Shirt

Assemble objects that tell the story of how clothes are made from sheep shearing to the finished product. You might use a sheepskin, a spinning wheel, or spindle borrowed from local spinners, a variety of looms, and handwoven material. Since spinning and weaving have become popular crafts, you should be able to find different objects from local craftspeople. You can even turn this display into a "living display" by inviting the craftspeople to demonstrate their skills for children. This would be a wonderful program to have outside and invite the entire family!

Blue Jeans Book Bag

Make cutoffs out of old blue jeans and sew the legs closed. Use this bag to display books on recycled clothing or to carry the books for the day's program.

Recycled Laundry Bags

Sew the sleeves closed on a shirt or sweater, the top of the legs on pants, or the bottom opening of a jacket to form recycled laundry bags and demonstrate good use of old clothes.

This Is the Way We Wash Our Clothes

For many young children washing clothes means putting them in an automatic washing machine. Assemble laundry aids to inform children about the way clothes were washed during earlier times. Old washboards and laundry tubs, different kinds of clothespins, and maybe even an old wringer-type washing machine (if you can find one!) would be good selections. You could also display antique irons.

3
Umbrellas, Boots, and Swimming Suits

INTRODUCTION

If children live in a part of the world where the weather is consistent year-round, the idea of seasonal clothing may be new to them. But as many children do experience seasonal changes of weather, we have organized the materials in this chapter around the following subthemes: "All Seasons and In Between"; "Pitter, Patter, Splish, Splash"; "Suits to Swim and Sun"; and "Bundle Up." You may wish to use these subthemes throughout the year as the weather changes.

We have used a broad interpretation of "clothes" in this chapter to include weather-related paraphernalia, such as umbrellas and sand covering the skin. Numerous picture books and the story "For Rain or for Shine" take us beyond the strict weather-related use of the umbrella. "Samuel Strand" becomes a sand monster by wearing sand on his skin, and Harry in *Harry by the Sea* sports a covering of seaweed.

Selecting and wearing appropriate clothes for the weather can be a nuisance. Young children will identify with the young rabbit in *Thumpity Thump Gets Dressed* and Mrs. O'Hanna in "March Weather," both of whom dress and undress many times during the day because the weather changes.

Winter weather adds other frustrations: bundling up, getting everything on in the right order, keeping jackets and boots fastened, and not losing something. Such problems are faced by Lewis in *Oh, Lewis*, Tommy in *Tommy Goes Out*, and the twins in *Too Many Mittens*. We have added activities and stories to extend these themes, including "New Red Mitten" and "My Brand New Snowsuit."

On the other hand, many children eagerly anticipate wearing those items of clothing set aside for rain, snow, or sun. The classic story *Umbrella* and the newer picture book *A Walk in the Rain* illustrate this enthusiasm. And there's a joy in shedding layers and layers of clothing for summer fun, which the poems "Summertime Clothes" and "Summer's Coming" celebrate.

Skills taught by the stories and activities in this chapter include sequencing and classification. Seasonal changes provide natural sequencing. Matching the clothes to the weather aids in classification and identification. Verbal skills are expanded when children learn different words for the same articles of clothing (for example, boots, galoshes, and overshoes).

INITIATING ACTIVITY

Clothes the Year-Round

Say the poem through once. Repeat only the last two lines as you point to a child to give his name. Then help the group clap out the syllables of the name. For example: Jennifer is three claps.

Clothes in Winter,
Summer, Fall,
Spring, or any
Time at all.

Puddle jumpers
Put on boots.
Winter funsters
Wear snowsuits.

Pull on mittens,
Stocking cap.
Say your name and
Let's all clap!

LITERATURE-SHARING EXPERIENCES

Books about All Seasons and In Between

Allen, Marie Louise. **A Pocketful of Poems**. Illustrated by Sheila Greenwold. Harper & Brothers, 1957.

Poems about mittens, zippered snowsuits, rubber galoshes, and winter-wear suit a young child's seasonal changes of clothes and feelings about dressing appropriately.

Fisher, Aileen. **Runny Days, Sunny Days**. Abelard Schuman, 1958.

Poems about clothes for all four seasons include a wide variety of choices, from going barefoot in the spring to ducks wearing snowshoes in the winter.

James, Diane. **My Clothes**. Rourke, 1981.

A young child illustrates the steps in getting dressed and undressed, and in choosing the appropriate kinds of apparel for rainy, cold, and sunny summer weather.

Kuskin, Karla. **Sand and Snow**. Harper & Row, 1965.

Annabella Peach delights in summer fun while Joseph T. Tempestossed prefers winter in this book in verse. Apparel includes jaunty sun hats and suits, mittens, and layers of clothing to enjoy each season.

La Fontaine, Jean. **The North Wind and the Sun**. Illustrated by Brian Wildsmith. Franklin Watts, 1964.

Wildsmith's brilliantly colored illustrations vividly retell this familiar old fable of the contest between the sun and the wind in trying to see which can make a man take off his cloak.

Surprises. Selected by Lee Bennett Hopkins. Illustrated by Megan Lloyd. Harper & Row, 1984.

A collection of easy-to-read poems includes several weather-related rhymes in the section "Rain, Sun, and Snow" (pp. 44-52). Examples are "Sudden Storm"—umbrellas grow "like flowers ... when it showers"; "In August"—"We don't wear much in the way of clothes/And squirt ourselves with a garden hose."

Szekeres, Cindy. **Thumpity Thump Gets Dressed**. Golden Press, 1984.

A young rabbit must get dressed and undressed many times during the day because of changes in the weather. He's glad to go to bed where, in his dreams, he can wear anything he likes.

Ziefert, Harriet. **Bear Gets Dressed**. Illustrated by Arnold Lobel. Harper & Row, 1986.

Foldout picture pages and text ask a young child to choose the appropriate clothing for Bear to wear on chilly, rainy, snowy, sunshiny, and windy days.

Related Activities about All Seasons and In Between

Reasons and Seasons for Clothes

(An Action Verse)

Older children may suggest articles of clothing and the weather in which to wear them to create new verses.

I have a hat I like to wear
   (Touch head.)
When it's cool outside.
I wear my hat upon my head
   (Touch head.)
When it's cool outside.

With a hat on my head,
   (Touch head.)
For the wind that blows,
   (Wave arms at sides.)
And the snow that snows,
   (Flutter fingers.)
And the sun that shines outside.
   (Touch fingers over head.)

I have some boots I like to wear
   (Point to feet.)
When it's wet outside.
I wear my boots upon my feet
   (Point to feet.)
When it's wet outside.

With boots on my feet,
   (Point to feet.)
And a hat on my head,
   (Touch head.)
For the wind that blows,
   (Wave arms at sides.)
And the snow that snows,
   (Flutter fingers.)
And the sun that shines outside.
   (Touch fingers over head.)

I have sunglasses I can wear
   (Circle eyes with fingers.)
When it's bright outside.
I wear sunglass on my eyes
When it's bright outside.

Glasses on my eyes,
   (Circle eyes with fingers.)
And boots on my feet,
   (Point to feet.)
And hat on my head,
   (Touch head.)
For the wind that blows,
   (Wave arms at sides.)
And the snow that snows,
   (Flutter fingers.)
And the sun that shines outside.
   (Touch fingers over head.)

Drizzle, Brrrr, Whoosh, and Shine

(To the tune of "Good-Night Ladies")

Drip and drizzle,
   (Wiggle fingers by shoulders for rain.)
Drip and drizzle,
Drip and drizzle,
I'll put on my boots.
   (Bend over to touch shoes.)

Brrrr! It's freezing,
   (Hug self and shiver.)
Brrrr! It's freezing,
Brrrr! It's freezing.
I'll zip up my coat.
   (Run thumb from belt to chin.)

Whoosh! Wind blowing,
   (Wave arms over head.)
Whoosh! Wind blowing,
Whoosh! Wind blowing.
I'll put on my hat.
   (Hands to head.)

Sun is shining,
   (Touch fingertips over head.)
Sun is shining,
Sun is shining.
Go outside and play.
   (Run in place.)
Hey!
   (Jump.)

March Weather

This story can be told showing the articles of clothing for each type of weather as you mention them. It would be fun to get them out of a bag or box as Mrs. O'Hanna searches her closet.

You can also do the story on the flannel board with a simple female figure in a dress and all the articles mentioned. Place and remove them as Mrs. O'Hanna changes her mind.

The weather in March is very funny! At least that is what Mrs. O'Hanna says, and she should know. This is the story of how she knows.

One morning last March, Mrs. O'Hanna woke up knowing it was a very special day, and she should put on something very special. Now what was that special day? Mrs. O'Hanna couldn't quite remember, but she knew she should wear something special.

So Mrs. O'Hanna looked out the window to see if she could remember the special day. The sky was light gray, and it was snowing. "That must be it!" said Mrs. O'Hanna. "It is a special snowy day. I need to wear my warm jacket and my boots." Well, Mrs. O'Hanna looked through her closet for her warm jacket and her boots. Then she put them on. "Now," she said, "I am ready for this special snowy day!"

But when Mrs. O'Hanna looked out the window again, the sky was darker gray and it was raining. "I was wrong," said Mrs. O'Hanna. "It is not a special snowy day. It is a special rainy day. I will need my raincoat and my umbrella." So Mrs. O'Hanna put away her warm jacket and her boots. Then she looked through her closet for her raincoat and her umbrella. She put them on. "Now," said Mrs. O'Hanna, "I am ready for this special rainy day."

But when Mrs. O'Hanna looked out the window again, the sky was not so gray and the wind was blowing. "I was wrong," said Mrs. O'Hanna. "It is not a special rainy day. It is a special windy day. I will need my heavy sweater and my scarf." So Mrs. O'Hanna put away her raincoat and her umbrella. Then she looked through her closet for her heavy sweater and her scarf. She put them on. "Now," said Mrs. O'Hanna, "I am ready for this special windy day."

But when Mrs. O'Hanna looked out the window again, the sky was light and the sun was shining. "I was wrong," said Mrs. O'Hanna. "It is not a special windy day. It is a special sunny day. I will need my sunglasses and my funny hat." So Mrs. O'Hanna put away her heavy sweater and her scarf. Then she looked through her closet for her sunglasses and funny hat. She put them on. "Now," said Mrs. O'Hanna, "I am ready for this special sunny day."

Mrs. O'Hanna went to the front door and opened it wide. The air was warm and the sun was shining bright. "That must be it," said Mrs. O'Hanna. "It is a special sunny day."

"That it is!" said the voice of her good friend, Mrs. Shannagan. "And are you forgetting that this very special day is St. Patrick's Day? Put on your new green dress, and let's go to the big parade!"

Then Mrs. O'Hanna remembered. She was supposed to wear her special new green dress. As quick as a leprechaun, Mrs. O'Hanna took off her sunglasses and funny hat and put on her new green dress. They made it to the St. Patrick's Day Parade just in time.

The weather in March is very funny. Just ask Mrs. O'Hanna. She knows!

Books about Pitter, Patter, Splish, Splash

Blance, Ellen, and Ann Cook. **Monster and the Magic Umbrella.** Illustrated by Quentin Blake. Bowmar, 1973.

Monster's umbrella keeps the sun off his face and as the day gets hotter, the umbrella grows until it's big enough to turn upside down and catch the rain. Monster and all the children use it for a giant swimming pool.

Bright, Robert. **My Red Umbrella**. Morrow, 1959.

A little girl finds her red umbrella grows big enough to cover a dog, two kittens, three chickens, four rabbits, a woolly lamb, two goats, three pigs, four foxes, and a big wet bear. They all sing until the rain stops, each crawls out, and goes home.

Demi. **The Leaky Umbrella**. Prentice-Hall, 1980.

Once upon a time in Japan, a man named Wako, who likes to daydream, goes out for a walk. He borrows an umbrella, as it starts to rain, but by mistake he takes a broom. He offers to share it with a friend, but wonders why they end up wet.

Feczko, Kathy. **Umbrella Parade**. Illustrated by Deborah Colvin Borgo. Troll Associates, 1985.

A kitten, dog, bunny, pig, and even a duck go walking int he rain with their umbrellas, each one a different color.

Friedrich, Priscilla, and Otto Friedrich. **The April Umbrella**. Illustrated by Roger Duvoisin. Lothrop, Lee and Shepard, 1963.

On a rainy April morning, Nicholas finds an old green umbrella in his attic and wishes for a dog. When a little black dog appears and tells Nicholas the umbrella is a magic wishing umbrella, Nicholas wishes for a million dollars, piles of candy, and so many toys he trips over them all. He wishes it all away, except for the dog. The umbrella drifts on to the house of another little boy, waiting for another April and another wish to be made.

Hurd, Edith Thacher. **Johnny Lion's Rubber Boots.** Illustrated by Clement Hurd. Harper & Row, 1972.

Johnny Lion cannot go out to play in the rain because he doesn't have boots. To amuse himself he plays with blocks, draws wild animals, and sings songs. At last Father Lion brings him red rubber boots so he can go out to play.

Kessler, Ethel, and Leonard Kessler. **Splish Splash!** Parents, 1973.

Signs of spring and the approach of summer are shown as the snow melts, seeds sprout, and robins build nests. Appropriate changes in clothing show what is "no more"—earmuffs, big boots, furry hats, snowsuits, heavy scarves, warm mittens—and what comes next—slickers, barefeet, swimsuits. Not a clothing book so much as a change of seasons book. The clothing changes are clearly pictured.

Pinkwater, Daniel. **Roger's Umbrella**. Illustrated by James Marshall. Dutton, 1982.

Roger doesn't like the ways his umbrella behaves—it turns itself inside out, catches a gust of wind and makes him tiptoe, then lifts him off the ground, and at night it pops open and flaps around like a bat. So Roger has to stick it in the closet. Roger asks for a new umbrella, but his mother won't listen. The umbrella continues to misbehave. Finally, three old ladies teach Roger how to talk to umbrellas. And it listens. After that Roger is in perfect control.

Rand, Ann, and Jerome Snyder. **Umbrellas, Hats and Wheels**. Harcourt, Brace and World, 1961.

A catalog of the many unique differences in the world includes umbrellas that are plain, striped like candy, flat like Chinese hats, and those carried by a jungle prince. Hats include English ones, Uncle Sam's top hat, and a maharajah's turban. All these differences make the world more fun.

Scheffler, Ursel. **A Walk in the Rain**. Illustrated by Ulises Wensell. Translated by Andrea Mernan. Putnam, 1986.

Josh loves to walk in the rain with his grandmother. She gives him a bright yellow raincoat and matching hat, and his grandfather gives him shiny rubber boots. In his new rainwear, Josh and his grandmother explore the wonders of nature on their rainy day walk.

Yashimo, Taro. **Umbrella**. Viking, 1958.

Momo, a Japanese-American little girl, receives red boots and an umbrella for her third birthday, but she has to wait many, many days for rain. The sound of the rain on her umbrella and the girl's independence in walking by herself will be remembered for a long time.

Related Activities about Pitter, Patter, Splish, Splash

Rain Gear
(A Fingerplay)

You'll want to tell the children in advance that a bumbershoot is another word for umbrella. They will have great fun saying it!

It's raining outside.
(*Wiggle fingers near shoulders.*)
So I'll pull on my boots.
(*Point to feet.*)
I'll zip up my coat.
(*Run thumb from waist to chin.*)
Open my bumbershoot!
(*Place palms together overhead, separate hands so just fingertips are touching to form umbrella.*)

I'll splash in the puddles,
(*Tap ground beside you or march in place.*)
And have lots of fun,
(*Clap hands or jump.*)
And I'll be wearing
(*Point to self.*)
A smile like the sun.
(*Point to happy smile.*)

Frog Fog
(A Flannel-board Story)

For this story you will use flannel-board pieces of a frog, school bus, yellow car, yellow motorcycle, and man in yellow slicker. Put them on the board and move the frog as indicated in the story. You may wish to indicate the road by stretching two pieces of yarn the length of the flannel board.

In early spring the sun begins to warm the earth. Sometimes when it is cool at night and warm in the day, in the morning we see a low cloud all around us. We call that fog. Cars drive more slowly in the fog because drivers cannot see where they are going. This story is about Frog and his adventures in the fog.

In spring, Frog and his friends gathered at the pond at the first light of morning. They sang and sang in the croaky way frogs have, until the sun came up. The frogs were silly, but they thought that their singing made the sun come up. Of course, the sun would have come up without them, but the frogs did not know that.

One morning in early spring, Frog opened one big gold eye. Then he opened the other big gold eye. Then he blinked and opened them again. Frog didn't see the first light of morning. He couldn't see anything but fog. Thick fog.

"Ribbbbit?" croaked Frog. "What is this fog? How can I get to the pond to sing? Only frogs can make the sun come up!"

Now Frog lived in a ditch by the side of the road. He had to cross the big road to get to the pond. Usually he looked to the right and the left and then hopped across carefully. On this morning when he looked to the right, he saw fog. When he looked to the left, he saw fog. There was nothing to be done but hop out carefully and hope for the best.

So Frog hopped and hoped his way about two jumps across the road. Suddenly, out of the fog came something big and yellow. It was the big yellow school bus! Frog turned around and in two jumps was back in his ditch by the road.

"Ribbbbit?" croaked Frog. "What is this fog? How can I get to the pond to sing? Only frogs can make the sun come up!"

So Frog climbed back up to the road. When he looked to the right, he saw fog. When he looked to the left, he saw fog. There was nothing to be done but hop out carefully and hope for the best.

So Frog hopped and hoped his way about three jumps across the road. Suddenly, out of the fog came something big and yellow. It was a big yellow motorcycle! Frog turned around and in three jumps was back in his ditch by the side of the road.

"Ribbbbit?" croaked Frog. "What is this fog? How can I get to the pond to sing? Only frogs can make the sun come up!"

So Frog tried again to cross the road. When he looked to the right, he saw fog. When he looked to the left, he saw fog. There was nothing to be done but hop out carefully and hope for the best.

So Frog hopped and hoped his way about four jumps across the road. Suddenly, out of the fog came something big and yellow. It was a big yellow sports car! Frog turned around and in four jumps was back in his ditch by the side of the road.

"Ribbbbit?" croaked Frog. "What is this fog? How can I get to the pond to sing? Only frogs can make the sun come up!"

Well, Frog knew he had to try once more to get to the pond on the other side of the road. This time he had gone five jumps across the road, when he saw something coming that was big and yellow. And five jumps was too many to turn back in time. Frog closed his gold eyes as the big yellow thing came closer and closer, until ....

"Hello! What is this? A frog out in the middle of the road?" said the big yellow thing, and it scooped Frog up. Frog opened one gold eye. Then he opened the other gold eye, and he saw that the big yellow thing was really a nice man in a big yellow raincoat. "Say, little Frog," said the nice man in the big yellow raincoat, "you might get hurt out here in the road. Let me put you down by this pond." And he set Frog down by the pond where the other frogs were waiting.

Frog was so happy to get to the pond that he led the singing in his best croaky voice. Those frogs sang and sang in the croaky way frogs have, until the sun came up. The frogs were silly, but they thought that their singing made the sun come up. Of course, the sun would have come up without them, but the frogs did not know that. And to this day, if you are out in the country by a pond on an early spring morning, you will hear the frogs singing to make the sun come up.

Umbrella Flowers
(A Poem)

Umbrellas
Pop out like flowers
On days
When there are showers.

Pop!
Here comes
A yellow one!
Pop!
A spotted red—
That's fun!

Gardens sprouting
Springtime flowers.
Umbrellas growing
In the showers.

For Rain or for Shine

(An Object Story)

Tell this story with a blue umbrella and stick it in a box of sand for the sandbox, hook it over a chair for the lemonade stand, and prop it open on the floor for the playhouse. Then, open it up and parade around joyfully for the last part of the story when Carrie gets to use her umbrella in the rain.

Carrie got a new umbrella for her birthday. A bright blue umbrella. It was bright as a summer day when there's not a cloud in the sky. Carrie loved her umbrella, but she could hardly wait for the day when it would rain.

On Monday when Carrie woke up, she ran to her window. The sun was bright, there wasn't a cloud in the sky. It was as blue as her new umbrella. So Carrie took her umbrella outside, opened it up, and planted it in her sandbox. She pretended she was playing on the beach by the ocean.

On Tuesday Carrie looked outside. The sun was bright, there wasn't a cloud in the sky. It was blue as her new umbrella. So Carrie set up her umbrella on the sidewalk and made a lemonade stand for hot, thirsty customers. She had a lot of fun, but she still wanted it to rain so she could use her umbrella.

On Wednesday Carrie looked out her window. The sun was bright, there wasn't a cloud in the sky. Carrie was tired of playing outside, so she made a little playhouse in her room with her new umbrella. When the umbrella was opened up, there was enough room for all her teddy bears and baby dolls to fit inside!

On Thursday Carrie looked outside and maybe you've already guessed—yes, the sun was bright, there wasn't a cloud in the sky. Carrie put her umbrella in the corner. She sang a little "waiting for rain to come" song:

> Waiting for the rain,
> Oh, go away sun!
> I've got a new umbrella
> And I want to have fun!

On Friday when she woke up, Carrie sang her "waiting for the rain to come" song again. And, do you know what? The song must have been magic, because when Carrie looked out her window, the sun was not bright, and there were clouds in the sky. Hooray!

So Carrie ran right outside, opened up her bright blue umbrella, and she had fun all morning in the rain.

I Have a Red Umbrella

(To the tune of "Turkey in the Straw")

This is a perfect rain song to sing after you read the book *My Red Umbrella* (p. 68).

Oh, the rain keeps comin' down
But we really don't care.
I've got my umbrella
For us all to share.
It is big and it is shiny
And it can open up so wide.
We will keep very comfy
If we hide inside.

Comfy inside,
Hide inside,
Comfy inside,
Hide inside.
We will keep so comfy
If we hide down inside.
We will keep so very comfy
If we hide way down inside

Open Your Umbrella

Open your umbrella
Up like a bowl,
So you can catch
Your own rainbow!

Umbrellas Are Fine

An umbrella's fine
To take to the beach.
An umbrella's good
For crawling beneath.
An umbrella makes
A hide-and-seek spot.

An umbrella keeps
The raindrops off.
I have my own umbrella—
It's shiny and new.
I'll share my umbrella
With you and you and you!

Inside Out

I have a new umbrella.
It opens up wide.
What a nifty place
For me to hide.
Listen to the raindrops:
Plop! Plop! Plop!
Uh-oh! My new umbrella
Just came down—PLOP!

Boots, Galoshes, Overshoes
(To the tune of "Mulberry Bush")

Boots, galoshes, overshoes,
Tell me which one will you choose—
When it's wet
Or when it snows—
To keep your tootsies dry?

A slicker, raincoat, mackintosh
Keep you dry—by gosh, by gosh!
Rainy days don't make me hide—
I'm waterproof outside!

Bonnie's Rain Boots
(An Object Story)

Tell this story with a pair of boots and two plastic bags big enough to fit over your feet.

Bonnie got a brand new pair of rain boots to keep her feet dry when it rained. They were shiny red rain boots. But they were hard to pull on over her shoes.

"Don't forget to wear your boots today," said Bonnie's mother. "I think it's going to rain."

"Ah, gee, do I have to?" asked Bonnie.

"Yes, you have to," said Mother.

"But they're hard to pull on over my shoes," said Bonnie.

"Try," said Mother.

Bonnie tried. She pulled and pulled until she got all red in the face. Red as her shiny red rain boots. Finally Mother pulled. Mother's face got red, too. But the rain boots went on.

The next day it rained again.

"Don't forget to wear your boots today," said Mother. "It's raining cats and dogs outside."

"Good," said Bonnie, "if it's raining cats and dogs, I won't have to wear my boots. Cats and dogs aren't wet!"

"Bonnie, wear your boots," said Mother.

"But my boots are hard to pull on," said Bonnie.

"Try," said Mother.

"No," said Bonnie. "No boots!" And she sat down on the floor.

Bonnie's mother took the boots and put them in the closet. Then she went over to a drawer and got out two plastic bags and two strings.

"Here," said Mother, "bags are not hard to pull on."

And Mother slipped the bags on Bonnie's feet. She tied them around Bonnie's ankles with the strings.

"Now your feet will not get wet."

Bonnie looked down at her feet. The bags were not shiny and red. They were bunchy and ugly and looked awful.

So Bonnie went to the closet and got out her boots. She sat down and she pulled. And do you know what? The boots went on over her shoes just as slick as a whistle.

Then Bonnie went right out in the rain. She was whistling herself. She was wearing the bags tied on with strings and she was wearing her brand new shiny red rain boots. She had pulled them on all by herself, too!

Sing a Song of Puddles
(To the tune of "Sing a Song of Sixpence")

Sing a song of puddles
Made for splashing in.
Don't be shy and tiptoe,
Put your whole feet in.
Now squat down like froggies —
You know what to do.
Jump right in the middle!
    (Spoken) Wait!
I forgot my overshoes!
    (Spoken) SQUISH!

Duck Parade
(An Action Poem)

Before doing this poem, teach the children to waddle. Place hands on hips for wings, then walk in place while swinging hips. They will enjoy this motion while they "quack and quack and quack, quack, quack."

I wear my yellow slicker
When there is a rainy day.
I look just like a yellow duck.
I waddle and I sway.
With a quack and a quack,
And a quack, quack, quack.

The other kids who walk with me
Wear yellow slickers, too.
We waddle and we jump and splash
Until the sky turns blue.
With a quack and a quack,
And a quack, quack, quack.

I wonder what would happen,
As we waddle down the street,
If there would be some real live ducks
That we would chance to meet.
With a quack and a quack,
And a quack, quack, quack.

Perhaps then we would all line up
Through puddles we could wade.
Big ducks and the small ones waddle
In a yellow duck parade!
With a quack and a quack,
And a quack, quack, quack.

Ducks Should Not Complain
(A Poem)

Ducks should not complain
When it rains.
Rain rolls right off their backs—
So why do they have to quack?

They don't wear galoshes
To wade through sloshes.
What luck
To be a duck!

Books about Suits to Swim and Sun

Fisher, Aileen. **Going Barefoot.** Illustrated by Adrienne Adams. Thomas Y. Crowell, 1960.

Through the happy rhythms of verse, a child looks forward to a morning or afternoon in June so he can go barefoot like kittens, squirrels, mice, and rabbits, who "never wear slippers with straps or zippers."

Lobel, Arnold. "A Swim" from **Frog and Toad Are Friends.** Harper & Row, 1970.

Toad makes Frog agree not to look at him until he gets into the water because he is self-conscious of his appearance in his bathing suit. Frog agrees, but all the other animals come to look and laugh.

Ueno, Noriko. **Elephant Buttons.** Harper & Row, 1973.

This wordless picture book is full of surprises. Elephant is unbuttoned to reveal a horse, who is unbuttoned to reveal a lion. This continues, revealing a monkey, duck, mouse, and then an elephant again!

Zion, Gene. **Harry by the Sea.** Illustrated by Margaret Bloy Graham. Harper & Row, 1965.

Harry the dog is a hot dog in the summer sun. Because his owners won't let him under their sun umbrella, he wades into the water and finds seaweed will keep him cool. Unfortunately, the people at the beach think he's a sea monster.

Related Activities about Suits to Swim and Sun

Summer's Coming!
(A Poem)

Make this poem come alive by showing the different types of shoes as they are mentioned.

All fall I wear my sneakers
And slippers warm my feet.
I wear big boots in winter snow.
Spring dress-up shoes are neat.

Yesterday the grass was green,
The sun was warm and gold.
We bought me some new sandals—
Just two straps and a sole.

In winter boots are fun to wear.
My new spring shoes have bows.
But I know summer's coming
When my sandals show my toes!

Summer Hats
(A Flannel-board and Action Rhyme)

You can do this action rhyme with the children acting out the animals indicated, as they buy their funny summer hats.

For more fun use animal cutouts and draw five simple hats, decorated as indicated in the rhyme. Back these with felt and use the poem for a flannel-board story by placing the hats on the board at the beginning and matching them to each animal. If these pieces are sturdy enough, the children will enjoy having the set for a matching game to use on their own.

Five funny summer hats,
But people don't wear these.
These are for the animals.
Watch now, if you please.

Five funny summer hats:
There's a red one by the door.
A monkey came and bought it,
Then there were four.
        (Make monkey sounds: eep-eep-eep.)

Four funny summer hats:
The yellow one has bees!
A kangaroo just bought it,
Now there are three.
        (Jump.)

Three funny summer hats:
One is big and blue.
An elephant just bought it,
Now there are two.
        (Join arms in front and swing
        like trunk.)

Two funny summer hats:
The green one's good for sun.
A camel came and bought it,
Now there is one.
        (Make sounds like a camel walking:
        galoompa-galoompa.)

One funny summer hat:
It's very, very small.
A lady bug just bought it,
The last one of all.
        (All sit quietly.)

The Day the Hippo Unzipped His Zipper
(A Mask Story)

For this story you will need the cutout masks of a hippo, cow, dog, duck, mouse, and a second hippo mounted on craft sticks. Give each child a different mask and line up the children behind each other. As each animal unzips his skin, move that child out of the way to show the animal inside. This is a good story to use with the book *Elephant Buttons* (p. 74).

This is a story about a very, very hot summer. One that was so hot that it was too hot to wear clothes. One that was so hot that it was too hot for the animals to wear their skin. And this is what happened when the Hippo Unzipped His Zipper.

One day a hippo was looking for some cool mud to wade in. Slurp-slurp. Slurp-slurp. It was a hot day, and the hippo got so hot that he decided to unzip his skin and take it off. Zzzzzzzzzzzip! The hippo took off his skin, but inside was a cow.

So the cow set off to find a cool shade tree. Moo-moo. Moo-moo. But it was still a hot day, and the cow got so hot that she decided to unzip her skin and take it off. Zzzzzzzzzzzip! The cow took off her skin, but inside was a dog.

So the dog set off to find a cool doghouse. Arf-arf. Arf-arf. But it was still a hot day, and the dog got so hot that he decided to unzip his skin and take it off. Zzzzzzzzzzzip! The dog took off his skin, but inside was a duck.

So the duck set off to find some cool water to swim in. Quack-quack. Quack-quack. But it was still a hot day, and the duck got so hot that she decided to unzip her skin and take it off. Zzzzzzzzzzzip! The duck took off her skin, but inside was a mouse.

So the mouse set off to find a cool nest to curl up in. Squeak-squeak. Squeak-squeak. But it was still a hot day, and the mouse got so hot that he decided to unzip his skin and take it off. Zzzzzzzzzzip! The mouse took off his skin, but inside was a little tiny hippo!

And the little tiny hippo found a little tiny mud puddle. Slurp-slurp. Slurp-slurp. Ahhhh. That was a nice cool place to spend a hot, hot day.

Summertime Clothes

It's summertime, so I will roll
My jeans up to my knees.
Then I can go wading
Into the bright blue seas.

I'll pull my sandals off, of course,
So I can leave some tracks
All along the sandy beach,
Running up and back.

Summertime's a fun time,
'Cause everybody knows
You get to run around
Without a lot of clothes!

Green Magic

Tell this story with a story wheel (see illustration) that has a green acetate overlay. When the different objects become green, pull the green acetate over the pictures.

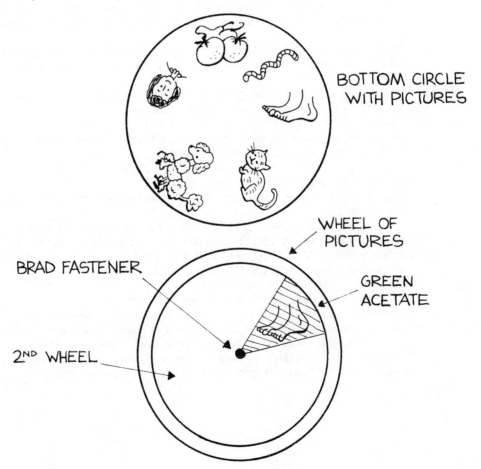

BOTTOM CIRCLE WITH PICTURES

WHEEL OF PICTURES

BRAD FASTENER

GREEN ACETATE

2ND WHEEL

Gary loved to play outside in the sun during the summertime. He loved to wear only his shorts and feel the hot sun on his arms and his legs. But sometimes he stayed out in the sun too long. His skin got bright pink and then it got bright red.

Gary's mother told him to put on a T-shirt when he went outside so he wouldn't get sunburned. But his hands and arms and his feet still got bright red.

One day his mother brought home a bottle of Special Magic Formula Sun Tan Oil. It was guaranteed to keep skin from turning red.

"Be sure you put plenty of this Special Magic Formula Sun Tan Oil all over your arms and legs," she said. "Then you won't get red."

So Gary poured the magic oil all over his arms and legs and even on his toes. Then he put on his shorts, his T-shirt, and his sunglasses and went out to play.

First he walked up and down the rows in the garden. Little tomatoes were growing from the vines.

"Green tomatoes sure look weird," said Gary.

A little garden snake slithered through the garden. "Yipes!" said Gary. "I'm sure glad my skin isn't green like that," he said.

Then Gary looked down at his toes.

"Oh no," he cried. His toes seemed to be turning green. "Maybe I got too much of that magic oil," he said.

Just then Fluff, his pretty yellow cat, ran through the garden.

"Fluff, look at my toes," called Gary.

Fluff ran over and started to lick Gary's toes. She liked the taste of the greasy oil. She liked the magic oil so much that she licked and she licked.

"Stop!" laughed Gary. "You're tickling!"

Then he reached down to pick Fluff up, and he saw that Fluff was green.

"Oh no! Fluff, look what you did! You ate that stuff off my toes. Now you're green all over!"

Well, when Fluff heard that, she took off running. The little poodle dog next door chased her. 'Round and 'round they ran—so fast that all Gary could see was a great, green, blurry glob.

Gary ran over to catch the green glob before it could get away. But when he reached out, he noticed that his hand was green all over.

"Mom! Mom! Help!" he yelled. "It's catching!"

Mom came running out of the house. Gary threw his arms around her. Then he looked up and said, "Oh no! Mom, it's got you, too!"

"What's got me? You look like you've seen a ghost," she said.

"It's a glob—a great, green, greasy glob."

Gary's mother started to laugh. "I think you've been out in the sun too long. You're starting to see things."

"Yeah! Just look at me!" It's that magic oil. It's turned my toes green. Fluffy licked them and now she's green, and the dog next door, and now my hands, and when I touched you, it got you, too. What's going to happen? What are we going to do?" he cried.

Well, Gary's mother laughed again. "I know just what to do."

"You do? Will it hurt?" Gary asked.

"Not one bit," she said. "Just hold still."

Then Gary's mother reached over and very carefully she took off Gary's sunglasses. And do you know what? His skin wasn't green anymore, but it was bright pink.

"I'm taking this oil back to the store right now," she said. "It doesn't work at all."

"I don't care," said Gary, petting his pretty yellow cat and the fluffy white poodle dog from next door. "At least the great, green glob didn't get us after all."

Sunglasses

(A Fingerplay)

This morning is hot and the sun's shining bright.
(Touch fingertips overhead.)
The trees rustle as the wind passes.
(Wave arms in air.)
And when we go down to the grocery store,
(Walk in place.)
I get to pick out new sunglasses.
(Circle eyes with fingers.)

My sunglasses sometimes will slip down my nose
(Point to nose.)
And everything looks kind of green.
(Arms wide to indicate "everything".)
I wonder when I have my sunglasses on
(Circle eyes with fingers.)
If people will know that it's me!
(On word "me" quickly take fingers away from eyes.)

The Tale of Samuel Strand

(A Story-Poem)

Tell this story-poem with a two-sided hand puppet. On one side show Samuel in shorts. The other side shows Samuel as the Sand Monster. Glue globs of sand (or use pieces of sandpaper) to this side of the puppet. Turn to the appropriate sides as the words in the story dictate.

PIECES OF SANDPAPER

There once was a boy named Samuel Strand,
Who was ever so fond of playing in sand.
Samuel dug tunnels, Samuel made moats.
He filled them with water to sail his boats.

One day the boy named Samuel Strand
Covered himself with cool wet sand.
He smeared it on from his head to his toes.
He even covered his sunburned nose.

He wore that sand like a second skin.
Not even his mother recognized him.
The kids on the block started to run.
"Monster!" they shouted. "Here IT comes!"

Oh, the sand monster caused a terrible fright.
"Wait," said his father. "Something's not right.
Those shorts he's got on are Samuel Strand's."
Then Father got water to wash off the sand.

Well, the sand monster melted right then and there.
Water came dripping down from his hair.
The kids all cried—Why, it's Samuel Strand,
The boy who always plays in sand.

You could be famous—you're something to see,
The neighborhood kids all shouted with glee.
Now Samuel wears sand instead of his clothes.
He's the Sand Monster Star of a TV show!

Swimming Suits and Trunks Fall Down
(To the tune of "London Bridge")

Young children often experience swimming attire that won't stay up when they plunge into the water. Just like London Bridge, the falling swimsuit problem can be remedied in a number of ways. Sing this song and supply appropriate actions as you teach it to preschoolers. Other solutions may be added before the final verse.

Swimming suits and trunks fall down,
Trunks fall down, trunks fall down.
Swimming suits and trunks fall down
When you swim.

Tie them up with strings and ties,
Strings and ties, strings and ties.
Tie them up with strings and ties
When you swim.

Strings and ties can come untied,
Come untied, come untied.
Strings and ties can come untied
When you swim.

Paste them on with sticky glue,
Sticky glue, sticky glue.
Paste them on with sticky glue
When you swim.

Sticky glue can come unstuck,
Come unstuck, come unstuck.
Sticky glue can come unstuck
When you swim.

Let's go home and sew 'em up,
Sew 'em up, sew 'em up.
Let's go home and sew 'em up
So we can swim!

Let It All Hang Out!

When summer comes
And it gets hot,
You don't want
To wear a lot.

Cut your jeans off
To your knees.
Tie your shirt up,
If you please.

Now your tummy's
Hanging out,
So you can wiggle
All about!

Books about Bundle Up

Alborough, Jez. **Bare Bear**. Knopf, 1984.

"To keep warm in the arctic air a polar bear wears polar wear." A rhymed text and jaunty illustrations tell what a polar bear wears under his polar suit—right down to his pink behind.

Kay, Helen. **One Mitten Lewis**. Illustrated by Kurt Werth. Lothrop, Lee and Shepard, 1968.

Lewis loses so many mittens that he has to wear mismatched ones and is nicknamed "One Mitten Lewis." He is teased by the other children, but meets a new friend who has the same problem. They swap mittens from each other's "lonesome mitten" boxes, so everything comes out matching in the end.

Kellogg, Steven. **The Mystery of the Missing Red Mitten**. Dial, 1974.

A little girl retraces her steps in looking for a lost mitten. She finds a boat, a sock, and a sweater. She fantasizes that a hawk has her mitten, then she grows a mitten tree, but finds the missing mitten buried in the heart of her snowman.

Rice, Eve. **Oh, Lewis!** Macmillan, 1974.

On a winter outing with his mother and little sister, Lewis's clothes are a problem: his boots are unbuckled, his jacket is unzipped, he loses his mittens, and his hood comes untied. Mother helps him so he stays all "done-up," but then Lewis has to learn how to take everything off again when he gets home.

Singer, Bill. **The Fox with Cold Feet**. Illustrated by Dennis Kendrick. Parents, 1980.

Fox tries to protect his feet from the cold snow with various kinds of "boots"—a bird's nest, a bucket, a pair of earmuffs, and a scarf. These are all too cumbersome, so he learns to run through the snow instead!

Slobodkin, Florence, and Louis Slobodkin. **Too Many Mittens**. Vanguard Press, 1958.

Grandmother takes care of twins, Ned and Donny, when their parents go on a trip. A red mitten is lost and it is returned. Soon all the neighbors, the postman, the garbage man, the grocer, the delivery man, and a host of people bring all the red mittens everyone has lost to the house. Before long, there are so many red mittens the boys hang out a "Lost Mitten Line" for everyone to share the mittens.

Todd, Kathleen. **Snow**. Addison-Wesley, 1982.

A young child enjoys playing in the snow when he is bundled up in warm clothes and boots.

Tresselt, Alvin. **The Mitten.** Illustrated by Yaroslava. Lothrop, Lee and Shepard, 1964.

A boy loses one of his mittens in a snowdrift and a host of animals move in, one by one, to keep warm: mouse, frog, owl, rabbit, fox, wolf, wild boar, and then bear. All manage to squeeze in, but when a little black cricket tries, the mitten splits open. The boy hurries home for the new mittens his grandmother has been knitting. Authentic Ukrainian designs adorn the costumes of the animals, adding to this tale.

Walde, Gunilla. **Tommy Goes Out.** Houghton Mifflin, 1971.

Mother insists that Tommy dress warmly to go out to play, so he puts on everything—not always in the right order—but he finally is ready.

Related Activities about Bundle Up

It's Not That Cold Outside
(To the tune of "Mary Had a Little Lamb")

I don't want to wear my coat,
wear my coat,
wear my coat.
I don't want to wear my coat.
It's not that cold outside.

I don't want to wear my gloves,
wear my gloves,
wear my gloves.
I don't want to wear my gloves.
It's not that cold outside.

I don't want to wear my cap,
wear my cap,
wear my cap.
I don't want to wear my cap.
It's not that cold outside.

SNEEZE!

The Scarf
(A Story with Props)

Tell this story using a long, long scarf. You may wish to make one of felt. Cut the scarf in three pieces and attach the sections with Velcro®, so you can "rip" the scarf in pieces and still have it to tell the story another time. Show the scarf as indicated in the story.

Aaron's grandmother did not want him to get cold outside. He had a warm coat and fuzzy mittens and a snug hat. But Grandmother did not think that was warm enough for Aaron. So she made him a scarf.

First it was a little scarf. *(Hold hands up indicating a short distance.)* "Not warm enough for Aaron," said Grandmother.

Then she made a little longer scarf. *(Spread hands a little.)* "Not warm enough for Aaron," said Grandmother.

Then she made a still longer scarf. *(Spread hands a little more.)* "Not warm enough for Aaron," said Grandmother.

So she made Aaron the longest scarf anyone had ever seen! *(Show scarf.)*

Now Aaron loved his Grandmother very much, and he did not want to get cold outside. He always wore his warm coat and fuzzy mittens and snug hat. But as soon as Aaron saw that scarf, he said, "I don't know about the scarf, Grandmother. It looks long enough to collect a whole lot of trouble."

"Oh, knitting needles!" said Grandmother. "It is just the right size. Besides, what kind of trouble can a scarf get into?" And when Aaron did not have an answer for that, she tied the long, long scarf around and around and around and around him, and sent him outside to play.

At first it was a little hard for Aaron to move with that long, long scarf tied around and around and around and around him, but he finally started out on a walk.

Plop, plop, plop—went Aaron's boots on the sidewalk. Plop, plop ... STOP! Aaron's new scarf caught on a big stick that was stuck in the ground. Aaron pulled and pulled and pulled. *(You may have the children pretend to pull the scarf.)* Finally, the stick pulled loose from the ground and stuck in Aaron's scarf. The scarf was collecting a whole lot of trouble.

Aaron walked on with a stick stuck in his long, long scarf. Plop, plop, plop—went Aaron's boots on the sidewalk. Plop, plop ... STOP! Aaron's new scarf caught on a broom that was propped against a mailbox. Aaron pulled and pulled and pulled. *(You may have the children pretend to pull the scarf.)* Finally, the broom pulled loose from the mailbox and stuck in Aaron's scarf. The scarf was collecting a whole lot of trouble.

Aaron walked on with a stick and a broom stuck in his long, long scarf. Plop, plop, plop—went Aaron's boots on the sidewalk. Plop, plop ... STOP! Aaron's new scarf caught on his dog, who was sitting on the grass. Aaron pulled and pulled and pulled. *(You may have the children pretend to pull the scarf.)* Finally, the dog gave up trying to sit on the grass and stuck in Aaron's scarf. The scarf was collecting a whole lot of trouble.

Aaron walked on with a stick and a broom and his dog stuck in his long, long scarf. He walked all the way home and Grandmother saw him.

"Aaron!" she cried. "That scarf is collecting a whole lot of trouble. Let me help you out of it." So Grandmother pulled out the stick and the broom and the dog. She helped Aaron build a snowman with the stick for an arm and the broom by his side. Then she tore that long, long scarf in three parts. The first part she wrapped around the snowman, and it was just the right size. The second part she wrapped around the dog, and it was just the right size. The third part she wrapped around Aaron. It was just the right size to keep him nice and warm, but not long enough to collect any more trouble.

New Sweater

I have a new sweater.
What could be better
To wear when it's freezing
And I start in sneezing?
What could be better
Than a sweater?

Hot Dog

Tell this story with a sock puppet dog pulled over your arm. When the dog crawls inside the sweater, simply pull another part of a sock—a larger red one—over the sock puppet.

RED SOCK

DOG PUPPET
OF SOCK

Gretchen was a long, long, low, low, little, little dog. Some people call that kind of dog a "hot dog." But Gretchen was not a hot dog. She was a cold dog—and not just her nose—she was cold all over.

Most dogs like to go outside for a walk, but not Gretchen. When Mr. or Mrs. Grundy, her owners, got her leash to take her out for a walk, Gretchen hid in the corner. Gretchen shivered and shook on the walk until she got to come inside. Then she snuggled down in one of Mr. Grundy's old sweaters by the fire and went to sleep.

Well, one winter day just before Christmas, it was so cold outside that Mr. Grundy had to put on his big coat and cap and boots and gloves and a wool scarf. He called Gretchen to come for her walk, but Gretchen just howled.

"Come on, Gretchen," said Mr. Grundy. "All dogs need exercise even in winter."

But Gretchen howled. She refused to move.

The next day the wind howled. Mr. Grundy put on his coat and his cap and his boots and gloves and two wool scarves.

"Come on, Gretchen," he said. "All dogs need exercise even in winter." Gretchen howled and she howled. Then she got up, turned around, and crawled right inside Mr. Grundy's old sweater by the fire.

Then Mrs. Grundy got an idea. She got out her knitting needles and some thick red wool yarn. She knit and she knit all day long—right up until Christmas Eve.

The next day when the wind howled and howled, Mrs. Grundy said, "Come on, Gretchen. I know just what you need. You need a sweater so you can go outside and get your exercise."

So Mrs. Grundy gave Gretchen a beautiful thick red wool sweater. Gretchen crawled right inside. And Gretchen went out for a walk on Christmas morning. She didn't howl once!

After that, Gretchen didn't hide when Mr. or Mrs. Grundy got her leash. She just put on her sweater and went out for her walk the first time she was called.

Gretchen is still a long, long, low, low, little, little dog. But now Gretchen is also a hot dog besides!

Shout for Sweaters

Cardigan
Pullover
Turtleneck top
V-neck
Long-sleeved
Short and cropped
Tucked down in
Hanging out—
All for sweaters
Give a shout!

Keep Me Warm from the Storm

This story is a variant of the popular Russian folktale "The Mitten." After you read Tresselt's picture book, let children participate in telling this similar version. Provide children with small stick puppet figures to stuff in a red felt stocking cap that is attached at the seams by Velcro® . They will be fascinated as the stocking cap rips apart in the end, and the sound of the Velcro® will be most effective! The robin's nest can be a felt board piece to display in the end.

It was January, the coldest month of the year. The North Wind blew so hard that a little boy, Charlie, had to pull his red wool scarf up to his nose to keep it warm. He stuffed his mittened hands down in the pockets of his coat. And he started running backwards against the wind.

But just before Charlie got to his house, a big gust of wind pulled his red wool stocking cap right off his head. Up, up went the cap—so high that Charlie couldn't see it. Charlie ran to his house. And the stocking cap kept on going with the wind. Finally, the wind set the stocking cap down on a snowbank in the woods.

A little gray squirrel who was carrying a nut in her teeth saw the cap. She was so cold her teeth chattered, but she said to herself, "What a fine house to keep me warm from the storm. I shall just settle in for a spell." So Squirrel crawled inside the stocking cap.

Not long after the squirrel had settled in, along came a raccoon with a black-and-white striped tail. Raccoon was so cold that his tail was shaking. "What a fine house to keep me warm from the storm," he said. "I shall just settle in for a spell." So Raccoon crawled into the stocking cap, too.

Just then a big, brown owl flew by. Owl was so cold her wings quivered. So when she saw the stocking cap, she said, "Whoo whoo is there? What a fine house to keep me warm from the storm. I shall settle in there, too, for a spell." So Owl flew into the cap.

Now the next animal to come along was a red fox. His feet were cold and his nose was frozen. How glad he was to see the stocking cap! "What a fine house to keep me warm from the storm. I shall settle in there for a spell," he said. And Fox nosed his way into the cap.

By this time the stocking cap was getting crowded. But a big, black bear came along. Even though he had on a thick winter coat, Bear was cold. "Just look at that fine house," he said. "I could get warm inside. I shall just settle in for a spell and take a long winter's nap!" And Bear crawled into the red wool stocking cap, too.

Well, the cap was so crowded that there wasn't an inch left for anyone else, but someone else came along. It was a gray mouse. Her little body was shivering so much that she couldn't say anything. She just crawled inside the stocking cap. But, then the cap began to rip. And out came the gray squirrel, out came the raccoon with the black-and-white striped tail, out came the brown owl, out came the red fox, out came the big, black bear, and out came the small, gray mouse.

And what happened to the red stocking cap? No one ever saw it again that winter. But in the spring, Robin's nest had a bright red patch that the other animals said looked like a piece of the red stocking cap. And Robin's nest made a fine house to keep her babies warm all spring.

Winter Mittens
(A Poem)

Keep your fingers all together
And stick out your thumbs.
On go your mittens
For winter fun!
You can make a snowball,
Or a big snowman,
With warm wool mittens
On your little hands!

New Red Mitten

Follow the drawings to tell this story as a tear-and-tell story. Glue together two pieces of paper, one red and one white, so you can turn over the paper and hold up the red mitten in the end.

Peggy loved wintertime. She could hardly wait every year for it to snow so she could go out and play. She liked to lie down in the snow and wave her arms up and down to make snow angels. She liked to make round snowballs. And she liked to leave footprints in the snow.

One day just after the first snow, Peggy got all bundled up in her new red snowsuit and her two new red mittens. She went outside and made footprints in the snow. She climbed up a high, high hill to her friend, Pam's house.

Pam came out, so Peggy and Pam built a snow fort on the hill. They made snowballs and had a snowball fight. And then they slid down the hill into a deep snowbank on the other side of the hill.

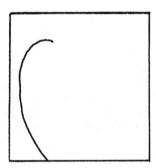

The snow was so deep, Peggy and Pam had to dig and dig the snow with their hands to get out.

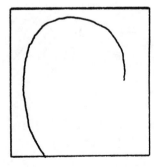

There was a lot of ice on the top of the snowbank, so Peggy and Pam fell down when they stood up.

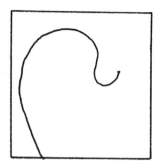

Finally, Pam took hold of Peggy's hand to help her up. Then they walked through the snow back to Peggy's house to get warm.

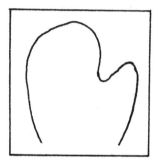

But when they got inside and took off their snowsuits and mittens, Peggy's mother said, "Peggy, you must have had so much fun that you forgot to bring everything back. Tomorrow please find your new red mitten."

So the next day when Peggy went out, she didn't make snow angels or snow forts or have a snowball fight. She looked and looked until she found her new red mitten. *(Turn over the shape and hold it up so the red side shows.)*

Gloves Are Hard to Put On

Gloves are hard to put on.
My fingers go in wrong—
Think that you could help me,
So it doesn't take so long?

Open up your fingers.
Stretch them out so wide.
Put them in their places:
1-2-3-4-5!

My Brand New Snowsuit

I have a brand new snowsuit.
It's nice and thick and warm.
It will keep me cozy
In any winter storm.

To put it on I first unzip
The legs and then the top.
Then I stick my feet down in,
And stand up next and hop.

Now I'm in the bottom part.
My arms go in the sleeves—
Ooo! This part is kinda tight—
Guess I'll have to squeeze!

Pull the hood up on my head,
Now I'm almost in.
Here comes the big, long zipper—
Ouch! I caught my chin!

The Runaway Snowsuit
(A Mask Story)

Tell this story with face masks held in front of the face—a mask for Barney, one for his mother, one for another little boy, and his mother. Use a stop sign for the crossing guard, and a big, red circle for the police light. Use a truck shape for the truck and orange and yellow circles for the oranges and grapefruit. All these props should be attached to craft sticks so the children can move them about easily. The leader holds the blue snowsuit—a stick puppet with the arms and legs attached to the main body part with brad fasteners so it will run and move about as the snowsuit runs away. You can make figures of people for other children to move as the people on the beach chase the snowsuit, or you can ask the other children to become these characters by standing up and running in place for that part in the story. Have a trash bag handy in the end to dispose of the snowsuit.

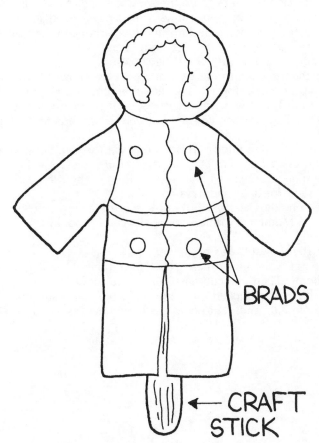

BRADS

← CRAFT STICK

Once there was a bright blue snowsuit that lived in Barney Brown's closet. It had lived in Barney's closet since late August when Mrs. Brown bought it at a department store back-to-school sale. Mrs. Brown brought the snowsuit home and told Barney, "What fun you will have with your new blue snowsuit this winter in the snow."

But winter was a long time away. August was hot. September was warm. October was cool. And November was cold. Then, early one December morning, Mrs. Brown said, "Barney, go get your new blue snowsuit. It's time to have fun in the snow."

Well, the snowsuit was so cozy in Barney's closet that it didn't want to go outside in the snow and get wet and dirty. Barney ran over to the closet, but just as he reached for the snowsuit, it popped off the hanger and jumped out of the closet.

"Stop!" yelled Barney. "I want to have fun in the snow."

"No!" cried the snowsuit. "Let me go! I'm too fine to play in snow!"

The snowsuit ran around Barney's room. It ran around the house. It ran out the door. Barney ran after the snowsuit, and Barney's mother ran after the snowsuit.

"Stop!" yelled Barney's mother.

But the snowsuit would not stop. "No! Let me go! I'm too fine to play in snow!" it shouted.

The snowsuit ran down the street past the crossing guard who held up her stop sign.

"Stop!" shouted the crossing guard.

But the snowsuit ran on and shouted, "No! Let me go!"

Before long the snowsuit got cold and tired from all that running. Up ahead on the road, the snowsuit saw a big truck. And on the side of the truck was a picture of a yellow sun and an orange tree.

"That," said the snowsuit, "is where I want to go! No snow!"

The snowsuit asked the truck driver if he could go along.

"No room up front," said the driver, "but I have the perfect spot for you in the back."

The truck driver picked up the snowsuit and threw it in the cold refrigerated compart-ment of the truck. The poor snowsuit had never been so uncomfortable before in its life. Dozens of oranges and grapefruits bounded around in the back of the truck. Oranges hit it in the arm and grapefruits bounded on its back.

"Ooooo! Let me go!" cried the snowsuit.

But the truck kept right on going with the snowsuit trapped in the back. Finally, after three days the truck stopped and the driver got out. He opened the back door of the truck. The snowsuit saw it was warm outside, so it jumped out and ran straight to the beach.

No one had ever seen a snowsuit on the beach before. Hundreds of people chased the snowsuit.

"Stop!" they shouted. "This is no place for you. Snowsuits go where there is snow!"

"NO! Let me go! I'm too fine to play in snow!" cried the snowsuit.

The snowsuit ran down the beach until it got so tired that it had to lie down on the sand. There it slept for days and days and days.

Then one day, another little boy found the snowsuit.

"Look, Mommy! A blue snowsuit! Maybe I could take it home with me on the plane tomorrow!"

But the snowsuit was no longer new.

"Oh no!" said the mother. "Not that old thing! We'll get you a nice new snowsuit when we get home. Then you can have fun in the snow."

So the mother picked up the not-new blue snowsuit and dumped it in a trash bin.

The old blue snowsuit never did have fun. The last thing it said was, "Oh no! Let me go!"

Bear Suit
(A Poem)

Bears don't have to wear
Boots
Or snowsuits
Or scarves
Or hats
Or lots of stuff
Like that
When it snows.
That's the way it goes
If you're a bear.
You just wear
Your fuzzy wuzzy hair!

GAMES FOR UMBRELLAS, BOOTS, AND SWIMMING SUITS

Weather Match Game

Divide a posterboard into four parts and on each draw simple pictures of different types of weather. You might show rain, snow, sunshine, and an autumn leaf. Cut clothing out of magazines or catalogs and mount on construction paper. You may wish to cover these with clear self-adhesive paper to make them last longer. As a group the children may each take a clothing picture and put it in the correct seasonal square. After this activity is done as a group, the children will enjoy having the board available to play individually.

Hot or Cold

Many children are familiar with the directions "Hot" or "Cold" in playing a treasure hunt game, but this game is a different kind of hot or cold activity. With children seated, the leader holds up clothes (or pictures of clothes) that people wear in different kinds of weather. As the article of clothing is held up, the leader says, "Hot? or Cold?" Children remain seated if the clothing is worn during cold weather and stand if the clothing is worn during hot weather.

Mitten Match Game

With children seated in a circle, play music and pass a mitten around the circle. When the music stops, the child holding the mitten gets to put it on. Begin passing another mitten around the circle (preferably one of another color) and start the music again. When the music stops, the child holding this mitten gets to put it on. Play continues until someone ends up wearing two matched mittens.

Bundle Up Game

To play this game, draw an outline of a child on a posterboard and cut out various articles of winter-wear—scarves, coats, earmuffs, stocking caps, mittens, and boots. Very young children will simply enjoy coming up and placing the clothes on the outline. (The clothes might have tape or plastic tack on the back.) Older children can play this game like "Pin the Tail on the Donkey" and enjoy the fun of seeing the clothes placed in odd places.

Your Duck Parade

Scatter the children throughout the room. Take the hand of one child and sing these words to the tune of "The Farmer in the Dell."

Here comes a duck parade,
Here comes a duck parade.
Now it's time to join the line.
Here comes a duck parade.

As you sing, walk to another child who joins hands with the first. Continue going from child to child until everyone is part of the duck parade. For more fun make duck feet (p. 93) to wear in the duck parade.

Raindrops

Sing these words to the tune "Bluebird, Bluebird," doing the actions as indicated.

Raindrops, raindrops falling gently,
    (Wiggle fingers overhead.)
Raindrops, raindrops falling gently,
Raindrops, raindrops falling gently.
Down come the dancing raindrops.

Raindrops, raindrops making puddles,
    (Join hands, walk in a circle for puddle.)
Raindrops, raindrops making puddles,
Raindrops, raindrops making puddles.
Rain dancing in the puddles.

Splishing, splashing in the puddles,
    (Drop hands, march to center of "puddle" and back out again.)
Splishing, splashing in the puddles,
Splishing, splashing in the puddles.
Boots dancing in the puddles.

CRAFTS FOR UMBRELLAS, BOOTS, AND SWIMMING SUITS

Mittens for All Seasons

Provide children with two mittens (you can glue together two pieces of white paper or inter-facing; the interfacing will be more expensive, but it is durable and you can draw on it with felt-tipped markers). On one side of one mitten, decorate with cotton balls for snow; on the other side, draw on a sun for summer. On one side of the other mitten, decorate with rain-drops or strips of waxed paper for spring rain; on the other side of this mitten, decorate with small leaves for autumn. After you make these mittens, teach children this simply rhyme and turn the appropriate side of the mitten as each season is mentioned.

Summer, fall, winter, spring—
Look what fun each season brings!

Glove Puppets

Provide work gloves or have children bring their own. They may stuff a small ball of cotton into each finger and tie a twist tie below it to form a head. Provide felt features to glue on to make five finger puppets on a glove.

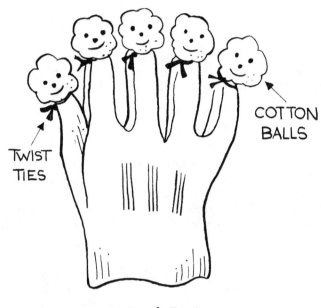

Duck Feet

Help the children trace and cut out two webbed feet from orange card stock. Punch holes in the instep and outer edge. Children can string yarn through the holes and tie the webbed feet over their own. Now have a Duck Parade (p. 92).

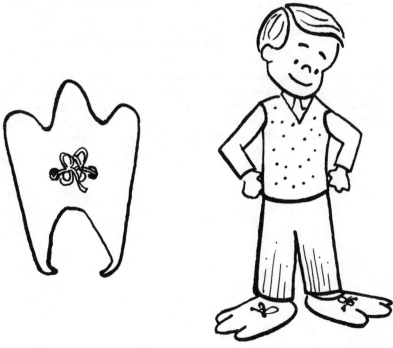

Red Umbrella

Cut out a 6-inch diameter circle of red paper and scallop the outer edge. Make a small slit and overlap edges. Glue in place. Push a pipe cleaner through the top of the cone and bend crooks in both ends.

Samuel Strand Craft

After you've told children the story of Samuel Strand in this chapter (pp. 79-80), give each child an outline drawing of Samuel. Then let them put glue on Samuel and sprinkle sand all over his body until they make their own sand monsters.

Sun Visor

Enlarge the two pattern pieces illustrated and photocopy them on card stock (construction paper will not work as well, since it's not quite stiff enough). Let children decorate their visors before taping together. To attach the two pices, begin taping in the middle, then at each end, so the two curved pieces will match up. With a small hole punch, punch holes on the top piece and use thin elastic cord knotted so it will not pull through.

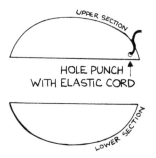

Runaway Snowsuit Puppet

After you have told the story of the runaway snowsuit in this chapter (pp. 89-90), give each child the opportunity to make a snowsuit puppet to take home. Photocopy the five pieces shown in the illustration (two arms, two legs, and main body piece) on card stock or construction paper. Let children cut out the pieces and attach them with brad fasteners. Tape or glue a craft stick to the back and jiggle the stick so the snowsuit puppet seems to be running away.

DISPLAYS FOR UMBRELLAS, BOOTS, AND SWIMMING SUITS

Turn over a New Leaf

On each of four pieces of paper, draw a large tree trunk and branches. Children will enjoy tearing pieces of paper and pasting on red, yellow, and orange leaves for the fall tree, white snow for winter, light green leaves for spring, and bright green leaves for summer. You may wish to do this for all four trees in the fall or save three trees and decorate each close to the date the season officially changes or on the first day it really feels like the new weather has arrived.

Sandy and His Rain Gear

On a bulletin board area, hang a cutout figure of a child named Sandy. You may wish to trace around one of the children in the group. Put the head and shoulder of the figure on the board and let the rest of the body hang down so that the feet are near the floor. Collect child-size rainwear from garage sales or secondhand stores. Dress this figure by pinning the slicker and hat to the board. Slip the feet into the boots and tape them to the floor. Hang the umbrella from the figure's hand. The children will enjoy helping you make this display by covering cutout clouds with cotton balls and hanging strips of tin foil for rain above the figure's head on the bulletin board.

March Weather—What Next?

Divide the bulletin board into thirty-one parts to represent a calendar. Using different clothing, indicate each day what the weather is like. You may use a snowsuit, umbrella, jacket, or sunglasses. How many different types of clothing did you use in the month? Were there any days where more than one was needed as the weather changed quickly?

Lucky Umbrellas

Place a variety of colorful umbrellas on the tops of shelves. You may wish to hang some from the ceiling by fishing line, which is nearly invisible and very strong.

Mr. and Ms. Snowperson

If you live in a climate with snow, step outside and help the children build snowpeople dressed in appropriate attire. This outdoor display will introduce the subtheme on winter clothes and will last as long as the cold weather does!

Lost Mitten Line

After you have read the book *Too Many Mittens*, give each child a red mitten cut out from construction paper and help the child write his or her name on the mitten. Using clothespins, attach the mittens to a small clothesline strung across the room and label the display "Lost Mitten Line."

4
Long Ago and Far Away

INTRODUCTION

This chapter features clothes children today probably have not worn except as costumes. Few picture story books have been written specifically about historical dress so you may wish to draw upon books in the resource bibliography to expand children's background. Children are exposed to fashions of the past indirectly through reprints of the books of Kate Greenaway and Beatrix Potter. Contemporary illustrators continue to retell folktales in dress appropriate to the historical period in which the stories were originally told. We have selected a few eras noted for distinct fashions of special interest to children. "A Showcase of Clothes" traces the story of dress from cave people to bloomers through songs and costumes so children can participate actively. Poems and songs about flapper dress and bobby socks introduce more recent fashion fads.

Since young children are just beginning to develop a sense of the past, you may wish to bring in old family photograph albums to see actual clothing from the past. Children will learn that past generations dressed children much like adults (and expected them to behave that way, too!).

Children the world over dress more alike today than they have in ages past. The names for articles of apparel may not be the same. The boy in *Not So Fast, Songolo*, for example, goes shopping with his grandmother in South Africa for tennis shoes that he calls *tackies*. An American child shopping for clothes in England may be surprised to learn that undershirts are called *vests* and underpants are *knickers*. Activities in this chapter will teach children names for clothing—dashiki, serape, rebozo, and jellaba—worn in other cultures. Exposure to cultural differences is important so children will grow in multicultural understanding.

Clothing traditionally associated with a specific culture such as the Japanese kimono is seldom worn everyday. We can use this opportunity to introduce children to unique clothing, but explain that it is often worn for festival occasions rather than as everyday dress.

Activities such as "African Clothing Chant," "Fan Dancing," and "Buffalo Clothes" preserve some of these special differences and recreate the rhythms and moods of the appropriate cultures.

These are not easy concepts to grasp, but the opportunity to empathize with other cultures and learn from the past will help children broaden their understanding of the world beyond their own backyard.

INITIATING ACTIVITY

Togas to Turbans

Practice the new words in this poem and then enjoy teaching them to the children. Have them join hands in a circle of friendship.

'Round the world and long ago,
Here are words you may not know:
Crinoline and saddle shoes,
Toga, bloomers, sombrero,
Dashiki, poncho, jellaba,
Clogs and turban, kimono.
Join your hands, and let's all go
'Round the world and long ago.

LITERATURE-SHARING EXPERIENCES

Books about Ages and Rages of Fashion

Babbitt, Natalie. **Phoebe's Revolt**. Farrar, Straus & Giroux, 1968.

Because Phoebe Euphemia Brandon Brown, age eight, lives in 1904, she wears frills and lace like other girls in those times. One day she revolts and insists on dressing like her father. Finally, her mother has a seamstress make Phoebe simple sailor dresses.

Lobel, Anita. **The Seamstress of Salzburg**. Harper & Row, 1970.

Long ago in Salzburg, Anna embroiders such fine dresses that all the ladies of the court demand her services. The quality of Anna's sewing deteriorates and the clothes begin to fall apart. When the prince intercedes and Anna teaches all the ladies of Salzburg to sew, the story ends happily.

St. George, Judith. **By George, Bloomers!** Illustrated by Margot Tomes. Coward, McCann & Geoghegan, 1976.

An easy-read text in six short chapters tells the story of eight-year-old Hannah, who wants to follow Mrs. Bloomer's fashion of wearing bloomers instead of petticoats, stockings, lace pantalets, and skirts. Since her mother won't buy her the bloomers, Hannah creates her own version. And, in her bloomers, Hannah saves the day by crawling out an attic window and onto the roof to rescue her brother. The story is accompanied by a historical note on the origin of bloomers.

Related Activities about Ages and Rages of Fashion

Clothes Long Ago
(To the tune of "Turkey in the Straw")

Clothes of long ago are fascinating to young children, but young children do not have a historical context to understand "times past" in any detail. You may wish to find some clothes or pictures of clothing to add to their knowledge. A trip to a local historical museum would be another possibility to extend this background.

Clap hands to keep the rhythm of this rollicking song, and then add actions as indicated.

Oh, the clothes worn long ago,
    (Thrust thumb backward indicating past time.)
Now they look so very strange
That I'm thinking I'm so glad
    (Point to self.)
That fashions change.
But before you start to snicker,
    (Point to children.)
And you giggle and you stare,
Think that one day you'll look
Just like the Old Gray Mare.
    (Pull imaginary beard.)
Handlebar mustache
    (Twirl imaginary mustache.)
Fashions of the past,
Pull that corset fast.
    (Pull.)
Fashions never last.
Looking sort of silly
    (Wiggle fingers overhead and dance.)
In some fashions of the past.
But I think it's fun to wear
Some silly fashions of the past.

Yankee Doodle Retold

(To the tune of "Yankee Doodle")

After singing this song, you may wish to make Yankee Doodle hats from the pattern in chapter 6, "Hats and More Hats" (p. 185).

Yankee Doodle went to town
To buy some macaroni.
Put it on his favorite hat,
And fed it to his pony.

Yankee Doodle, what a guy!
Dressed up like a dandy.
Is that feather in your hat
A stick of sugar candy?

One of a Kind Big Wig

(A Flannel-board Story)

For this story you will use a lady's face, a big powdered wig, a butterfly, bluebird, bunch of flowers, red-and-white striped bow, and a cow. Place the items on the board as they are mentioned in the story. Teach the children to help you tell the story by reaching "tall," reaching "wide," and wiggling fingers for "curls" each time they are mentioned in the story.

Once upon a time it was considered very elegant for a lady to wear a wig. One lady, called Madam Poofapuff, thought she would have the finest wig in the land. So she got a wig that was tall and wide and had curls. Then Madam Poofapuff thought she had the finest wig in the land.

But soon all the other ladies got wigs that were tall and wide and had lots of curls, so Madam Poofapuff looked for something else to put on her wig. She found a butterfly. A real, live butterfly! She put him on her wig and Madam Poofapuff thought she had the finest wig in the land.

But soon all the other ladies got wigs that were tall and wide and had lots of curls, and a butterfly, so Madam Poofapuff looked for something else to put on her wig. She found a bluebird. A real, live bluebird! She put him on her wig and Madam Poofapuff thought she had the finest wig in the land.

But soon all the other ladies got wigs that were tall and wide and had lots of curls, and a butterfly, and a bluebird, so Madam Poofapuff looked for something else to put on her wig. She found some flowers. Some real, live flowers! She put them on her wig and Madam Poofapuff thought she had the finest wig in the land.

But soon all the other ladies got wigs that were tall and wide and had lots of curls, and a butterfly, and a bluebird, and some flowers, so Madam Poofapuff looked for sometthing else to put on her wig. She found a big bow. A red-and-white striped bow! She put it on her wig and Madam Poofapuff thought she had the finest wig in the land.

But soon all the other ladies got wigs that were tall and wide and had lots of curls, and a butterfly, and a bluebird, and some flowers, and a big bow, so Madam Poofapuff looked for something else to put on her wig. She found a cow. A mooing, milk-giving cow! She put it on her wig and Madam Poofapuff thought she had the finest wig in the land.

She also had the heaviest wig, the messiest wig, and the most uncomfortable wig in the land. But finally Madam Poofapuff had a wig that no one would copy. And if it was not the finest wig in the land, at least it was one of a kind.

And that is what fashion is all about!

Flapper

(A Poem)

You may wish to teach the children a simple Charleston step or simply sway to the rhythm of this 20s celebration!

'Round and 'round,
Twirling beads.
Rolling stockings,
Wiggling knees.
Painting cheeks,
Bobbing hair.
Wearing skirts
Short as they dare.
Raccoon coats,
Tapping canes.

Pocket watches
Swung on chains.
Cat's pajamas,
Coochie-coo!
All decked out—
23 skidoo!
Charleston kick
Around the floor.
Flappers made
the 20s roar!

Bobby Socks and Blue Suede Shoes

(A Poem)

Here is the time to dig out the old yearbooks, class ring, pull your hair back in a pony tail, and take the kids back to the 1950s. With movies and TV shows reminiscing about the "good old days," today's children will identify with these articles of clothing—now over 30 years old!

Significant in this era was the development of clothing uniquely for the teenager. No longer did young people move directly to adulthood, but they developed a separate subculture with their own literature, music, and fashions.

Slicked down hair and short crew cuts,
Blue jeans at the soda shop.
Bobby socks and saddle shoes,
Poodle skirts to bunny hop.

Blue suede shoes and pony tails,
Letter sweaters and class rings.
Jukebox playing rock and roll,
50s teens could really swing!

A Showcase of Clothes
Or
How People Have Dressed Down through the Ages

Tell the story of how people have dressed throughout different times by putting on a fashion show with children trying on the kinds of dress described in this story. Prepare large costumes from posterboard for the children to hold up in front of them. You will need the following costumes: bearskin suit for a cave person, mummy costume, King Tut's costume, Roman toga, suit of armor, fair lady's dress, Renaissance man's costume, Renaissance lady's dress, and bloomers. Distribute these costumes for the children to hold up as you tell the story. You might like to teach the songs to the children before you begin or use them as followup activities.

Once upon a time, a long, long time ago, people didn't dress up in clothes like you wear. At first people didn't have clothes at all. Cave men and women must have been very cold. But then they looked at the animals. Why, animals were wearing nice warm clothes. Bears had heavy fur coats. And that gave people a good idea! *(Give bearskin costume to first child.)*

Song of the Cave People
(To the tune of "When Johnny Comes Marching Home")

I'll get me a great, big, bearskin suit
Tonight, tonight!
I'll get me a great, big, bearskin suit
Tonight, tonight!
It'll keep me warm from my neck to my toes,
Bearskin makes the snuggiest clothes.
So I'll just go get me
A bearskin suit tonight!

Well, animal skins were a good idea. But they got smelly, and they didn't fit very well either.

After a long time, people learned how to make their own cloth. Cloth was a wonderful invention. You could stretch it and wrap it and wind it around and around your body to fit just like a second skin.

Long ago and far away in ancient Egypt, people came up with a new way to dress their bodies. This is the way you might dress if you were a mummy. *(Give mummy costume to second child.)*

Mummy Song
(To the tune of "Mulberry Bush")

Wrap and wrap and wrap and tie
'Round your leg and 'round your thigh,
'Round your waist and 'round your chest.
That's the way a mummy's dressed!

Cover up your neck and chin,
Wrap it like a second skin.
Cover up your head and nose.
Now you're wearing mummy clothes!

Of course people didn't really dress like mummies until after they died. Most Egyptian everyday clothes were plain and simple. But rich people like Pharaohs and their queens got all decked out in wigs and makeup. They simply dripped with so much gold and jewels that it would make you drool! King Tut's wardrobe looked like a treasure trove.

King Tut's Song
(To the tune of "The Farmer in the Dell")

I'm the famous King Tut:
Just watch me when I strut.
My crown is made of gold and jewels.
I love to make you drool!

King Tut was a fancy king, all right! But most people didn't live like that.

Over in Rome people went back to the idea of wrapping themselves up in cloth. But they didn't look like mummies. They wrapped and draped their bodies in yards and yards of cloth until they almost looked like they were carrying a bedsheet around them. The Romans called their big robes *togas*. *(Give toga costume to another child.)*

Toga Song
(To the tune of "Mulberry Bush")

Wrap and wrap and tuck and tie,
Wrap it low and wrap it high.
Just be careful when you skip—
In a toga you might trip!

Some togas took so much time to wrap that people had to have a servant just to help them get dressed for the day! And togas weren't very practical if you were going to fight in a battle.

The ancient Romans came up with some metal armor and helmets to protect them when they fought. But it took many years before poeple designed a full set of clothes made out of iron. A suit of armor could cover you from your head to your toes, but it might weigh as much as you would! *(Give knight's suit to another child.)*

Knight Song
(To the tune of "She'll Be Comin' 'Round the Mountain")

I'll be wearing iron plates upon my chest.
I'll be wearing an iron helmet and a vest.
Oh, I'll carry a shield and dagger.
When I walk I nearly stagger,
'Cause a suit of armor
Isn't really light *(Speak:)* for a knight!

When knights were off fighting dragons in their heavy suits of armor, their fair ladies stayed home to take care of the castle. And when the ladies dressed up, they put on long gowns and high, high headdresses. First they put wire mesh on their heads, and then they piled and piled their long, long hair on top. And then, they had to make their hats tall and pointed so they covered up all their hair. If you were a fair lady back in fairytale days, you'd really hold your head up high! *(Give fair lady's costume to another child.)*

Fair Lady Song
(To the tune of "I'm a Little Tea Pot")

I'm the fairest lady
In my clothes.
See my tall headdress
Above my nose.
Heads will turn around when
I go by,
'Cause my hair is
Piled this high.

People got a little carried away with their clothes in those days. But, as time went by, both men and women became big show-offs. King Henry VIII thought his legs were so good-looking that he wore fancy knitted stockings, or hose, so everyone would notice his legs! In those days men wore stiff ruffles around their necks. They cut off their fancy puffy pants at the knees so they could show off red and yellow stockings. *(Give Renaissance man's costume to another child.)*

Renaissance Man's Song
(To the tune of "Skip to My Lou")

Starch in my collar, fancy lace,
Hose on my legs, I walk with grace.
Fancy and puffy knee-high pants,
Makes me want to do a dance!

Oh, the men were dandies in those days, but women tried all kinds of contraptions. Underneath their enormous jeweled gowns, women wore metal hoops that looked like bird cages. And, when they put on their dresses over the hoops, they looked like fancy tops ready to spin around and around. *(Give Renaissance Lady's costume to another child.)*

Renaissance Lady's Song
(To the tune of "Skip to My Lou")

Hoop skirts go around and around,
Spin like a top, but don't fall down.
'Cause I'm a lady in fancy dress
Wearing nothing but the best!

Clothes were certainly fancy in those days. But hoops—oops!—were almost impossible to sit down in. Still, women wore iron hoops on and off for many, many years.

Finally, women decided hoops were uncomfortable. They couldn't breathe very well in hoops and corsets. They couldn't ride horses as well as men. Hoops just didn't feel as good as they looked. Great-great-grandmother looked at great-great-grandfather. And what was he wearing? Pants! Why you could ride a horse or a bicycle if you were wearing pants!

So women crawled out of corsets and hoop skirts and they decided to have fun, too. Great-great-grandmother put on big roomy pants that they called *bloomers*. Now bloomers look kind of silly to us today, but in 1880 they were a revolution! *(Give bloomer costume to another child.)*

Bloomer Song
(To the tune of "She'll Be Comin' 'Round the Mountain")

I'll be wearing roomy bloomers,
That's for me!
'Cause I'm a modern woman,
As you see—
I can jump and I can straddle
On a horse's leather saddle.
In my roomy bloomers I am
Feeling free! (Whee!)

Now today we can wear all kinds of clothes: clothes to stay warm; clothes to dress up; and clothes to just pretend. But mostly, we wear clothes to be comfortable and have fun.

Clothes for Fun Song
(To the tune of "Twinkle, Twinkle Little Star")

Tell me what you'd like to be?
Knight in armor, wrapped mummy?
Lady in a fancy gown?
Queen with jewels on her crown?
Let us make a fashion show—
Try on clothes from long ago!

Books about Worn in the U.S.A. and Far Away

Aardema, Verna. **Who's in Rabbit's House**. Illustrated by Leo and Diane Dillon. Dial, 1977.

This Masai folktale of Rabbit's efforts to get "The Long One" out of her house is told as a drama with villagers wearing typical Masai clothing. The animal masks the villagers wear are the Dillons' own creation, but suggest the color and mood of African art.

Baylor, Byrd. **They Put on Masks**. Illustrated by Jerry Ingram. Scribners, 1974.

The text evokes the mood of native American cultures in which masks were worn to gain power over the spirits of the gods. Although the entire book may be too long to share with young preschoolers, the chants and handsome illustrations may be used.

Daly, Niki. **Not So Fast, Songolo**. Atheneum, 1986.

A little boy in South Africa helps his old grandmother get on the bus to do her shopping, and she buys him new red *tackies* (sneakers), even though he goes so fast in them she has to warn him, "Not so fast, Songolo."

Matsuno, Masako. **A Pair of Red Clogs**. Illustrated by Kazue Mizamura. World, 1960.

A grandmother finds her old cracked clog and remembers when she was a young girl who goes shopping with her mother for a pair of clogs to start school. She decides on a red lacquer pair that talk and sing when she runs. Then she plays a game of throwing her clogs and they crack. It is too soon to ask for a new pair, so she tries to get them very dirty so her mother will buy her a new pair. But she cleans them and learns not to trick her mother again. The grandmother telling the story wonders if her granddaughter will play the same game with her clogs.

Prieto, Mariana. **When the Monkeys Wore Sombreros**. Illustrated by Robert Quackenbush. Harvey House, 1969.

Long ago in Mexico, two brothers were entrusted to sell the sombreros their parents made. They loaded the burros, but on the way, they met with catastrophes, resulting in monkeys wearing the sombreros and getting them stained. An old man gave them his recipe for a bleach to remove the stains. The sombreros turned white, which made them valuable at the market. The family ended up bleaching all their sombreros and became rich.

Steiner, Charlotte. **Karoleena's Red Coat**. Doubleday, 1960.

A long time ago in Austria lived a little girl, Karoleena. She could hardly wait for her first day of school, but when she goes to school, the children tease her because she is the only one in class with a red coat. Karoleena finally becomes accepted by the other girls and makes a new friend who asks for a red coat just like Karoleena's. The illustrations and old-fashioned charm of the story are similar to *Madeline*, though this story is told in prose rather than verse.

Yarbrough, Camille. **Cornrows**. Illustrated by Carole Byard. Coward, McCann & Geoghegan, 1979.

As the children have their hair braided, Grammaw and Mama tell the story of cornrows, an ancient African rite, and, later during slavery, a sign of disgrace. Black-and-white drawings complement the black African origins of this evocative text.

Related Activities about Worn in the U.S.A. and Far Away

Special Dress, Special Days

Clothes associated with other cultures often seem more colorful and interesting than the clothes we wear every day. Too often children get the impression that people in other lands wear festival clothes, many of them dating back hundreds of years, in their everyday life. The following poem celebrates the varieties of dress around the world, but also emphasizes that these kinds of clothes usually are worn just for special occasions.

A Scottish kilt is full of pleats.
Japanese clogs cover your feet.
Hawaiian grass skirts swing and sway.
A flower necklace is a lei.

Mexican sombreros are worn on the head.
In Arabia turbans are worn instead.
People dressing many ways
Throughout the world for special days.

A sari in India is a wrap-around dress.
A Mexican poncho covers your chest.
A shirt in Nigeria is called a dashiki.
Sarongs are worn in a place called Tahiti.

African Clothing Chant
(A Chant with Actions)

Turban
    (Touch head.)
Leaf fan
    (Wave hands by face.)
Bright shirt
    (Cross arms over chest, tap shoulders.)
Barefoot
    (Touch feet.)

The Pride of the Lion
(A Story with Masks)

Because masks are so important in the culture and clothing of Africa, you may wish to make some special ones for this story. Cut posterboard using the patterns shown. Cut on the slits indicated. Overlap and staple for a three-dimensional effect.

CUT NOSE ON
LINES AND FOLD UP

CUT OUT
EYES

CUT OUT SLIT AND OVERLAP-
THEN STAPLE FOR
3 DIMENSIONAL SHAPE

You will need an antelope with horns, an elephant with a trunk, a hippo, and a frog. Make a lion with a separate mane to attach with Velcro® at the end of the story. Give each to a child and have them move as directed in the story. Teach all the children this chant to repeat as the animals are running:

> Rumba rappa
>   *(Pat hands on knees.)*
> Rumba rappa
> Run, run, run.
> Rumba rappa
> Rumba rappa
> RUN! *(Clap.)*

Have the children line up on one side of the room. Hand them each a mask as their character is mentioned in the story.

When the world was new many of the animals looked like they do now. The antelope was very fast. The hippo was very strong. The elephant was very loud.

But there were some animals who did not look like we see them today. One of those was the lion. Oh, no, he did not look the same at all. He had thick fur all over this body and looked like a big, big, fluffy kitten.

And he acted like a big, fluffy kitten. Most of the time he spent by a peaceful pond. He was afraid of the antelope and the hippo and the elephant, who were so very fast and so very strong and so very loud. The other animals did not like the frightened, fluffy lion. *(Have the lion and frog stand a little apart from the others.)* The only friend the lion had was a frog. The two would talk for hours about someday doing something very brave, although as they sat by the peaceful pond, they both secretly hoped they would never have a chance.

And so they would have lived out their days, except for the rainstorm. Now the frog loved the rain, so he stayed in the pond during the rain, but the frightened, fluffy lion ran home to his cave when he saw the rainstorm coming. *(Have lion stand on the other side of the room.)*

First the sky got very black, then the rain began to pit-pat, pit-pat on the leaves. *(The children can imitate this sound by tapping the fingers of one hand into the palm of the other.)* The rain came down harder. *(Have children rub hands on knees for this rain sound.)* And harder. *(Have children tap knees lightly for the heavy rain.)* Then there was one bolt of lightning and crash of thunder. *(Everyone clap once.)* All was still.

Lion looked out of his cave. It was such a short rain that things were not very wet. Lion took a deep sniff. *(All the children may sniff deeply with the lion.)* Snnnnnnnnnnniff. Then he took a shorter one. *(Have children sniff.)* Snnniff-sniff-sniff. Something was wrong in the jungle. Sniff-sniff-sniff. The lion smelled fire. The lightning bold had hit an old tree, and a fire was starting deep in the jungle.

Lion did not stop to think that he was frightened. He ran to tell the other animals. *(Lion should move back to group of animals. Frog is still standing apart from them.)*

"Fire!" he said to the antelope. "You are fast. Run to the other side of the jungle."

But the antelope was too frightened to run. So lion led her as fast as he could to the other side of the jungle. *(Repeat the running rhyme, once slowly and once quickly, while the lion and antelope move to the other side of the room.)*

> Rumba rappa
>   *(Pat hands on knees.)*
> Rumba rappa
> Run, run, run.
> Rumba rappa
> Rumba rappa
> RUN! *(Clap.)*

The antelope was safe on the other side of the jungle. And Lion found out that he could run very fast—as fast as the antelope.

Lion went back to save another animal. "Fire!" he said to the hippo. "You are strong. Stomp over the trees to the other side of the jungle."

But the hippo was too frightened to stomp over trees. So Lion led her as fast as he could to the other side of the jungle. *(Repeat the running rhyme, once slowly and once with especially loud slapping on knees, as the lion and hippo move to the other side of the room.)*

Rumba rappa
 (Pat hands on knees.)
Rumba rappa
Run, run, run.
Rumba rappa
Rumba rappa
RUN! *(Clap.)*

The hippo was safe on the other side of the jungle. And Lion found out that he could be very strong, stomping over trees—as strong as the hippo.

Lion went back to save another animals. "Fire!" he said to the elephant. "You are loud. Make a lot of noise to warn the others as we go to the other side of the jungle."

But the elephant was too frightened to make a single sound. So Lion led him, roaring all the way, to the other side of the jungle. *(Repeat the running rhyme, once slowly and once loudly, as the lion and elephant move to the other side of the room.)*

Rumba rappa
 (Pat hands on knees.)
Rumba rappa
Run, run, run.
Rumba rappa
Rumba rappa
RUN! *(Clap.)*

The elephant was safe on the other side of the jungle. And Lion found out that he could be loud—as loud as the elephant.

Now the only one left to save was lion's friend, the frog. Lion turned to the antelope. "You are so fast. Please come with me to save the frog." But the antelope was too afraid.

Lion turned to the hippo. "You are so strong. Please come with me to save the frog." But the hippo was too afraid.

Lion turned to the elephant. "You are so loud. Please come with me to save the frog." But the elephant was too afraid.

So all alone the lion went back into the firey jungle to save the frog. *(Have lion move over to frog.)* All alone he ran through the flaming bushes and the burning trees. He saved his friend and brought him to the other side of the jungle. *(Repeat the running rhyme, twice very quickly, as the lion and frog move to the other side of the room.)*

Rumba rappa
 (Pat hands on knees.)
Rumba rappa
Run, run, run.
Rumba rappa
Rumba rappa
RUN! *(Clap.)*

The frog was safe on the other side of the jungle. And Lion found out he could be brave—braver than any other animal in the jungle.

The frog looked at lion. "Oh, no," cried Frog. "Look at your fluffy fur!"

All the animals looked. In the fire all of lion's fluffy fur had burned off—all but the very tip of his tail. And the only fur that ever grew back was around the lion's head. *(Add mane to the lion mask.)* Fur that was thick and looked like flames all around his face. Fur that reminded all the other animals of the jungle fire and of the day Lion became fast and strong and loud and brave.

So it was. So it is to this very day.

Fan Dancing
(To the tune of "The Farmer in the Dell")

Japanese storytellers use a fan in their storytelling. The fan is closed or opened and moved to simulate actions or characters in the story. For this song you may wish to give each child a simple paper fan to use as indicated.

My fan can make the waves,
(Wave fans in a horizontal line, waist high.)
My fan can make the waves.
When I move my fan like this,
My fan can make the waves.

My fan can make the wind,
(Wave fans from side to side overhead.)
My fan can make the wind.
When I move my fan like this,
My fan can make the wind.

My fan can make a bird,
(Flutter fans in the air.)
My fan can make a bird.
When I move my fan like this,
My fan can make a bird.

My fan can fall like leaves,
(Flutter fans to the ground.)
My fan can fall like leaves.
When I move my fan like this,
My fan can fall like leaves.

And then we sit right down,
(All sit down.)
And then we sit right down.
When I move my fan like this,
And then we sit right down.

Grandmother's Kimono
(A Story with Props)

The Japanese kimono is no longer worn every day, as nowadays, dress in Japan is becoming more westernized. Even older women are abandoning this traditional dress, but children still associate the kimono with Japanese dress. And what a wonderful garment it is! The sleeves are used to carry small objects—a purse or a handkerchief, but probably not as many "treasures" as this story suggests. This story is similar to "Hold This, Please" (pp. 218-19), in that Grandmother ends up carrying all the treasures a child finds.

Children will be introduced to some Japanese words and phrases in this story. The word *arigato* means "thank you" and the suffix *chan* at the end of a child's name denotes "child." Cherry blossoms and elaborate decorations are worn in the hair, and fans are traditional accessories to carry. The cricket cage is an authentic touch—children often make their own cages to keep crickets they catch. You may follow up the story by having children make cricket cages from berry baskets by securing the top to the bottom with twist ties or pipe cleaners (see illustration).

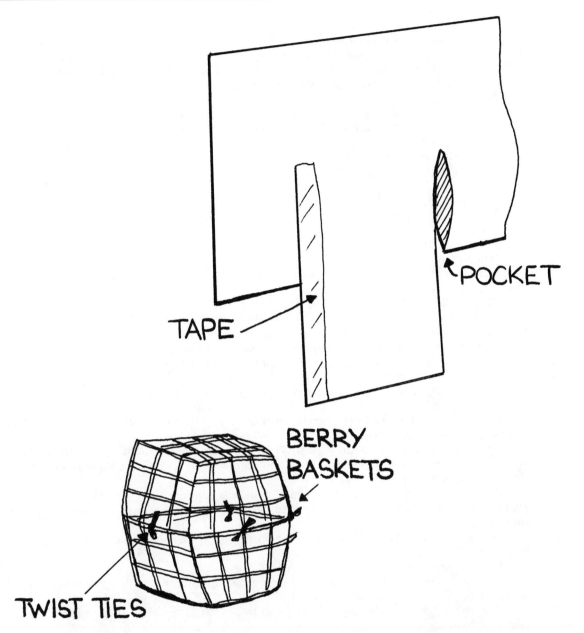

TAPE

POCKET

BERRY
BASKETS

TWIST TIES

To tell this story, make a kimono from paper (a dark blue wrapping paper will work nicely), following the illustration. Tape the "seams" together to hold the various objects. The cherry blossoms can be cut out from construction paper. Use a homemade cricket cage as described above for that part in the story.

Mukashi, mukashi, long, long ago, when Japanese women wore lovely, long kimonos every day, there lived a little girl named Jan-chan. Jan-chan lived with her mother and father in a small village. And, although she loved her parents dearly, she was never happier than when she was allowed to visit her grandmother far away in the city of Kioto.

Grandmother told Jan-chan stories and fed her delicious rice cakes. And Grandmother took Jan-chan along to shops and sometimes bought her little presents.

One day Jan-chan made the long trip to Kioto to visit Grandmother. When Jan-chan arrived, she saw that Grandmother was wearing a lovely, long kimono, dark blue as a midnight sky. The sleeves were long and full and big enough to hold all kinds of treasures.

"Oh, Grandmother! What a beautiful kimono. And such big sleeves it has!" said Jan-chan.

"Yes, my child, sleeves big enough for keeping treasures for Jan-chan," said Grandmother. "Today we will find something special to tuck inside."

And so Jan-chan and Grandmother began walking. They walked and they walked until Jan-chan's little feet were too tired to walk any longer. They rested by a cherry blossom tree.

"Oh, look, Grandmother, the first cherry blossoms! Cherry blossoms would be a treasure to keep," said Jan-chan.

"Yes, my child. Put the blossoms in Grandmother's kimono."

So Jan-chan carefully tucked the cherry blossoms in the sleeve of Grandmother's kimono.

After they had rested, Jan-chan and Grandmother went on walking. Before long Jan-chan stopped.

"Oh, look, Grandmother! A silver hairpin on the road! That would be a treasure to keep!" said Jan-chan.

"Yes, my child. Put the hairpin in Grandmother's kimono."

So Jan-chan put the silver hairpin in the sleeve of Grandmother's kimono, along with the cherry blossoms. Then Jan-chan and Grandmother continued their walk. Before long they came to the shops. So many stores! So many treasures inside the stores!

They stopped at the first stop that sold fans. Grandmother bought Jan-chan a lovely white fan with peach blossoms painted on the front side.

"Arigato, Grandmother. A fan is a treasure to keep," said Jan-chan.

"Yes, my child. Put the fan in Grandmother's kimono."

So Jan-chan tucked the fan in the sleeve of Grandmother's kimono, along with the silver hairpin and the cherry blossoms.

Next they stopped at a doll shop. There Grandmother bought Jan-chan the most beautiful koheshi doll in the whole shop. And the little girl tucked the koheshi doll in the sleeve of Grandmother's kimono.

Finally, they came to a shop where a man was selling cricket cages. Jan-chan had always wanted her own cricket cage to keep her own crickets, because crickets bring good fortune.

"Oh, look, Grandmother," said Jan-chan. "Cricket cages! A cricket cage can keep good fortune inside. A cricket cage is a treasure."

Grandmother laughed.

"Yes, my child. A cricket cage is a treasure. But Grandmother's kimono will not hold anything else."

"Perhaps I can carry the cage myself. And I will find a cricket to keep inside for you," said Jan-chan.

"That is a good idea," said Grandmother.

So Grandmother bought Jan-chan her very own cricket cage. On the way home Jan-chan caught one, two, three crickets. And she carried the cricket cage all by herself. Because Grandmother's kimono was already full of treasures.

Walk in My Shoes
(An Action Rhyme)

The expression "walk in my shoes" will be a new one for young children. It's not an easy concept to grasp, but the idea of empathizing with others, especially with people from other lands, is an important one today.

Teach children this rhyme and use the actions to begin a path to greater understanding.

I wear moccasins,
  (Point to self.)
You wear shoes.
  (Point to another.)
You don't dress like me.
  (Shake head.)
My skin is golden,
  (Point to self.)
Yours is not.
  (Point to another.)
You don't look like me.
  (Shake head.)

But I have feet,
  (Point to self.)
And you do, too.
  (Point to another.)
We both can run and play.
  (Run in place.)
So walk in my shoes,
Learn how I feel.
  (Hands over heart.)
We can be friends that way.
  (Arms out as if offering friendship.)

Buffalo Clothes
(A Chant)

Hunting the buffalo for the native American was a way of life. It was not for the sport of hunting, but for survival: each part of the buffalo was used completely. In this chant, dressing for the hunt is preparation for the hunt itself. The animal hides would be worn reverently later. This chant evokes a thoughtful tone about the native American and his ceremonial dress.

Show the children how to set the beat of Indian drums by pounding fists on the floor. Accent the first syllable of each line and all three of the last line.

Deer skin leggings
Feathered headdress
Woven blanket
Beaded necklace
Painted faces
Fringe and leather
Bow and arrow
Buffalo

A Feather in His Cap

Once upon a time, when the earth and sky were new, there lived a young boy, who was native American. The members of the tribe called him "Talkety-talk," because he talked all the time. He talked from the moment the great sun rose in the eastern sky, and he talked until the moon and stars came out in the night sky. Talkety-talk, talkety-talk, talkety, talkety, talkety-talk!

He talked so much that one day the squaws told him, "Talkety-talk! Talkety-talk! You're worse than the crows with your squawkety-squawk!"

But he didn't stop talking.

He talked so much that one day the braves said to him, "Talkety-talk! Talkety-talk! Go hide in the woods with your talkety-talk!"

So the boy left his tribe and went to the woods. The woods were dark and lonely. There was no one to talk to. But soon the boy met Deer. He was so happy to find someone to talk to! So he began—talkety-talk, talkety-talk, talkety, talkety, talkety-talk! Deer was such a quiet animal that he ran away.

The boy walked on through the woods until he met Rabbit. At last! Someone with big ears to hear him! So the boy began—talkety-talk, talkety-talk, talkety, talkety, talkety-talk! Well, Rabbit perked up her ears and hopped away.

The boy was all alone again. Then he looked down and saw a little chipmunk chattering away to herself. The boy was so happy that he answered—talkety-talk, talkety-talk, talkety, talkety, talkety-talk! All that talk was too much even for Chipmunk. Before you could say, "Jack Rabbit," Chipmunk swished her tail and ran away.

Now the boy was all alone. The moon and the stars came out. He sat down by a stream and just listened to the night.

The moon rose many times before the boy heard someone coming. It was the Chief of the Big Feather Headdress, his father.

When the Chief of the Big Feather Headdress saw his son just sitting quietly by the stream, he said to him, "My son, I see you have learned the lesson of silence. Even the animals of the woods do not listen to a talkety-talk."

The boy looked up, but he did not talk.

"Come, my son. I have a present for you," said the Chief of the Big Feather Headdress. Still the boy said nothing.

The chief took one white feather out of his big feather headdress and handed it to his son.

"This is a talking feather," the chief explained. "When you hold it in your hand, you may speak. But if you are wise, you will wear it in your headdress and be silent."

The boy took the feather and put it in his headdress. He went back with his father to the tribe.

Sometimes he used the talking feather to talk, but only when the squaws and braves were ready to listen. Most of the time he wore the feather in his headdress and was silent.

Everyone said he became wise in the end. You might even say that he had earned a feather in his cap for the great lesson he had learned.

Made in the U.S.A.

(To the tune of "Paw Paw Patch")

We wear snowsuits in Alaska,
We wear snowsuits in Alaska,
We wear snowsuits in Alaska.
Sing about the things we like to wear.

We wear big hats down in Texas,
We wear big hats down in Texas,
We wear big hats down in Texas.
Sing about the things we like to wear.

We wear grass skirts in Hawaii,
We wear grass skirts in Hawaii,
We wear grass skirts in Hawaii.
Sing about the things we like to wear.

Different kinds of outside clothing,
Different kinds of outside clothing,
Different kinds of outside clothing.
We can wear them in the U.S.A.

Feet 'Round the World

(A Foot-Clomping Chant)

Wooden Dutch shoes—
Clomp, clomp, clomp,
Clomp, clomp, clomp,
Clomp, clomp, clomp.
Wooden shoes are fun.

Japanese clogs—
Plop, plop, plop,
Plop, plop, plop,
Plop, plop, plop.
Clogs are so much fun.

Indian moccasins—
Creep, creep, creep,
Creep, creep, creep,
Creep, creep, creep.
Moccasins are so fun.

'Round the world
I clomp and creep,
Plop and creep,
Creep, creep, creep.
'Round the world
Go my two feet.
Shoes are so much fun!

Fiesta Finery

(To the tune of "Mexican Hat Dance")

If you or someone you know has traveled south of the border, be sure to bring in some colorful Mexican clothing for the children to see. Then sing this song.

A poncho's a cloak like a blanket.
A serape can look, oh so snappy.
A rebozo can carry a baby
And keep your bambino so happy!

A sombrero can look very dashing
And keep off the sun on a hot day.
Let's put on our Mexican clothing
And have a fiesta today.
Ole!

Desert Clothes and Eskimos

If you lived in the desert
Where it was hot,
Would you wear lots of clothing?
No, you would not!

The air would blow through
Your full robe of white.
You'd use a wool jellaba
To wrap you at night.

With a cloth on your face
To keep out the sand,
You'd ride on a camel
Across the hot land.

If you lived in the arctic
Where it could freeze,
Would you wear a bikini?
If you did you would sneeze!

Parkas are fur coats
For some Eskimos,
Who wear sealskin mukluks
To cover their toes.

Wear polar bear mittens
To keep out the chill,
And two pairs of pants
When you slide down the hill.

Arctic cold and desert sands,
Different clothes for different lands.

GAMES FOR LONG AGO AND FAR AWAY

Yankee Doodle Round
(To the tune of "London Bridge")

Set this game up in the usual manner for "London Bridge Is Falling Down." On the word "macaroni" the child under the bridge is caught and gets to wear a Yankee Doodle-style hat. Continue play for several rounds and give everyone a hat at the end.

Yankee Doodle come to town,
Come to town, come to town.
Yankee Doodle come to town
On your pony.

Put a feather in your cap,
In your cap, in your cap.
Put a feather in your cap:
Macaroni!

Mummy Wrap

Divide into teams. Give each team a roll of toilet paper to wrap one child as a mummy from head to toe. Give each team a small prize for their efforts: "Fastest Wrap," "Most Wrapped," "Most Toilet Paper Used," etc.

Feather Frolic

Give a bright paper feather to each child and have them all sit on the floor Indian-style. The leader has a headdress full of colored feathers, each with a simple trick written on the back (for example, jump three times, make a funny face, etc.) The leader pulls one feather and has all the children with the same color stand up. Together they all do the tricks written on the back of the feather and then sit down. Game continues until all the headdress feathers are gone.

Scarf Dance
(To the tune of "Good-Night, Ladies")

In the Mediterranean area many circle dances are done with the participants holding scarves between them, rather than joining hands. You can use scarves or simply give each child a strip of material to hold between him and his neighbor. Move in a circle using the movement indicated.

Dance by hopping,
Dance by hopping,
Dance by hopping,
Dance a dance of scarves.

Dance by running,
Dance by running,
Dance by running,
Dance a dance of scarves.

Other verses might include walking, jumping, or skipping.

'Round the World

Make a paper hat from another culture—a Dutch hat, an Alpine hat, or a Chinese coolie hat, for example—for each child. Give a hat to one child, the rest sit in a circle. The child puts on the hat and walks around the circle as the others chant:

'Round the world and back again
'Round the world and back again
Come with me around the world:
I pick YOU!

On the word "you" the child taps the nearest child without a hat who is seated in the circle. They both run around the circle and the one who gets back first sits in the empty space. If the one left standing does not have a hat, give him one; play continues by repeating the chant. Each time the child must choose the nearest child who does not have a hat, so eventually everyone has a turn—and a hat!

CRAFTS FOR LONG AGO AND FAR AWAY

Egyptian Mask

Start with a simple eye mask of pink paper, using the design shown in costume party masks (p. 157). Cut out the eyes for the children. Add eye makeup with markers. Glue a three-piece headdress in place as shown in the illustration. Add thin elastic cord to the back, so children can wear the masks.

Knight's Helmet

Use an ice cream carton cylinder for the basic shape of this knight's helmet. Cut out an eye opening approximately 6 x 2 inches. Then attach a visor piece to move down over the eye opening with brad fasteners. Let children cover the helmet with aluminum foil so it will look like a shining suit of armor. Paper plumes may be inserted in the top.

Colonial Costumes

Mother Hubbard-Style of Colonial Cap

Girls can make a simple colonial cap from a large circle (about 24 inches in diameter) of fabric. An old sheet will do nicely. Cut out the circle and make slits evenly spaced around the cap just a few inches from the edge. Provide children with a long ribbon to thread through the slits and pull the ribbon so the cap fits the head. Tie the ribbon ends together.

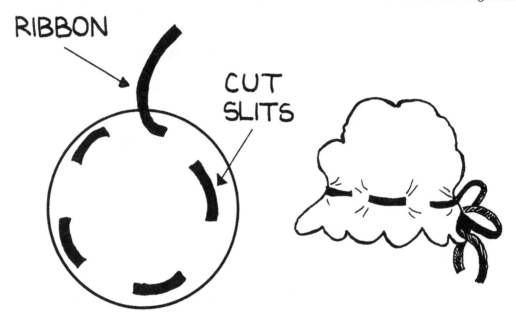

Tricorner Hat

Girls and boys will enjoy making the patriot hat described in chapter 6 (p. 184).

Handlebar Mustache

After you sing the song "Clothes Long Ago," children will enjoy making their own handlebar mustaches from card stock or tagboard. Simply cut out the mustache shape using the pattern and let children color the mustache with crayons. The mustache fits in the nostrils.

African Animal Masks

You can make a variety of three-dimensional animal masks. Try your favorite picture book of African folktales for inspiration. Cut posterboard using the patterns shown in the story "The Pride of the Lion" (p. 109). Add features with colored pencils, crayons, or magic markers, as well as parts such as trunks and horns cut from posterboard and stapled on. Cut on the slits indicated. Overlap and staple the edges.

Japanese Kimono Crafts

Simple Kimono

Following the illustration, cut kimono shapes from flowered wrapping paper and let children arrange the pieces on construction paper. You might cut the kimono from plain paper and let the children draw their own designs.

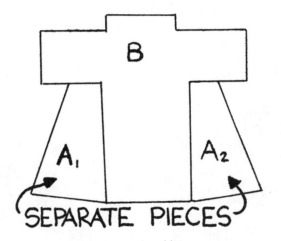

Kimono Doll

Make a kimono doll by following these instructions to fold the kimono:

Start with a 6-inch square of wrapping paper.
Fold paper diagonally.
Fold the diagonal edge down 1/2 inch.
Fold each end down to form the arms of the kimono, as shown in the illustration.
Glue in place.

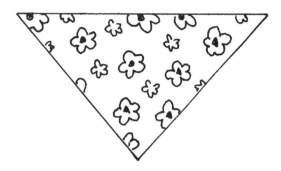

FIRST FOLD

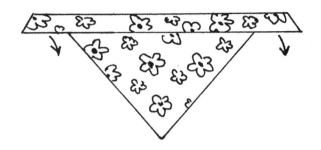

2ND FOLD

3RD FOLD

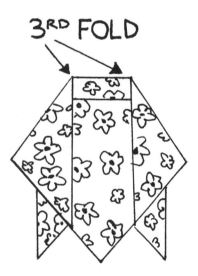

ADD HEAD

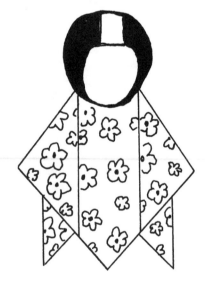

Japanese Bunraku Puppet

A Japanese Bunraku puppet is a large puppet manipulated by three puppeteers—one moves the feet, one moves the left arm, and another moves the head and right arm. Movement becomes lifelike, so the puppeteers move right along with the puppet.

Children can make a version of this kind of puppet that is easier to manipulate, because the "puppet" is attached to the child's body. Thus, the child becomes the puppet.

Make the head of the puppet from a paper plate and attach it to the main body piece with a brad fastener. Make the arms and legs as separate pieces, and attach with brad fasteners. The legs swing free, but the arms of the "puppet" are attached to the child's arms with big rubber bands. Hang the puppet around the child's neck with thin elastic cord.

The puppet may become a woman in a kimono or a character from a Japanese folktale. The wicked Oni from "Funny Little Woman" is a popular choice.

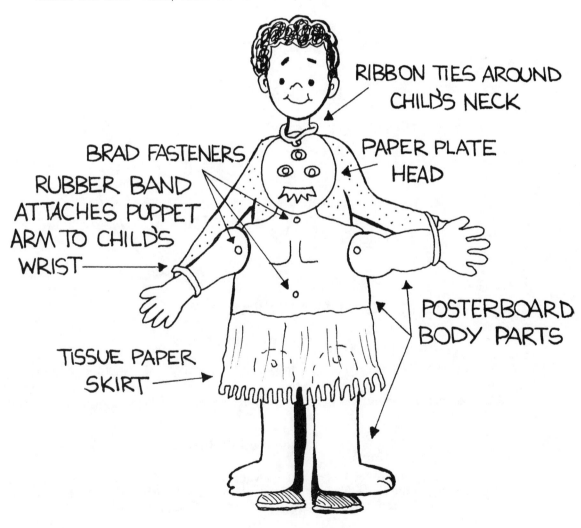

RIBBON TIES AROUND CHILD'S NECK

BRAD FASTENERS

PAPER PLATE HEAD

RUBBER BAND ATTACHES PUPPET ARM TO CHILD'S WRIST

POSTERBOARD BODY PARTS

TISSUE PAPER SKIRT

Feather in My Cap Craft

After you have told the story "A Feather in His Cap" (pp. 115-16), invite children to make their own feather headdresses. Cut a length of corrugated cardboard the length of the child's head and let them color the headband with crayons or felt-tipped markers. Staple the headband at the ends. Insert a real feather or one cut from paper in the corrugated band.

Eskimo Spirit Mask

Eskimos wear masks in their dances, to honor the "spirits," and even to change into the "spirits." From paper plates, children can make simple spirit masks to wear or just for display. If the masks are worn, staple thin elastic cord to the sides of the plate. Cut eye and mouth holes. With tape or brad fasteners, attach feathers for bird spirits or fish shapes for fish to the sides of the mask.

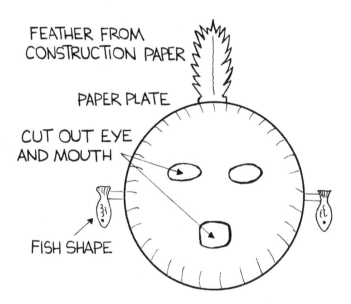

DISPLAYS FOR LONG AGO AND FAR AWAY

Now and Then

Arrange to borrow clothes from a historical society—or grandmother's trunk! Divide the bulletin board or display case into two parts with the old clothes on one side. On the other, put their modern counterparts. String colorful ribbons from the old clothes to the new ones.

The Good Old Days

Create a hands-on display by collecting a variety of 50s clothes from saddle shoes to letter sweaters to poodle skirts. Place them in an old suitcase along with 45rpm records and yearbooks of people from the "old days"—their parents and grandparents!

Cobbler, Cobbler, Mend My Shoe

In days of old, the cobbler repaired shoes and the shoemaker made new ones, but today children will know only about shoe repair shops and shoe stores with ready-made shoes. Expand children's knowledge of shoemaking and shoe care with a display of shoe tools and accessories. Ask a shoe repair shop for unusual tools, rummage through attics for high button shoes and boot jacks, and collect shoe trees and shoe horns from people in your community. An old cobbler's bench or a modern reproduction would make a fascinating addition to this display.

Pompadours and Pigtails

Decorate your bulletin board with pictures of unusual hairstyles from the past and present day. Some examples might be pompadour styles from the eighteenth century, crew cuts, pigtails, Afro cuts, periwigs, ancient Greek or Roman styles, pony tails.

To make this display interactive, make masks of the different hairstyles that the children can try on. Put a mirror close by.

Travel to the Orient

Ask local world travelers to loan kimonos for display. Or make a life-sized kimono by enlarging the pattern in the story "Grandmother's Kimono" and making it out of a long roll of wrapping paper. Display several of these kimonos with some bunraku puppets in the craft section of this chapter (p. 123).

Dolls the World Around

Invite collectors of dolls from around the world to display their collections in a glass display case. Be sure to identify the countries and display books from the cultures represented.

Putting Our Heads Together

Set out a number of wig stands. (Make easy ones out of papier-mâché over balloons. Break the balloon when dry and paint on a simple face. Place upside-down over pop bottles for stands.) On each put a different type of head covering—sombrero, turban, top hat, crown, ten-gallon hat.

All over the World

Put a large world map on a bulletin board. Cut out people in native costume (children when possible) from *National Geographic* or other travel magazines and mount them on the board near the country they represent.

5
Fairytale, Fantasy, and Just-Pretend

INTRODUCTION

Since earliest times, people have donned masks and costume to tell stories of experiences in the world around them. Children respond to this human need to order the events in their lives by creating a world of make-believe. Clothes become the natural vehicle for that imaginative experience.

The three subsections of this chapter include fairytales, modern fantasy, and "just-pretend" stories in which costume assumes a central role. There is some overlap with clothes included in chapter 4, "Long Ago and Far Away." But the dress in this chapter involves the costume a child might wear in imaginative play rather than clothing actually worn in the past or in another culture.

The books and activities in the fairytale section include the familiar folktales about Red Riding Hood, Rumplestiltskin, and Cinderella. We have adapted these tales to emphasize the articles of apparel and to make the stories more accessible to young children. We have not found a picture book of Cinderella that is simple enough to read in its entirety to young children and still include the essentials. "Cinderella on a Tube" will help you tell the story for young children by focusing on the magic clothes transformation. *Red Riding Hood* and *The Frog Prince* are retold through stories and action rhymes to give children an opportunity to take active roles.

Modern fantasy books from Edward Lear's *The New Vestments* to Nancy Willard's *The Nightgown of the Sullen Moon* show unusual clothes or clothes worn in unlikely situations. Extend these books by singing "Mr. Glop," chanting the "Clothesline Fantasy," and telling "Why the Stars Dance in the Sky" with a sequined story cape.

Costume and "just-pretend" picture books abound, especially books about Halloween costumes. We have annotated our favorites and anticipate many more excellent choices in the future. Shy children identify with Thomas in *A Tiger Called Thomas* and worry about finding just the right costume like Emily in *Emily's Bunch* or Arthur in *Arthur's Halloween Costume*. Invite children to participate in "Magic," a creative dramatics activity, sing "Ten Trick-or-Treaters," and enjoy the "just-pretend" activities in this chapter as you help children explore these possibilities.

INITIATING ACTIVITY

Dress-Up Clothes for Play
(To the tune of "Mary Had a Little Lamb")

Clothes for every kind of fun,
Party suits, every day!
Funny clothes and holidays,
Clothes worn many ways.

Halloween and fairytales,
Costume plays, special days.
Clothes to help us just pretend,
Dress-up clothes for play.
Yea!

Glad Rags

(A Poem)

Put your Glad Rags on
And come out tonight
All gussied up
In your fancy tights!
Fine full feathers,
Spangles that shine—
You are dressed up
To the nines!

LITERATURE-SHARING EXPERIENCES

Books about Once-upon-a-Time Clothes

Andersen, Hans Christian. **The Emperor's New Clothes**. Retold and illustrated by Nadine Bernard West-cott. Little, Brown, 1984.

The Emperor in this retelling of the popular tale loves nothing better than trying on new clothes. When two swindlers promise to weave him a suit of clothes that will appear invisible to those foolish or unfit for their office, the Emperor is easily duped. As the Emperor parades down the street in his magnificent new clothes, no one speaks out until a small child reveals the truth. The Emperor may look foolish, but he carries on wisely to the cheers of the crowd. Westcott's droll cartoon-style illustrations that sport a pink-bottomed Emperor match perfectly the joie de vivre of the text!

De Regniers, Beatrice Schenk. **Red Riding Hood**. Illustrated by Edward Gorey. Atheneum, 1972.

The classic fairytale of the little girl with the red hood who is accosted by a wolf, told in verse.

Galdone, Paul. **The Elves and the Shoemaker**. Clarion, 1984.

A poor shoemaker with only enough leather left to make one pair of shoes is secretly helped by two elves. In return for their faithful service, the shoemaker and his wife make fine suits for the naked little spirits. And though the elves never return, the shoemaker and his wife prosper as long as they live.

Galdone, Paul. **Puss in Boots**. Seabury, 1976.

The miller's youngest son inherits Puss. Puss asks for a pair of boots and a sack with a cord and tells the son he will never be unhappy again. With these accoutrements, Puss outwits the giant, acquires a castle and fields and the king's daughter for his grateful master.

Grimm Brothers. **The Twelve Dancing Princesses**. Illustrated by Errol Le Cain. Viking, 1978.

Twelve lovely princesses wear out their dancing shoes each night until a clever soldier with a magic cape that makes him invisible learns their secret and claims the eldest for his own.

Jacobs, Joseph. **Tom Tit Tot**. Illustrated by Evaline Ness. Scribners, 1965.

In this English variant of Rumplestiltskin, a girl must spin flax. She gets help from a little black imp, but must guess his name or become his. Ness's woodcut illustrations capture the flavor of the Cornish text.

Jeffers, Susan. **Cinderella**. Dial, 1985.

Jeffers's jewel-like illustrations intensify the magic of this popular fairytale, though the text may be a bit long in its entirety for younger children. You might use the book and just read portions of the text for them.

Myers, Bernice. **Sidney Rella and the Glass Sneaker**. Macmillan, 1985.

This "unorthodox" fairytale updates the Cinderella tale. Sidney Rella is left to do the chores while his brothers run off to football practice. But a fairy godfather comes to his aid by doing the chores and turning his clothes into a football uniform and glass sneakers, so Sidney can go on to become a winning football player.

Zelinsky, Paul. **Rumplestiltskin**. Dutton, 1986.

In this retelling of the Grimm Brothers' tale of the miller's daughter who spins straw into gold with the help of a little man, Zelinsky's oil paintings richly detail the medieval setting. The straw spun into gold glows with fairytale magic.

Zemach, Harve. **Duffy and the Devil**. Illustrated by Margot Zemach. Farrar, Straus & Giroux, 1973.

In this variant of Rumplestiltskin, Squire Lovel of Trove finds a maid to help his old housekeeper with spinning and sewing and knitting his clothes. The young woman Duffy must rely on the devil to help her spin squire's stockings. In payment for his work, he'll take her away at the end of three years, unless she guesses his name. When the three years are almost up, Duffy has help to guess the devil's name: Tarraway. When the devil disappears into a puff of smoke, all of his knitting turns to ashes. The squire, out on the moors at the time, suddenly finds he has no clothes. Duffy swears never to knit again. And she never does.

Related Activities about Once-upon-a-Time Clothes

Magic Up Your Sleeve
(To the tune of "Yankee Doodle")

Cinderella got her wish:
    (Hands clasped to heart.)
She became a princess.
    (Curtsy.)
Magic turned her dirty rags
    (Flick hands in disgust.)
Into a gown of riches.
    (Hands up in delight.)

Mind your manners with a frog—
    (Shake warning finger.)
You can never tell:
He might be a prince inside
    (Bow.)
A witch's nasty spell.
    (Hands up in surprise.)

Fairytales can still come true,
    (Hands to heart again.)
If only you'll believe.
Close your eyes and dream a dream—
    (Hands over eyes.)
There's magic up your sleeve!
    (Hands up in surprise.)

Cinderella on a Tube

Tell this very simple version of the traditional Cinderella story. Mount the figures of Cinderella (both in her rags and in her ball gown), the fairy godmother, and the prince on cardboard rings around a paper towel tube. Flip each character up as indicated in the story.

PAPER TOWEL ROLL   PAPER RINGS

(Flip poor Cinderella up.) Once upon a time there was a poor girl named Cinderella. She was very kind to everyone, but she was still very, very poor.

So when Cinderella heard there was to be a fancy dress ball at the palace where the prince lived, she knew she could not go. She had no nice clothes or fancy slippers to wear to such a nice ball.

Now someone knew what Cinderella was thinking. It was someone who knew how kind Cinderella was and wanted her to be happy. That someone was her Fairy Godmother.

(Flip up Fairy Godmother.) Poof! The Fairy Godmother appeared by Cinderella and granted her a wish. Of course, Cinderella wished to go to the ball. So with a wave of her magic wand, the Fairy Godmother "poofed" off Cinderella's rags and dressed her in a beautiful ball gown. *(Flip down poor Cinderella, flip up fancy one.)*

As Cinderella started off to the ball, her Fairy Godmother called after her, "Be sure to be home by midnight or your beautiful clothes will turn back to rags."

(Flip down Fairy Godmother, flip up prince.) Cinderella went to the ball and danced and danced all night with the prince. How happy they were together. Then suddenly, Cinderella heard the clock strike. *(Have children count with you.)* 1-2-3-4-5- ... Cinderella said good-bye to the prince and ran out of the ball. *(Flip down prince.)* 6-7-8-9- ... Cinderella ran down the steps and lost a slipper. 10-11- ... Cinderella had no time to stop for the lost slipper. She ran on into the night. 12- ... *(Flip down fancy Cinderella. Flip up poor one.)* Cinderella's beautiful clothes turned back into rags ... all except for the other glass slipper.

(Flip down poor Cinderella. Flip up prince.) The next day the prince looked everywhere for the beautiful girl from the ball. The only clue he had was one glass slipper. When he came to the last house, he saw Cinderella. *(Flip up poor Cinderella.)* "Is this your slipper?" he asked and he showed her the glass slipper. Cinderella pulled the other glass slipper out of her pocket. Just at that moment the Fairy Godmother appeared. *(Flip up Fairy Godmother.)* She changed Cinderella back into her beautiful ball gown. *(Flip down poor Cinderella, flip up fancy one.)* Cinderella and the prince were married. They ruled the kingdom with kindness and lived happily ever after.

How to Marry a Prince

Have even more fun with this poem by having the children roll one hand over the other to suggest spinning for the first stanza on *Rumplestiltskin*, wave a magic wand over the pumpkin in the second stanza about *Cinderella*, and pretend to look into the magic mirror for the last stanza about *Beauty and the Beast*.

Marry a prince?
That's a cinch!
Name an elf
All by yourself.
Spin the flax into gold—
That's the way the story's told.

Marry a prince?
That's a cinch!
Just act kindly to a beast,
Dine with him and have a feast.
Look into a mirror of gold—
That's the way the story's told.

Marry a prince?
That's a cinch!
Get yourself a magic friend—
She knows how to just pretend.
Find a pumpkin round and gold—
That's the way the story's told.

Prince-less Princess
Or
Mind Your Manners with a Frog

Tell this story with hand puppets. You will need puppets for the King, Princess, and Frog, but not for the prince since the frog does not turn into a prince in this version.

You may wish to read a picture-book version of the Frog Prince before you tell this story, but it will stand on its own even if you don't. The original tale is a story about keeping promises, and this version retains that theme but adds one about vanity and dress.

Once upon a time there lived a Royal Princess. She lived in a palace with more than enough gowns and crowns to wear a new one every day of the year. But she wanted more because she was spoiled rotten. Her father, the King, always gave her everything she wanted.

One ordinary day the Royal Princess said to her father, the King, "Daddy, I want a golden gown. This old gown looks like a rag!"

So the King ordered the Royal Seamstress to make the Princess a golden gown.

The next day the Princess said, "Daddy, I want golden slippers. I'm not fit to be seen in these old sandals."

So the King ordered the Royal Cobbler to make the Princess some golden slippers.

And the next day the Princess said, "Daddy, I want a golden crown to match my golden slippers and my golden gown. I'll never find me a prince if I look like this!"

So the King ordered the Royal Crown Maker to make the Princess a golden crown.

And so the days went on like that. The Princess kept on asking for new gowns and crowns, and her father, the King, ordered the Royal Seamstress or the Royal Crown Maker to make them. Of course, the Princess was so spoiled that she never bothered to say "Please" or "Thank You" or things like that.

Finally, one day the King went on a holiday so the Princess could not ask him for anything. That day the Princess went out in the royal garden to admire herself in the garden pond. Just as she leaned over to admire herself in the water—PLOP!—her crown fell off her head and disappeared in the pond.

"YOWWWWWWWW!" cried the Princess. "My crown! I've lost my beautiful crown!"

Of course, the Princess had 364 other crowns, but she was so spoiled she cried anyway. The Princess cried so loudly that a big frog in the pond fell off his lily pad and splashed into the water.

"Hey you!" cried the Princess.

"Ribbit?" said the Frog.

"Yeah! I'm talking to you, Pop Eyes," snapped the Princess.

"Ribbit?" said the Frog.

"Is that all you can say for yourself?" asked the Princess.

"Pardon me," said the Frog (who really could talk quite well).

"I thought you could talk," said the Princess. "Well, don't just sit there with your tongue hanging out. Get down there and bring me my crown!"

"Pardon me, Princess. You should mind your manners with a frog!"

"Mind my manners! How dare you tell me what to do. Just watch out or I'll tell my daddy, the King, on you!"

The next night when the King returned from his holiday, the Princess told him all about her crown and the frog.

"You mean you met a talking frog?" asked the King. "You must always mind your manners with a frog."

"Why?" asked the Princess.

"Because you can never tell about frogs," explained the King. "He just might be a prince inside a witch's magic spell."

"Really?" asked the Princess. "But he is such an ugly frog. If he is a prince inside, I'll bet he's an ugly one. Oh well, I suppose I could have said 'please' to him just to be on the safe side."

So the next day the Princess went out to the garden and called, "Froggie. Here, Froggie. Hey get off your pad and get me my crown. Uh, I almost forgot—Please!"

The Frog almost fell off his lily pad again because he was so surprised that the Princess had said "Please."

"Ribbit! What do I get in return for getting your crown?" he said.

"What do you get? Oh, I dunno, I guess I could find you a few fat flies."

"Yuck! Flies! Just what kind of a frog do you think I am?"

"Oh yes, I suppose you're really a prince turned into a frog by a wicked witch."

"Yeah, well, you can never tell," said the Frog.

"Very well, if you get me my crown, you can come to dinner," said the Princess.

"Now you're talkin'. But you have to promise—no flies for dinner. And then I'd like a good night's sleep on your best bed."

Well, the Princess could hardly stand the sight of him, but she wanted her crown back, so she promised. And just as quick as a frog can catch a fly, this frog jumped down into the pad and brought back the royal crown. Now the Princess was pleased, but, like always, she forgot her manners. She didn't say "Thank you." She just ran into the palace and slammed the door.

Before long, the Frog came squishing his way up the steps and called out, "Princess, let me in. You promised!"

So the Princess let the Frog in.

Then the Frog said, "Princess, you promised to feed me dinner."

So the Princess shoved him a plate of leftover peas and prune whip.

"And don't burp!" said the Princess. "Your table manners make me sick!"

After dinner, the Frog asked to go up to the bed chamber.

"But you'll get my bed all wet and squishy."

"Princess, you promised!"

"Oh very well, but you'd really better turn into a handsome prince by morning!"

So the Princess showed the Frog up to her bed chamber. The Frog jumped up on her pillow, and, of course, he made a big puddle.

"Now look what you've done!" screamed the Princess. "You've wet my bed and splashed all over my lovely golden gown. I don't care if you are a prince inside. Get out of here immediately!"

And that's just what the Frog did. He decided he didn't want to turn back into a prince. He just went back to the pond and lived happily ever after.

As for the Princess—well, she was a princess, but she never found a prince. You might say she was a prince-less princess. All she had in the end were her gowns and crowns and bad manners.

Frog King
(An Action Rhyme)

Have all the children squat like frogs for the first stanza. Point to each child as you say every word in the second stanza. The child you point to on the word "king" stands up to become the first king. Repeat the second stanza, counting only the children squatting, until everyone is standing.

Froggy in the lake,
Froggy in the pond,
See I've got
A magic wand.

Hop, hop, froggies,
Sing, sing, sing.
One froggy now
Becomes the king!

Little Red Riding Hood Retold
(A Circle Story)

This version of the old folktale focuses on Red Riding Hood's red cape and hood. It uses a "story wheel" to help you tell it. To make a story wheel, cut two paper circles the same size. On the top circle draw a picture of Red Riding Hood's cape and hood on one side, and a picture of Granny's nightcap and granny gown on the other. Then cut out face holes so the different faces will appear in the clothes as you turn the wheel. On the under circle draw the faces of Red Riding Hood, Wolf, and Granny. Fasten the circles together with a brad fastener and turn the story wheel as you tell the story.

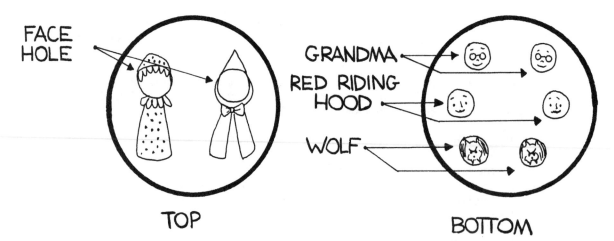

Once upon a time there lived a little girl with her mother in a small cottage at the edge of a dark forest. The little girl loved the color red so, on her birthday, the mother made her a beautiful red velvet cape and hood. The little girl loved her red cape with the hood. She wore it night and day. She never took it off. So her mother called her "Little Red Riding Hood."

One day the mother said to her, "Red Riding Hood, your granny is sick in bed. Please take this basket of little cakes to her so she will be comforted. The woods are dark and danger may be waiting. Do not talk to strangers along the way."

So Red Riding Hood took the basket of cakes. She tied up her hood. And she promised to be careful.

Now the journey was long, for Red Riding Hood had to go all the way around the forest to reach Granny's house. It was deep and dark and scary.

As Red Riding Hood walked she sang a little song:

The woods are dark,
Deep, and scary.
Something's there,
Huge and hairy!

But, Red Riding Hood was a brave little girl, so she went on. Then she sang this little song:

But I'll be brave.
I'll be good,
Because my name's
Red Riding Hood!

When Red Riding Hood got to the darkest part of the forest, something huge and hairy was waiting. That something was a wolf!

Wolf smelled the cakes. Then he saw Red Riding Hood. (She looked good, too!) And THEN he saw the beautiful red velvet cape and hood!

Wouldn't I look good in that hood? he thought.

So Wolf sang this little song:

Um, those cakes
Smell warm and good,
But I'd rather have
That cape and hood!

Of course, Wolf might have grabbed the hood right away, but he didn't want it to get torn. Instead, he asked Red Riding Hood where she was going with her basket.

"Why, I'm on my way to Granny's house, all the way around on the other side of the woods. But I'm not supposed to talk to strangers, so I must be right on my way," she said.

Hmm—Wolf thought to himself. All the better. Surely she'll take off her hood when she gets to Granny's house. And then I can take it! (He could just picture himself in that hood!)

Well, Wolf said good-bye to Red Riding Hood. Then he ran straight through the woods while Red Riding Hood was walking around the woods.

When Wolf got to Granny's, he barged right in. He stuffed Granny in the closet. He slipped on her granny gown and nightcap. And he crawled into her bed.

Before long Red Riding Hood knocked at the door of Granny's house. The old wolf was inside in Granny's bed. He didn't look much like Granny, but he scrunched down in her bedclothes and called out in his sweetest voice,

Come in, come in!
Don't be afraid.
Come show me that hood
You mother has made!

So Red Riding Hood came in and went up to the bed. "Oh, Granny," she said, "such big eyes you have."

"All the better to see you with, my dear," said Wolf.

"Oh, Granny," said Red Riding Hood, "such dark hairy arms you have."

"All the better to hug you with," said Wolf.

"Oh, Granny," said Red Riding Hood, "such big teeth you have. And they're chattering, too!"

Well—thought Wolf to himself—this is my chance. So he said,

Come closer, my dear.
Don't be afraid.
Give Granny that hood
Your mother has made!

So Red Riding Hood put her hood on the wolf's head, and then she saw his long hairy ears. But it was too late!

The wolf jumped out of bed and ran out of the house. He ran and he ran back through the woods with the hood on his head!

But Red Riding Hood ran after him. This time she ran straight into the woods. And Red Riding Hood and Wolf had a terrible fight. 'Round and 'round they fought over the cape. In the end Red Riding Hood must have won, because she came out wearing the hood on her head!

Then she ran back to Granny's and helped her out of the closet and told her the whole story. In the end they all lived happily ever after. (As for Wolf, he was too embarrassed to ever show his face again!)

Magic Things

(To the tune of "The Farmer in the Dell")

The first verse is for *Cinderella*, the second is for *The Twelve Dancing Princesses*, and the third is for *Big Anthony and the Magic Ring*.

I've got a magic wand,
I've got a magic wand.
Puff! Puff!
It's done its stuff—
My rags are gone, you see!

I've got a magic ring,
I've got a magic ring.
Puff! Puff!
It's done its stuff—
I'm handsome as can be!

I've got a magic cape,
I've got a magic cape.
Puff! Puff!
It's done its stuff—
Invisibility!

Books about Dreams and Schemes

Barrett, Judi. **Animals Should Definitely Not Wear Clothing**. Illustrated by Ron Barrett. Atheneum, 1971.

A series of absurd conclusions follows the statement: "Animals should definitely not wear clothing ...." Some of the results include "It would be disastrous for a porcupine" who pokes holes through a dress; a hen lays an egg in a pair of pants; a moose tangles suspenders in his antlers; and an elephant wears a flowered dress, like a woman—embarrassing!

De Paola, Tomie. **Big Anthony and the Magic Ring**. Harcourt Brace Jovanovich, 1979.

Big Anthony borrows Strega Nona's magic ring so he can turn himself into Handsome Big Anthony, but he soon learns that he may be getting more than he bargained for.

Hadithi, Mwenye. **Greedy Zebra**. Illustrated by Adrienne Kennaway. Little, Brown, 1984.

Long ago all the animals in the world were a dull color. They had no coats, horns, or spots and stripes until they discovered a cave of treasures. All went except greedy Zebra, who kept on eating until only a few strips of black material were left. He had a terrible time squeezing into his coat. After one more snack, he burst through the seams, so "to this day his chubby stomach shines through his coat because he is so greedy."

Lear, Edward. **The New Vestments**. Illustrated by Arnold Lobel. Bradbury, 1970.

In this story in verse an old man in the Kingdom of Tess invents a purely original dress—a hat of a loaf of brown bread, a shirt of dead mice, shoes and drawers of rabbit skins, a waistcoat and trousers of pork chops, buttons of chocolate drops, a coat of pancakes, and a cloak of cabbage leaves. As he walks down the street, a tumult of beasts and boys descend upon him and make mincemeat out of his garments as he runs home with no clothes on and declares he will *never more* wear a similar dress!

Reinach, Jacquelyn. **Me Too Iguana**. Illustrated by Richard Hefter. Holt, Rinehart and Winston, 1977.

Iguana had a lovely green color, but wants to be like everyone else. She ties a rubber hose on her nose to look like Elephant, sticks yellow wool on her head to look like Lion, paints on stripes to look like Zebra, and shakes on feathers to look like Goose. All the animals recognize her problem so they invite her to a costume party. When she arrives at the party, she discovers everyone is dressed as an iguana! But Iguana gets the prize for being the best iguana and likes herself that way.

Seuss, Dr. "What Was I Scared Of?" from **The Sneeches and Other Stories**. Random House, 1961.

On a walk in the woods, a typical Seuss creature spies a pair of green pants walking with nobody inside them. The spooky pants follow him until the creature and the pants admit their mutual fears.

Small, David. **Imogene's Antlers**. Crown, 1985.

Imogene wakes up to discover she's grown a pair of antlers. Dressing is difficult, and her mother decides the antlers must be hidden, so a milliner creates a special hat. The next day the antlers are gone, but Imogene has grown peacock feathers instead.

Sutton, Jane. **What Should a Hippo Wear?** Illustrated by Lynne Munsinger. Houghton Mifflin, 1979.

Bertha the hippopotamus can't find a large enough dress to wear to the jungle dance, so she decorates herself with body paint, but she discovers her friends like her just the way she used to be.

Watson, Paulene. **The Walking Coat**. Illustrated by Tomie De Paola. Walker, 1980.

Cousin Charley gives Scott his old hunting coat which he snuggles into when it gets cold. The coat is so big that Scott is lost inside, so everyone calls it "the walking coat." The coat has its picture taken for the newspaper, catches a thief, and enjoys the attention of amused crowds before it returns home for lunch.

Willard, Nancy. **The Nightgown of the Sullen Moon**. Illustrated by David McPhail. Harcourt Brace Jovanovich, 1983.

Ellen Fitzpatrick leaves her blue flannel nightgown stitched with stars on the clothesline on the billionth birth night of the full moon. The moon watches the nightgown in envy and goes to earth to find one herself. She tries on many until she finds one like Ellen Fitzpatrick's and wears it home. People and animals now cannot find the moon when they look for her. The moon hears people crying for her, so the moon hides the gown in a drawer at the back of the sky. But, on nights when you see no moon, you can be sure the moon is trying on the gown and dreaming she is back on earth.

Williams, Linda. **The Little Old Lady Who Was Not Afraid of Anything**. Illustrated by Megan Lloyd. Thomas Y. Crowell, 1986.

When a little old lady goes out walking on a windy afternoon, she sees two big shoes going CLOMP, CLOMP. She declares she's not afraid, but before long she meets pants that go WIGGLE, WIGGLE, a shirt that goes SHAKE, SHAKE, gloves that go CLAP, CLAP, and a head that goes NOD, NOD. She continues to declare she's not afraid, but she pacifies the whole perambulating wardrobe with a clever solution.

Related Activities about Dreams and Schemes

The Happiest Animal
(A Story with Props)

Tell this story with a cape, large bow, scarf, hat, and one mitten. (You can change the colors in the story to match the clothing you have.) Select five children to wear paper bag masks of a lion, hippo, giraffe, monkey, and mouse. As you tell the story, place the article of clothing on the animal that claimed it for his own. You may use a finger puppet mouse for the smallest mouse at the end of the story.

Plod-umpa-plod, plod-umpa-plod went the feet of the ox as he walked along the road to town. The ox was pulling a cart loaded with boxes and bags up a long, long hill. Plod-umpa-plod, plod-umpa-plod. He gave one last pull at the top of the hill, and off rolled a box full of old clothes. "Oh, well," said the owner of the ox, "those were old clothes anyway. Maybe whoever finds them can use them." And he led the ox down the hill to the town.

So the box rolled and tumbled down the hill off the road into the jungle where it hit a tree and popped open. The first one to find the box was a lion. He poked through the clothes looking for something royal. After all, he was the king of the jungle. He found one big red bow, but it was for someone very fat. He found one blue scarf, but it was for someone with a very long neck. He found a funny yellow hat, but it was for someone who was always up to tricks. And he found one green mitten, but no one could use just one mitten. Then he found a beautiful purple cape. That was just right for the royal king of the jungle. He put in on his royal back, held his head high, and said, "Now I am the happiest animal in the jungle." And he was.

After the lion left, a hippo waddled by on her way to the water hole. She saw the box of clothes and began to root around for something to make her beautiful. After all, she was the loveliest hippo at the pond. She found a long blue scarf, but it was for someone with a very long neck. She found a funny yellow hat, but it was for someone who was always up to tricks. And she found one green mitten, but no one could use just one mitten. Then she found the big red bow. That was just right for the loveliest hippo at the pond. She put it on her huge head, just over one ear, and said, "Now I am the happiest animal in the jungle." And she was.

After the hippo left, a giraffe galloped by on his way to a new tree to eat. He saw the box of clothes and began to kick with his hoof for something to keep his neck warm. After all, he was the tallest giraffe at the tree-feeding spot. He found a funny yellow hat, but it was for someone who was always up to tricks. And he found one green mitten, but no one could use just one mitten. Then he found the long blue scarf. That was just right for the tallest giraffe at the tree-feeding spot. He wrapped it around and around his neck, and said, "Now I am the happiest animal in the jungle." And he was.

After the giraffe left, a monkey came swinging by on his way to the treetop playground. He saw the box of clothes and began to reach down into them for something to make the other monkeys laugh. After all, he was the funniest monkey at the treetop playground. He found one green mitten, but no one could use just one mitten. Then he found the funny yellow hat. That was just right for the funniest monkey at the treetop playground. He put it on his head, and said, "Now I am the happiest animal in the jungle." And he was.

Now all that was left in the box was the one green mitten. No one can use just one green mitten, so it sat there a long time. Then one day a mouse scurried by and saw the box with the one green mitten left inside. She pulled and tugged that mitten until she had dragged it all the way home where her five baby mice were shivering in the cool evening. "Come in here, my children," she said. "I found one green mitten that is perfect as a house for us." They all snuggled inside the one green mitten, and, as they fell asleep, the smallest mouse of all said, "Now I am the happiest animal in the jungle."

And she was.

Silly Clothes
(A Chant)

Teach the children to respond "No, that's silly!" after each suggestion of clothes that the animals don't need. Explain to the children that the animals don't need these particular items because they are already built in.

Animals don't need
A lot of fancy clothes.
They have them built right in.
Here are some of those.

Does a kangaroo need a pocketbook?
No, that's silly!

Does an armadillo need a suit of armor?
No, that's silly!

Does a duck need galoshes?
No, that's silly!

Does a bear need a fur coat?
No, that's silly!

Does a fish need a swimsuit?
No, that's silly!

Does a frog need flippers?
No, that's silly!

Animals don't need
A lot of fancy clothes.
They have them built right in.
We've named some of those!

Monkey's Birthday
(A Flannel-board Story)

For this flannel-board story, use a felt monkey. Separate the head, legs, and tail. Then make a bear and an extra tail, a giraffe and an extra neck, a duck and an extra pair of webbed feet, a rabbit and a monkey head with long rabbit ears. Place the pieces on the board as directed in the story.

(Place monkey on board.) It was Monkey's birthday. "Chip-chee, chip-chee!" he sang as he jumped from tree to tree in the forest. "Chip-chee, chip-chee! Happy birthday to happy me!"

Mama Monkey had planned a party for all the animal friends. As Monkey ran from tree to tree he could see his friends as they got ready for his party. "Chip-chee, chip-chee!" said Monkey as he landed in a tree by a cave. "Bear's ready for my party!"

(Place bear on board.) Bear was brushing his thick hair. "Grrrrump," said Bear. "Grrr-rump, grrrrump." Bear brushed and brushed and brushed all the way down to his stubby tail. Monkey thought, "What a cute stubby tail. Chip-chee! I wish I had a stubby tail like Bear." And Monkey ran from tree to tree to see more of his friends as they got ready for his party. *(Remove bear.)*

"Chip-chee, chip-chee!" said Monkey as he landed in a tree by an open field. "Giraffe's ready for my party!"

(Place giraffe on board.) Giraffe was licking his spotted coat. "Laaaaaama," said Giraffe. "Laaaaaama, laaaaaama." Giraffe licked and licked and licked by bending his long, long neck. Monkey thought, "What a graceful long neck. Chip-chee! I wish I had a long neck like Giraffe and a stubby tail like Bear." And Monkey ran from tree to tree to see more of his friends as they got ready for his party. *(Remove giraffe.)*

"Chip-chee, chip-chee!" said Monkey as he landed in a tree near the pond. Duck's ready for my party!" *(Place duck on board.)* Duck was flapping his webbed feet. "Quaaack, quack," said Duck. "Quaaack, quack, quack. Quaaack, quack, quack." Duck flapped and flapped and flapped his orange webbed feet on the grass. Monkey thought, "What fine orange webbed feet. Chip-chee! I wish I had webbed feet like Duck and a long neck like Giraffe and a stubby tail like Bear." And Monkey ran from tree to tree to see more of his friends as they got ready for his party. *(Remove duck.)*

"Chip-chee, chip-chee!" said Monkey as he landed in a tree near a hole in the ground. "Rabbit's ready for my party!"

(Place rabbit on board.) Rabbit was waving his long ears. "Whoosh, whoosh," said Rabbit. "Whoosh, whoosh, whoosh." Rabbit waved and waved and waved his beautiful long ears. Monkey thought, "What beautiful long ears. Chip-chee! I wish I had long ears like Rabbit and webbed feet like Duck and a long neck like Giraffe and a stubby tail like Bear." *(Remove rabbit.)*

Now Monkey did not see the Tricky Birthday Fairy sitting nearby. When the Tricky Birthday Fairy heard Monkey's wish, she decided to have some fun. So she gave Monkey the tail of a bear *(replace monkey tail with bear tail)* and the neck of a giraffe *(move monkey head so long neck can be inserted)* and the feet of a duck *(remove monkey feet and replace with duck feet)* and ears of a rabbit *(replace monkey head with one that has rabbit ears)*.

And that is how Monkey looked for his birthday party! Monkey greeted his friends at the door. *(Place all other animals on board again.)* He planned to do some tricks for them, and then they would all eat cake and ice cream.

But when Monkey tried to swing by his tail, the stubby bear tail was too short to wind around the branch and he fell down. When he tried to hop up and down on his leaf bed to do a back flip, his long giraffe neck made his head bump the ceiling. When he tried to do a dance and clap his hands, he tripped over the webbed duck feet. And when he went to put on his new birthday hat, the long rabbit ears were in the way.

"Chip-chee," sighed Monkey. "Chip-chee, chip-chee. All these things are not right for me!"

Right then Mama Monkey brought out the ice cream and cake with the candles. "Make a wish!" all his friends called. "Make a wish and we'll all blow the candles out!"

So Monkey wished as hard as he could. "Chip-chee, chip-chee. I wish I was just plain me!" *(Have children blow as you take off the wrong pieces and put monkey back together again.)*

Poof! Off came the stubby bear tail. Back came the monkey tail.

Poof! Off came the long giraffe neck. Back came the monkey neck.

Poof! Off came the webbed duck feet. Back came the monkey feet.

Poof! Off came the long rabbit ears. Back came the monkey ears.

"Chip-chee!" said Monkey. "Chip-chee, chip-chee! I'm happy when I am just plain me!"

Why a Turtle Doesn't Wear a Turtleneck Sweater
(A Poem)

A turtle doesn't wear
A turtleneck sweater
Because his shell
Fits him better!

Puttin' on the Dog
(A Story with Props)

If you wish to let children become characters in this story, prepare face masks, and attach to craft sticks for them to hold up as each character is mentioned in the story.

Hen had invited all her friends in the barnyard to a dress-up party. Bullfrog and Cricket were coming to play the music. Hen had baked a big cake for the occasion. And everyone was looking forward to a grand time. But Dog was in a dither about what to wear. He went around asking everyone what they were going to wear, just so he could look the best.

First he asked Horse.

"Horse, what are you going to wear to Hen's party? It's a dress-up party, you know!"

"I dunno," said Horse. "I'm kinda used to work clothes, but I guess I'll wear my horse shoes if it's a dress-up party."

"Those old clodhoppers?" laughed Dog. "They're not the latest fashion."

Then Dog asked Pig.

"Pig, what are you going to wear to Hen's party. It's supposed to be a dress-up party, you know," said Dog.

"Uh, I dunno," said Pig. "Maybe I could wear a wig if it's a dress-up party."

"A wig?" laughed Dog. "Wigs are certainly not the latest fashion."

Then Dog asked Goat.

"Goat, what are you going to wear to Hen's party? It's supposed to be a dress-up party, you know."

"Hmm, a dress-up party you say? I suppose I could wear my frock coat," said Goat.

"That old rag?" laughed Dog. "A frock coat is not the latest fashion."

Finally Dog asked Cat.

"Cat, what are you going to wear to Hen's party? I suppose you know it's a dress-up party."

"Well," said Cat, who really loved fine clothes herself, "I have been saving my spats. Spats are high fashion, you know."

"Spats?" laughed Dog. "Spats went out with high button shoes. Cat, spats are certainly not the latest fashion."

On the day of the party all the animals got dressed up in their clothes. They went to Hen's house—just waiting to see what Dog would wear.

When Dog strutted in, he was wearing a long coat with tails, a black tie, a top hat, and high button shoes with spats. He was even swinging a cane!

"Oh Dog," they all laughed, "you look like you are going to the circus!"

Well, Dog got so mad when the other animals laughed at him that Dog began to chase Cat in her spats. That started a terrible fight. Cat began to chase Goat in his coat. Goat began to chase Pig in her wig. And Pig began to chase Horse, who was wearing her horse shoes, of course. Then Hen began flapping her wings. Hen's fancy ball had turned into one big barnyard brawl.

So the next time Hen gave a party, she had a plain old-fashioned picnic because she didn't want anyone to wear the latest fashion and try to "put on the dog."

Mr. Glop
(To the tune of "Mulberry Bush")

For extra fun, draw a simple figure on paper and spread on the "clothes" as they are mentioned in the song.

Mr. Glop wears ketchup shirts,
Ketchup shirts, ketchup shirts.
Would you wear a ketchup shirt
Just like Mr. Glop?

Mr. Glop wears mustard shoes,
Mustard shoes, mustard shoes.
Would you wear some mustard shoes
Just like Mr. Glop?

Mr. Glop wears jelly pants,
Jelly pants, jelly pants.
Would you wear jelly pants
Just like Mr. Glop?

Mr. Glop wears honey hair,
Honey hair, honey hair.
Would you wear some honey hair
Just like Mr. Glop?

Mr. Glop wears pickle hats,
Pickle hats, pickle hats.
Would you wear some pickle hats
Just like Mr. Glop?

Dress for Dinner
(To the tune of "Did You Ever See a Lassie?")

Did you ever dress a salad,
a salad,
a salad?
Did you ever dress a salad for dinner
like this?

Does it wear a coat?
Does it wear a tie?
Does it wear a shirt?
Does it wear a skirt?

Did you ever dress a salad for dinner
like this?

Did you ever dress a chicken,
a chicken,
a chicken?
Did you ever dress a chicken for dinner
like this?

In a turtleneck?
In dungarees?
In a saggy bag?
In glad rags?

Did you ever dress a chicken for dinner
like this?

The Pants That Danced
(An Object Story)

To tell this story with a prop, cut out a pair of pants from paper with jointed legs (attach pant parts with brad fasteners). Secure a craft stick to the pants and jiggle them around whenever the pants dance in the story.

Kids sometimes love a favorite pair of pants so much that they want to wear them every day. Parents plead for a change. They might even tell kids that the pants will get up and walk all by themselves if they aren't washed. We've heard such stories, so we've created this improbable tale for fun. Teach children the song "Saggy, Baggy Pants" to the tune of "Be Kind to Your Web-Footed Friends" so they'll be prepared to sing it along with you.

Troy had a favorite pair of pants. They were corduroy pants. Brown corduroy pants. Soft, brown corduroy pants. They were soft because Troy had worn his corduroy pants everyday for almost a year.

Troy loved his soft, brown corduroy pants better than he loved his blue jeans, because dirt never showed on his brown pants. And Troy didn't want to take off his pants long enough for his father to wash them. He didn't want to take off his pants long enough for his mother to mend them. The pants were soft, but they were also saggy, baggy, sort of raggy pants. But Troy didn't care. He loved his soft, brown, saggy, baggy, sort of raggy, corduroy pants.

One day after he'd worn his pants for 364 days, Troy's father said, "Troy, if you don't take off your pants and let me wash them, those pants are going to start walking all by themselves."

"That's silly," said Troy. "I never saw pants walk all by themselves."

"Please take off your pants," said his father. "And give them a 'breathing spell.' You've probably worn them out. Even pants need time to rest."

Maybe Dad's right, thought Troy to himself. So that night when he went to bed, he took off his soft, brown corduroy pants and hung them over the rocking chair in his room. Then he turned on his radio so he could go to sleep. The radio station was playing rock music, and before you knew it, the rocking chair started rocking all by itself. Troy didn't notice the rocking at first, because he was so sleepy. But then the radio station started playing ragtime music.

Suddenly, the saggy, baggy, sort of raggy pants lifted up their legs and started tapping out a rhythm on the floor.

Troy popped up in bed and watched the pants dance and sing a ragtime tune right before his eyes. Troy rubbed his eyes just to be sure he wasn't dreaming. But the pants kept on dancing.

This was the ragtime song the pants danced to (to the tune of "Be Kind to Your Web-Footed Friends"):

We're saggy, baggy old pants.
We've been worn through the dust and the rain,
Over and under the fence.
Now get up and down again.
You might think that we're all worn out—
Well we are!

With that, the music stopped. The pants collapsed in a heap on the floor.

The next morning when Troy got up, he found his pants on the floor. Troy wasn't sure if he had really seen the pants dance or if he'd been dreaming. But he told his father to wash them right away. And then he told his mother to mend them. And after that he didn't wear his soft, brown corduroy pants every day. Only every other day. In between he wore his jeans and gave the pants a chance to rest.

Clothesline Fantasy
(An Action Chant)

Do the actions indicated for each item of clothes. This makes a good flannel-board set; use a string for the clothesline and add the clothes as mentioned.

Out on the clothesline in the sun,
Listen to the clothes all having fun!
First the pants
   Will start to dance. *(Tap feet.)*
On the clothesline in the sun.

Out on the clothesline in the sun,
Listen to the clothes all having fun!
First the pants
   Will start to dance. *(Tap feet.)*
Then the skirt
   Will start to flirt. *(Wave.)*
On the clothesline in the sun.

Out on the clothesline in the sun,
Listen to the clothes all having fun!
First the pants
   Will start to dance. *(Tap feet.)*
Then the skirt
   Will start to flirt. *(Wave.)*
Then the tie
   Will start to cry. *(Run finger down cheek
     from eye to chin.)*
On the clothesline in the sun.

Out on the clothesline in the sun,
Listen to the clothes all having fun!
First the pants
   Will start to dance. *(Tap feet.)*
Then the skirt
   Will start to flirt. *(Wave.)*
Then the tie
   Will start to cry. *(Run finger down cheek
     from eye to chin.)*
Then the gown
   Will start to frown. *(Frown.)*
On the clothesline in the sun.

Out on the clothesline in the sun,
Listen to the clothes all having fun!
First the pants
   Will start to dance. *(Tap feet.)*
Then the skirt
   Will start to flirt. *(Wave.)*
Then the tie
   Will start to cry. *(Run finger down cheek
     from eye to chin.)*
Then the gown
   Will start to frown. *(Frown.)*
Then the cap
   Will start to flap. *(Wiggle fingers on
     top of head.)*
On the clothesline in the sun.
What fun!

Why the Stars Dance in the Sky

The ancient Mayans of Mexico told many myths about the origins of people and of the sun. One legend tells of a man who puts on a cape and begins dancing. He dances to the edge of the world, then dances off the world and up to the sky until he becomes the sun.

In this tale a girl catches moonlight in her cape until she dances into the sky. Then she stretches out her cape and dances as pieces of moonlight become the stars. Add sequins or spangles to the underside of a dark cape to use as a storytelling prop to make this legend come alive.

A more elaborate cape is shown in the illustration. The top part of this "Sherlock Holmes"-type cape is flipped up when the girl becomes the stars. Beads or sequins are sewn to the underside of the top cape.

"SHERLOCK HOLMES" STYLE CAPE

UNDERSIDE OF TOP CAPE IS FLIPPED TO SHOW SEQUIN STARS

Long, long ago when the earth and sky were just beginning to be, there lived a girl. A girl who never danced.

The girl's sisters called to her, "Come, come dance with us in the sun."

But the girl only waited until the great sun fell behind the earth. Then the girl watched the moon dance over her shoulder. In its dance, pieces of the moon fell like jewels down to earth and danced upon the dew on the grass. The girl stretched out her cape upon the grass. The moon danced upon the girl's cape. Pieces of the moon fell like jewels on the girl's cape. And then the moon danced away. Over her shoulder. Over the earth. Over and gone again. The girl gathered up the moon's jewels in her cape and put it away.

The next morning the girl's sisters called again to her, "Come, come dance with us in the sun. You dream by the moon too long. Come, dance in the sun."

But the girl only waited until the sun fell behind the earth. Then the moon danced over her shoulder. Pieces of the moon fell like jewels upon the dew on the grass and danced. The girl stretched out her cape for the moon to dance upon. And then the moon danced away. Over her shoulder. Over the earth. Over and gone again. The girl gathered up the moon's jewels in her cape and put it away.

Once again the next morning the sisters called, "Come, dance with us in the sun. Do not dream by the moon. The moon will not last. Your dreams will not last. Come, dance in the sun."

The girl waited until the sun fell. But, that night the moon did not come.

The girl took out her cape. Around her shoulders she stretched the cape. And then she danced. She danced and she danced until she danced to the edge of the world. She danced off the edge of the world. But she did not fall. She danced and danced up, up into the sky.

The girl stretched out her cape across the sky. From her cape pieces of the moon fell like jewels across the sky. They became the stars.

So on those nights when the moon does not come to earth, the girl stretches out her cape to dance, so part of the moon will always come back to earth and last.

Cape Dance
(To the tune of "Twinkle, Twinkle Little Star")

Sing the first verse, then hum or la-la the tune several times for the children to move to, before singing the second verse.

Dance in the sun.
Dance by the moon.
Put on your cape and
Dance to my tune.

Tra-la-la-la-la-la-la.
Tra-la-la-la-la-la-la.

Dance by the moon.
Dance in the sun.
Take off your capes—
Our dance is done.

Books about Make-Believe

Balian, Lorna. **Humbug Witch**. Abingdon, 1965.

A little witch with a big nose, crooked teeth, and long stringy hair who wears a tall hat, orange gloves, a shawl, plaid apron, red-and-white striped stockings, and shoes with buckles is a horrible witching witch, but her witchy behavior and magic don't turn out quite the way they're supposed to. Her brew doesn't explode, it just makes Fred, her cat, sick. So she takes off her clothes, right down to her hair and mask, and goes to bed. The illustrations reveal a little girl in this humorous play of just-pretend that will appeal to young children who can sort out the different between reality and fantasy on a simple level.

Barton, Byron. **Hester**. Greenwillow, 1975.

Hester discovers an unusual place to trick-or-treat—at a house of witches and spooks—and she returns home just as her friends come in costume for another festive Halloween party.

Cauley, Lorinda Bryan. **The Animal Kids**. Putnam, 1979.

A group of kids decide to crash an animal party by donning costumes and fooling the animals. They succeed, only to be bested by the animals who peel out of their animal costumes and become other animals!

Charlip, Remy, and Burton Supree. **Harlequin and the Gift of Many Colors**. Illustrated by Remy Charlip. Parents, 1973.

At the time of Carnival, just before Lent, a time of giving up one's favorite things, Harlequin watches from his room as preparations are made in the town square for Carnival that night. As his friends call to him, Harlequin comes down and hears about everyone's costumes. When he announces he isn't coming, his friends understand why—he has no costume. Each cuts off a part of his or her costume and takes the pieces to Harlequin, who gets an idea. He asks his mother to sew the scraps on his old costume and he wears his rainbow-colored suit with happiness, because he is "clothed in the love of his friends."

Claverie, Jean. **The Party**. Crown, 1986.

A young boy encounters the difficulties and frustrations of deciding what to wear to a costume birthday party.

Craig, Helen. **The Night of the Paper Bag Monsters**. Knopf, 1985.

Two friends get into a fight while making their Halloween costumes, so they separate to add the final touches. The final results are scary enough to win double first prizes at a Halloween party.

Feczko, Kathy. **Halloween Party**. Illustrated by Blanche Sims. Troll Associates, 1985.

Children dress up as monsters, princesses, clowns, and other colorful creatures for a Halloween party. Each child takes off the disguise so the others can identify their friends. A reassuring book for children who are unsure of Halloween disguises.

Giff, Patricia Reilly. **The Almost Awful Play**. Illustrated by Susanna Natti. Viking Penguin, 1984.

Ronald, who is cast as a cat in the school play, tries to help make costumes and scenery, but nearly ruins the final performance until his quick thinking saves the day.

Hoban, Lillian. **Arthur's Halloween Costume**. Harper & Row, 1984.

Arthur the chimpanzee worries that his Halloween costume won't be scary enough, but he ends up winning a prize for the most original costume of all, the Spirit of Halloween.

Johnston, Tony. **The Witch's Hat**. Illustrated by Margot Tomes. Putnam, 1984.

A witch's hat falls in her magic pot. When she reaches for it, the hat turns into a bat and flies into the attic. There the bat gets mixed up with other bats. When the witch cleverly finds her bat hat, it turns into a rat, then a cat. The witch succeeds in turning her "hat" back to its original form only to have it become a frog in the final illustration.

Lionni, Leo. **The Greentail Mouse**. Pantheon, 1973.

A community of field mice decide to have a Mardi Gras and make costumes. They become so involved that they begin to believe they are ferocious animals, and the once-peaceful community becomes a place of hate and suspicion. They burn their masks and forget about the Mardi Gras, at least the bad part, as if it had been a bad dream.

Marshall, Edward. **Space Case**. Illustrated by James Marshall. Dial, 1980.

The thing from outer space is welcomed by kids trick-or-treating, but it is disillusioned about life on earth when it discovers that Halloween only comes once a year.

Numeroff, Laura Joffe, and Alice Numeroff Richter. **Emily's Bunch**. Illustrated by Laura Joffe Numeroff. Macmillan, 1978.

Emily can't decide on an appropriate Halloween costume until she enlists the aid of her friends. Wearing paper bags painted purple, the bunch of friends become a bunch of grapes.

Ormerod, Jan. **The Story of Chicken Licken**. Lothrop, Lee and Shepard, 1985.

When an acorn falls on Chicken Licken's head, she assumes the sky is falling. Her barnyard friends join her only to be led into Foxy Woxy's cave. Ormerod's retelling of this familiar folktale takes the form of a class play with children assuming the roles in costume.

Park, W. P. **The Costume Party**. Little, Brown, 1983.

At Shirley's costume party, everyone has a good time until they unmask. Inside the bear suit is a real bear who ruins the party until he learns proper party behavior.

Patience, John. **The Fancy Dress Party Counting Book**. Outlet Book Co., 1985.

One little girl gets dressed up as a fairy for her birthday party. At the party there are two clowns, three musketeers, four cowboys, five witches, six deep-sea divers, seven tigers, eight firemen, nine pirates, and ten royal rulers.

Peek, Merle. **Mary Wore a Red Dress and Henry Wore His Green Sneakers**. Clarion, 1983.

Each animal wears clothing of a different color to a birthday party in this book, based on the traditional folk song. Children can add their own articles of clothing in the manner of the song after you read this book.

Seuling, Barbara. **Just Me**. Harcourt Brace Jovanovich, 1982.

Three easy-to-read stories capture the imaginative play of a little girl who becomes a horse (on "horse shoe" blocks with a yarn tail), a dragon (with spikes taped to a jump rope tail and egg-carton jaws tied to her head), and a robot (in a box with a colander for her head). After each adventure the little girl decides she is happiest when she is "just me."

Wegen, Ron. **The Halloween Costume Party**. Clarion, 1983.

Kelly Comet loves to make Halloween costumes, so she expects to win first prize at Nancy Moonstar's party. But the competition is stiff. Kelly doesn't win, but looks off at planet Earth and sees some good disguises for next year's competition.

Zolotow, Charlotte. **A Tiger Called Thomas**. Illustrated by Kurt Werth. Lothrop, Lee and Shepard, 1963.

A little boy, Thomas, is afraid that no one will like him in the new neighborhood, so he doesn't venture from his porch. Then comes Halloween and he trick-or-treats as a tiger, only to discover that everyone recognizes him despite the costume—and likes him!

Related Actitivies about Make-Believe

Too Big for Your Britches!

Tell this story with posterboard cutouts of the various articles of clothing. Attach the clothing to elastic cord (the kind you use for masks) to hang around children's necks. The cowboy hat can have a band of elastic to fit around the back of the head. When you get to the part of the story where Shelby puts on many costumes, simply place one "costume" on top of another. Clap hands to make the sound of Shelby's pants popping off. Ask five children to wear the costumes—a superhero T-shirt, a cowboy hat, a fire fighter outfit, an astronaut suit, and a clown suit. You can distribute these costumes as they are mentioned in the story. You will also need to have another set of costumes: a matching superhero T-shirt and cape, a cowboy hat, a fire fighter outfit, an astronaut suit, a clown suit, and a rock star costume for Shelby; then you, as leader, can become Shelby the Show-off.

POSTER BOARD
COSTUMES

Shelby was a show-off. Whenever anyone got anything like a new superhero T-shirt, Shelby said, "That's nothin'! I've got a superhero T-shirt and a superhero cape to match!"

All the kids said, "Shelby, you're a show-off."

But Shelby just said, "Pooh! Pooh! I'll show you!"

And then Shelby went home and put on his superhero T-shirt and his superhero cape to match. And he flew around the whole neighborhood.

One day the kid down the street got a big cowboy hat for his birthday. Everyone thought it was a neat cowboy hat. But not Shelby.

Shelby said, "That's nothin'! I've got a cowboy hat and cowboy boots and cowboy chaps AND A GENUINE COWBOY LASSO, TOO!"

All the kids said, "Shelby, you're a show-off!"

But Shelby said, "Pooh! Pooh! I'll show you."

And then Shelby went home and put on his cowboy hat and his cowboy boots and his cowboy chaps. And he got his genuine cowboy lasso. He even lassoed the kids in the neighborhood and wouldn't let them go until dinnertime.

One day the teacher at school told everyone to come dressed as something they would most like to be when they grew up. One kid dressed up like a fire fighter. Another kid dressed up like an astronaut. And another kid dressed up like a circus clown.

The teacher said they all looked so splendid that the next day they would have a parade all around the school gym for the whole school.

"That's nothin'," said Shelby. "I'll show you!"

The next day Shelby came to school with his costume. But he didn't bring just one costume. He brought a whole trunk full of costumes!

The other boys and girls paraded around the gym as fire fighters and astronauts and clowns. Everyone cheered. All except Shelby. He was too busy putting on his astronaut suit, and his fire fighter suit, and his clown suit, and on top of all that, he put on his rock star spangly bangly pants.

Then Shelby paraded around the gym, saying, "I'll show you! Pooh! Pooh! Pooh!"

And then, Shelby's pants went pop-pop-pop! Everyone looked at Shelby, because all of Shelby's suits and pants popped right off. He was standing right in the middle of the gym in his next-to-nothings!

"Shelby," said all the kids, "you really are a show-off, but this time you showed off too much!"

Shelby didn't say "Pooh! Pooh!" this time. He said "Boo! Hoo! Hoo!"

So Shelby's teacher helped him pick up all of his suits and pants and said, "That's O.K., Shelby. This time you just got a little too big for your britches."

And, because Shelby had on next-to-nothing, he went right home. But after that, Shelby never tried to show off again.

Magic
(Creative Dramatics)

Guide the children through a series of imaginary experiences suggesting costume and then give them a chance to act out the situation. Whenever the refrain is said, all activity stops and everyone listens for the next direction.

Refrain:
Close your eyes. I do believe
You've got magic up your sleeve!

Think of a lion tamer in the circus. What does his hat look like? What does he have in his hand? What expressions does he have on his face? Now show me a lion tamer.

Refrain

Think of a ballet dancer. What does her costume look like? How does she move her arms? What kind of shoes is she wearing? Now show me a ballet dancer.

Refrain

Think of a fire fighter. What does she have on her feet? What is she holding in her hand? What is on her head? Now show me a fire fighter.

Refrain

Think of a clown. What color is his suit? Is he riding on something? What does he have in his hand? Now show me a clown.

Refrain

The Monster Who Didn't Even Wake Up

Young children love to play monster, but sometimes find nighttime monsters scary to have around. Dress up a child in your group as you tell this story to dispel their worries. The whole group will delight in being "let in on" the make-believe. Another way to tell the story is to use flannel-board figures. This way you won't reveal the "identity" of the monster until the end. Either way, this is a good way to show children that the monsters we create may only be scary children after all!

There was once a monster who lived in a dark hideout. It was so dark in that hideout that you couldn't even see the monster. But it was in there all right. It made a terrible sound like this: UGH!
And if you took a flashlight, and if you shined it into the hideout, this is what you would see:

You would see a big brown head.
   (Put grocery bag over child's head.)
And on that head was black hairy hair—all over.
   (Tape black yarn on bag head.)
On its hands it had sharp claws.
   (Put claws—cut from paper—on child's hands.)
On its feet it had sharp, SHARP claws.
   (Put paper claws on child's feet.)
And it had two holes—where its eyes SHOULD have been.
   (Cut two eyes in paper bag.)

One evening the monster crawled out of its hideout. It made a truly terrible sound like this: UGHHHHHH!
It scared the cat, who said, "Me-ow-ow-ow." It scared the dog, who said, "Bow-wow-wow." And it scared the little boy, who yelled, "MONSTER!"
So the little boy's mother made the monster go back in its hideout until dinner.
The monster started getting hungry in its hideout, so it crawled out and made a very hungry sound: UGHHHHHH!
It scared the cat, who said, "Me-ow-ow-ow." It scared the dog, who said, "Bow-wow-wow." And it scared the little boy, who yelled, "MONSTER!"
So the little boy's mother told the monster to go back to the hideout until bedtime.
Pretty soon it got dark. And quiet. So the little boy's mother opened the door. She reached into the hideout. And she picked up the monster. *(Lift monster child.)*

She took off its sharp claw hands.
  (Take off claws.)
She took off its sharp, SHARP claw feet.
  (Take off claws.)
And she took off its big brown head, with hairy hair all over.
  (Take off bag head.)

And do you know what? That monster didn't even wake up. Because the monster wasn't really a monster at all. It was just a little girl in disguise!

Ten Trick-or-Treaters

(To the tune of "Ten Little Indians")

Sing this song and hold up the appropriate number of fingers as you count up to ten. Add actions as you like. This song will teach children that Halloween costumes are disguises with children behind them, and hopefully dispel some of the scary part of seeing people in strange attire.

One little,
Two little,
Three trick-or-treaters.
Four little,
Five little,
Six trick-or-treaters.
Seven little,
Eight little,
Nine trick-or-treaters.
Ten trick-or-treaters on Halloween Night.

One dressed up in a pirate costume.
Two has a mask, and
Three has a hat on.
Four is a clown, and
Five is a skeleton—
All dressed up for Halloween Night.

Six is a ghost.
Seven is a cat.
Eight is a witch, and
Nine is a bat.
Ten is a monster—don't
They look spooky?
All dressed up for Halloween Night.

Take off the masks and
Take off the hats.
No more goblins,
No more cats.
All those spooks are
Just sleepy children,
Ready for bed on Halloween Night!

Halloween Dress Up

Chant the beginning stanza, then let the children guess each of the characters in the next three stanzas. This action rhyme may be followed by children acting out their own favorite Halloween dress-up creatures or by letting children make Halloween costumes.

Halloween! Halloween!
I can dress
Up like something
You won't guess!

I wear a cloak
And a tall black hat.
Sometimes I travel
With a cat.
What am I?

I'm dressed in white.
I moan and groan.
I'm found in every
Haunted Home!
What am I?

I wear green scales
And sharp red claws.
I have big teeth
Inside my jaws.
What am I?

Halloween! Halloween!
Fun to dress
Up like something
You *can* guess!

How to Make a Ghost

(To the tune of "Twinkle, Twinkle Little Star")

As you sing, do the actions suggested by the words.

Take a white sheet
From your bed.
Put it on your
Little head.

Cut two holes
For your eyes.
Make them just
About this size.

Now you know just
What to do:
Whisper softly
One word—Boo!

Whooo Are Youooo?

(A Prop Story)

Use a king-sized white sheet for the ghost. Invite five children to come be part of the ghost as you tell the story, using their names in place of the ones mentioned. Use a stuffed owl, one cut from paper, or an owl puppet. When the story tells about them leaving the ghost costume, all the children should run back to their seats. Teach the rest of the children to call "Whooo are youooo?"

One Halloween night Steve decided to dress up as a ghost. He got a big, big sheet and crawled under it. And he set out for trick-or-treat.

He walked a little way when he heard a voice, "Whooo are youooo?" There was Peter.

"It's a little ghost. Come have fun, too?" Steve answered. So Peter climbed under the sheet with Steve.

They walked a little way when they heard a voice, "Whooo are youooo?" There was Sara.

"It's a little ghost. Come have fun, too!" they answered. So Sara climbed under the sheet with the others.

They walked a little way when they heard a voice, "Whooo are youooo?" There was Alison.

"It's a little ghost. Come have fun, too!" they answered. So Alison climbed under the sheet with the others.

They walked a little way when they heard a voice say, "Whooo are youooo?" There was Bart.

"It's a little ghost. Come have fun, too!" they answered. So Bart climbed under the sheet with the others.

They walked a little way when they heard a voice, "Whooo are youooo?" But they didn't see anyone, so they were a little bit scared.

They walked a little way when they heard a voice, "Whooo are youooo?" But they didn't see anyone, so they were a little more scared.

They walked a little way when they heard a voice, "Whooo are youooo?" But they didn't see anyone. This time they were so scared that out from under the ghost costume ran Bart and Alison and Sara and Peter and Steve. They ran home as fast as they could.

And as the Halloween moon shone in the sky, all that was left was a big, white sheet and an owl that called "Whooo are youooo?"

BOO!

(A Fingerplay)

Who's behind the spooky mask?
   (Cover face with hands.)
Could it be a bear?
   (Hold hands up with fingers bent.)
Could it be a monster with
  Wild and crazy hair? *(Point to hair.)*
Could it be an anteater
  With nose of red and green? *(Hold one bent finger in front of nose.)*
No, it's just me in this mask.
   (Point to self.)
It's time for Halloween!
   (Cover face with hands.)
BOO!
   (Quickly peek out from behind hands.)

Clown Dress

(A Fingerplay)

Point to the parts of the body mentioned in this poem about getting dressed.

The clown puts on his clown face.
First he paints it white,
Then he draws around his eyes,
Big and round and bright.

He paints his mouth and nose
A rosy, rosy red.
His wig is green that he pulls on
His old round head.

His shoes are enormous.
His suit is immense.
It looks like he's wearing
A whole circus tent!

Treasure Trunk Dress Up

Do this little story poem with appropriate props, putting them on as you read the story. Or, you might tell the story with flannel-board figures. A good followup might be for children to play "dress up" with other old clothes and accessories.

Amelia was a girl
Who liked to play
In Grandma's attic
On rainy days.

And in that attic
She found a trunk,
A dusty, musty
Treasure trunk.

And in the trunk
She found a gown,
A spangly, jangly
Golden gown.

She found a hat
With a peacock feather,
Shiny shoes,
Made all of leather.

Two long gloves,
An old fur coat
She buttoned up
Around her throat.

Then—Amelia went
To visit the queen,
Who asked her to stay
For peppermint tea.

The queen said, "How lovely
You look, my dear!
Please stay on
At least for a year!"

But Amelia took off
The hat with the feather,
Gown, gloves, coat,
The shoes made of leather.

"Sorry," said Amelia,
"Another day.
Right now I'm going
Outside to play!"

Mask-erade

Put on a mask
To hunt a beast.
(A mask is good
For hiding beneath!)

Put on a mask—
Be a knight.
Now march bravely
Out to fight!

Put on a mask—
Let's play ball!
Or wear this mask
And dance at a ball!

Put on a mask
In Outer Space.
Now take it off—
And there's—your face!

GAMES FOR FAIRYTALE, FANTASY, AND JUST-PRETEND

Frog Prince

Seat children in a circle. One child walks around the outside of the circle tapping each child on the head and saying, "Frog, frog, frog, frog, PRINCE!" The child who is tapped on the word "prince" stands up and both race around the circle to the open space. The first one back sits down, the other continues the game, tapping children and repeating the line "Frog, frog, frog, frog, PRINCE!"

What Will They Think of Next?

Guide children in creating a strange new animal. Suggest parts for children to imitate, such as head, antennae, horns, feet, claws, and tail. Arrange the children to form a new creature, then dress it with hats, boots, and mittens.

Is This for Me?

In this creative dramatics game, articles of clothing are put in a variety of boxes. On each box put a tag indicating who the present belongs to. You may wish to have a stocking cap for a moose, a nose warmer for an elephant, a turtleneck sweater for a giraffe, earmuffs for a rabbit, sneakers for a centipede, mittens for an octopus, stretch pants for a hippo, and a tutu for a chicken.

Take one box at a time. Open the box to reveal the clothing and then read the tag. Invite the children to pretend to be the animal putting on this article of clothing. For example, "All right, all you giraffes, let's see you put on the turtleneck sweaters!"

This is a super game for holiday gift-giving time or birthday party celebrations. Use it as a followup activity after reading *Animals Should Definitely Not Wear Clothing* (p. 134).

Halloween Charade

Adapt the refrain from "Halloween Dress Up" on p. 152:

> Halloween, Halloween I can dress
> Up like something you can guess!

Then choose a child to act out a character he or she would like to be for Halloween while others guess.

Dress-Up Costume Relay

Fill two shopping bags full of clothes, jewelry, and shoes. The first child on each team draws an item out and must put it on before passing the bag on to the next child. The first team with all members wearing an article from the bag wins.

Let the children keep what they put on as a prize—and to get rid of your garage sale leftovers!

CRAFTS FOR FAIRYTALE, FANTASY, AND JUST-PRETEND

Fair Lady or Fairytale Hat

Fair ladies in fairytale times wore tall pointed hats that children can make from paper. Just roll a large rectangle of stiff paper into a cone and tape in place. Cut the base of the hat to fit the head, or make a smaller cone and attach to the head with bobby pins. Decorate the paper hat first with crayons or markers. Add a long, fringed strip of paper to the top of the hat so it trails down like a graceful plume.

Hat for a Prince
(When He's Not Wearing a Crown)

Adapt the Robin Hood hat in chapter 6, "Hats and More Hats," on p. 185, to put on the prince when he is not at royal functions.

Be a Fairy Godmother

Use the pattern below to make dress outlines for Cinderella's ball gown and decorate it with sequins, ribbon, and fabric scraps.

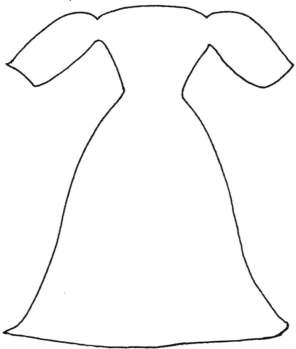

Croak, Your Majesty

Make simple frogs by stapling two paper plates together around the edge with bottoms to the outside. Cut one in half and fold them both to form the frog's mouth. There will then be places to put fingers and thumb to move the mouth. Staple egg-carton sections on top for eyes. Cut out a crown. Fold the bottom edge to paste on the plate so it stands up behind the eyes. Cut a red paper tongue and curl on a pencil before pasting inside the mouth.

Maybe one of these frogs will turn into a handsome prince as you make them!

RED PAPER PAPER PLATES

EGG CARTON SECTIONS

CUT TOP PLATE IN HALF FOR HAND

The Emperor's Real New Clothes

Give children a blank sheet of paper and catalogs or magazines. They will enjoy pasting pictures on the paper for the Emperor to wear, since he now has no new clothes.

Costume Party Masks

Even young children who are afraid of large masks that cover the face will enjoy wearing a small costume party kind of mask that just covers the eyes. Cut out masks for children in a variety of colors and provide sequins, stickers, feathers, fur, fringe, or other notions to glue to their masks. Attach masks with thin elastic cord.

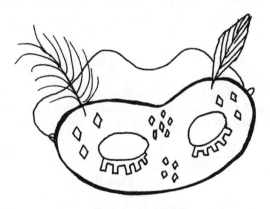

Clown Face Makeup

Children love to have their faces painted with clown makeup—even children who are afraid to wear masks. Mix up a batch of this homemade face paint and divide it into little margarine tubs. Tint the face paint different colors and let children make up their own faces. (Be sure that children wear old clothes when they do this.)

Measure about 1 teaspoon cornstarch and 1/2 teaspoon water in a dish. Stir in 1/2 teaspoon cold cream. Add food coloring, a drop at a time. This greasepaint will wash off with soap and water.

Paper Bag Costumes for Pretending

Paper bags were probably not invented for making costumes for children, but they certainly work superbly when children want to make inexpensive costumes for "just-pretend."

Large grocery bags work well if you cut them off about 10 inches long and curve the side panels to fit over a child's shoulders.

Make animal character costume masks by cutting out 10-inch diameter circles and different kinds of ears from different colors of construction paper. Children may choose what kind of animal they wish to become and glue the circles and ears on the bags. Help them cut out eye openings. Paper curls may be added for lions, paper strips for rabbit or cat whiskers, and triangles for noses.

Paper bag monsters are a natural followup activity if you read *The Night of the Paper Bag Monsters*. Children may use paint and pieces of torn paper, bits of string, and fake fur to glue all over the paper bags to their heart's delight. Cut out eye and nose openings and invite children to color around these openings to make the eyes and noses of their monsters more pronounced.

DISPLAYS FOR FAIRYTALE, FANTASY, AND JUST-PRETEND

Once upon a Magic Clothes

In a glass display case arrange copies of picture books and realia to complement them. A needle and thread (but no clothes!) could accompany *The Emperor's New Clothes*. You might also include plastic doll high-heeled shoes for *Cinderella*, tall leather dress boots out of your own closet for *Puss in Boots*, and a red hooded cape for *Red Riding Hood*. Use doll clothes if you cannot find full-sized ones.

Magic Umbrella Tales

In one of Hans Christian Andersen's lesser-known tales, a red umbrella is used by the sandman for bringing magic to good children. Open a red umbrella and fill it with books, some spilling out. Be sure to include some of the fantasy and "just-pretend" books from this chapter.

Masquerade

Ask children to donate some of the crafts and masks from this chapter or take pictures of the children in their finery and hang them with Halloween masks and costumes.

Role Play

Draw large character suits on posterboard or cardboard. Cut a half circle in the top edge near the neck of the garment for the children to place their heads. Attach two boards together at the top edge with short pieces of yarn.

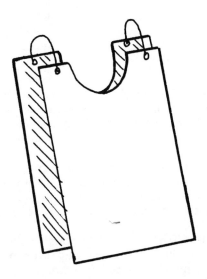

Animals Should Definitely Wear Clothing

Invite children to bring clothes to dress teddy bears or toy animals. You might have bears in striped knee socks or earmuffs on a stuffed bunny, a bathing cap on a fish, or boots on a duck!

Life-Sized Halloween

Make a life-sized doll from an old sheet, using the pattern from the "Child-Size Dress Me Doll" on p. 31, and dress it in a Halloween costume.

6
Hats and More Hats

INTRODUCTION

For fun, fashion, or necessity, people have always worn hats. But today most Americans seldom wear hats for everyday fashion or even for dress-up occasions. A young man is not taught to "tip his hat" because he probably doesn't wear one! And Sunday bonnets for girls may not be part of the once-popular "Easter Parade." Still, young children who enter into imaginative play find hats one of the most fascinating articles of apparel.

Throughout history, hats have been worn for protection against the weather. Our centrally heated homes no longer necessitate our wearing nightcaps, but we do instruct children to wear stocking caps in winter. Weather-related hats are covered more fully in chapter 3.

The focus of "Hats and More Hats" is the decorative, imaginative, and role-identifying properties of hats.

The first subtheme "Hat Tricks and Tricky Hats" explores hat journeys and transformations. Tomi Ungerer's top hat in *The Hat* is blown off a rich man's head to result in many merry adventures. Sometimes the adventure becomes even more far-fetched, for example, when hats multiply for Dr. Seuss's Bartholomew Cubbins or change form in Tony Johnston's *The Witch's Hat*. Our activities expand upon this theme as the hat in "Eat That Hat" travels to a jungle and a circus before it lands in the middle of a birthday cake where it ends up being eaten. Other hats grant wishes or cause animals to disappear.

A second subtheme "Pass the Hat" introduces different kinds of hats and the people or animals who wear them. Young children who role play in a fire fighter's hat or a space helmet will easily identify with the boy in *Martin's Hats*. The peddler who wears a stack of caps on his head in the classic story *Caps for Sale* invites children to become peddlers. Stories and activities about hats will help children to explore different occupations and learn about popular characters from baseball players to Yankee Doodle.

Since hairstyles may identify people as much as hats, a third subtheme "The Hair on My Head" has been included. The boy in Don Freeman's *Mop Top* is mistaken for a mop until he decides to get a hair cut. And the lion in *Dandelion* by the same author chooses an outlandish hairstyle before he decides just to be himself.

Young children will learn such basic skills in self-awareness, classification, and sequencing through these stories. And, activities using hat-related expressions—"pass the hat," "eat your hat," "bee in your bonnet"—will expand vocabularies and sensitize children to language. Certain precautions may need to be taken with children actually trying on a collection of hats, since head lice are a common problem among young children. For this reason, we recommend craft and game projects that allow each child to make his or her own creation.

A special effort has been made to encourage children to try on different roles so they become liberated from rigid gender associations of hats. Although girls generally enjoy the fancy bonnet in *Jennie's Hat* more than boys do, all children love trying on lampshades for hats. Our projects encourage children to make character and work-related hats from a witch's hat to a space helmet so boys and girls will explore choices in the roles they play.

INITIATING ACTIVITY

Hat Clap Chant

Here's a little chant to use with children as a warm-up activity. Begin with children standing in a circle and clapping their hands in time with the chant. As the leader comes to each child, the child says his or her name for everyone to repeat.

	Round and round
	We pass the hat.
	Say your name,
	And let's all clap.
First child:	Jennifer
Leader:	Let's all clap—
	Jenn-i-fer!
Second child:	Sam
Leader:	Let's all clap—
	Sam!

Proceed around the circle until everyone has been introduced.

LITERATURE-SHARING EXPERIENCES

Books about Hat Tricks and Tricky Hats

Asch, Frank. **Yellow, Yellow.** Illustrated by Mark Alan Stamaty. McGraw-Hill, 1971.

One day a boy finds a yellow hat and discovers a variety of uses for it from a step stool to a boat. The original owner claims the hat so the boy makes a new yellow hat folded from paper for his very own.

Barrett, Judi. **The Wind Thief.** Illustrated by Diane Dawson. Atheneum, 1977.

The wind decides he needs a warm cozy hat so he blows one off the head of a small boy. But the gust results in all sorts of hats getting lost in a hilarious confusion. The wind is sorry the boy is missing his stocking cap, and it discovers the boy's grandmother knitting a new one. In the end, both the boy and wind keep warm in identical stocking caps.

Fuchshuber, Annegart. **The Wishing Hat.** Translated by Elizabeth D. Crawford. Morrow, 1977.

One morning a man finds a hat on his table, decides it is a wishing hat, and consults fairytales on how to use it. He wishes for an apple tree, striped socks, a shopping basket, an umbrella to fly him anywhere he wants to go, a flute, and upside-down stairs. After each wish, someone tells him what he should have wished for. The man's final answer is to throw the hat out the window.

Iwamura, Kazuo. **Tan Tan's Hat.** Bradbury, 1983.

A playful monkey enjoys all the things he can do with his new hat—spinning it on a stick, throwing it, and catching a grasshopper. When he throws the hat so high it doesn't come down, he goes to sleep only to be awakened by the hat bringing down a falling star with it.

Johnston, Tony. **The Witch's Hat.** Illustrated by Margot Tomes. Putnam, 1984.

A witch's hat falls in her magic pot. When she reaches for it, the hat turns into a bat and flies into the attic. There the bat gets mixed up with other bats. When the witch cleverly finds her bat hat, it turns into a rat, then a cat. The witch succeeds in turning her "hat" back to its original form only to have it become a frog in the final illustration.

Lobel, Arnold. "The Hat" from **Days with Frog and Toad**. Harper & Row, 1979.

Frog gives Toad a hat for his birthday, but it's too big. Toad, determined to wear it anyway, goes to bed and thinks big thoughts so his head will grow. In the meantime, Frog takes the hat, shrinks it, and returns it to Toad's house. When Toad wakes up in the morning, the hat is just the right size.

Mark, Jan. **Fur**. Illustrated by Charlotte Voake. Harper & Row, 1986.

Simple text tells the story of "thin cat grew fat/she made a nest in my hat." The hat nest becomes filled with fur because it is full of kittens!

Nodset, Joan L. **Who Took Farmer's Hat?** Illustrated by Fritz Siebel. Harper & Row, 1963.

A farmer goes looking for his favorite old brown hat that has been taken by the wind. The farmer asks a number of animals about his hat. Finally the farmer finds his hat made into a bird's nest.

Seuss, Dr. **The 500 Hats of Bartholomew Cubbins**. Vanguard Press, 1938.

Bartholomew Cubbins appears to be defying the order of King Derwin's Captain of the Guards by not removing his hat when the king goes by. But each time Bartholomew removes his hat, another identical one appears on his head. The final one—number 500—turns out to be so magnificent that the king offers to buy it and preserve all of them in a case for posterity.

Ungerer, Tomi. **The Hat**. Parents, 1970.

A tall shiny top hat with a magenta sash blows off a rich man's head and goes on many adventures.

Related Activities about Hat Tricks and Tricky Hats

The Magic Hat
(To the tune of "The Farmer in the Dell")

Put on your magic hat. *(Touch head.)*
Put on your magic hat. *(Touch head.)*
Oh, you can do most anything *(Spread arms wide.)*
In a magic hat! *(Touch head.)*

(Do appropriate motions throughout the following.)

You can hop and hop.
You can hop and hop.
You can do most anything
In your magic hat!

You can make a face.
You can make a face.
You can do most anything
In your magic hat!

(Children can make their own suggestions. You can then end with a quieting verse.)

You can sit right down.
You can sit right down.
You can do most anything
In your magic hat!

Rabbit's Most Amazing Hat Trick
(A Flannel-board Story)

To tell this story, prepare felt cutouts of a rabbit, a hen, a deer, several frogs, a yellow cap, a green cap, a blue bonnet, a green bonnet, a fancy hat, a red hat for the hen, antlers with bright balls hanging from them for the deer, a tall black magician's hat, and a pair of earmuffs.

Once there was a rabbit who made amazing hats. *(Place rabbit on flannel board.)* She could turn a yellow cap *(place yellow cap on board)* into a green cap *(place green cap on top of yellow cap)*. She could turn a blue bonnet *(place blue bonnet on board)* into a bright green bonnet *(place green bonnet on top of blue bonnet)*. She could change a plain hat into a magnificent creation. *(Place fancy hat on board.)*

One day Hen *(place hen on board)* asked Rabbit to make her a hat to match Rooster's bright red comb. So Rabbit made a bright red hat for Hen. *(Place red hat on board.)* And that hat was so splendid that the next day all the barnyard hens came flocking to Rabbit's hole. They wanted red hats, too!

Then Deer wanted a headdress fancier than her husband's antlers. So Rabbit made her a headdress complete with all the trimmings. *(Place decorated antler headdress on board.)* All the animals became jealous. Even the frogs *(place frogs on board)* were green with envy. Soon the animals began to fight over which animal's hat was the grandest of all. *(Point to each animal on board as the name is mentioned in the story.)*

The frogs croaked, the hens cackled, and the deer butted headdress and antlers. They made such a commotion that Rabbit couldn't think.

Her head was splitting from all that noise. So she burrowed down in her hole. *(Place Rabbit on a far corner of the board.)* There she rested for three days and nights.

I must do something, she thought. I must stop all this racket. I will make a new hat. And she did. *(Place tall black hat on board.)*

"This," she told all the animals, "is my finest creation."

"But it is only a black hat," said Hen. "It's not as fancy as my bright red hat." *(Point to Hen.)*

"It is a very plain hat," said Deer. "It's not as beautiful as my headdress with all the trimmings." *(Point to Deer.)*

"It is not the kind of hat I would envy," said Frog. *(Point to Frog.)*

"It may not look amazing," said Rabbit, "but don't be tricked. This is a magic disappearing hat." *(Point to black hat.)*

"Doesn't look magic to me," said Hen.

"I don't believe in magic," said Deer.

"Well, I believe in magic," said Frog. "I used to be a handsome prince, until a wicked witch turned me into a frog with her magic."

Rabbit wiggled her ears and waved her arms over the hat.

"What are you doing?" asked Hen.

"Making the hat disappear?" asked Deer.

"Let's get out of here," said Frog. "Maybe she's going to make us all disappear!"

All the animals disappeared into the forest. *(Remove Hen, Deer, and Frog from board.)* They never stopped to find out if Rabbit's hat was really magic. They never came out again. And they never asked Rabbit to make another hat.

But Rabbit made one last hat just in case things got noisy again. She made herself a pair of big thick earmuffs! *(Place earmuffs on Rabbit's ears.)*

A Witch's Hat

This action rhyme is a good followup to Tony Johnston's *The Witch's Hat*. Children will love to jump in the pot and come out with this unusual hat on their heads.

A funny old witch
Had a tall black hat.
  (Arms up, hands form pointed hat.)
She also had
A small black cat.
  (Cradle imaginary cat in arms.)

On Halloween night
She stirred her brew.
  (Stir brew.)
But her hat fell in—
  (Bow head.)
What did she do?
  (Hands out, palms up.)

She jumped in the pot
  (Jump and crouch down.)
To find her hat.
But when she came out
  (Slowly rise.)
She was wearing a bat!
  (Flap hands over head.)

Eat That Hat!
(A Participatory Story with Masks)

To tell this story, prepare five face masks on craft sticks for children to hold in front of their faces. These masks represent the horse, the lion, the clown, the cake, and the dog. An additional prop is given to the dog: a brown "doggie" bag in which the hat will be thrown at the end. You will also need a fancy hat for each character to wear as the hat lands on each character's head. Before you begin the story, ask all children to help be the wind that takes the hat on its adventures.

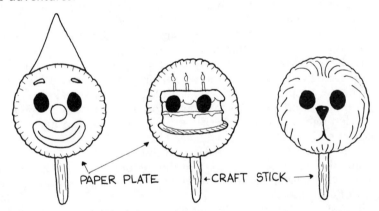

PAPER PLATE   ←CRAFT STICK →

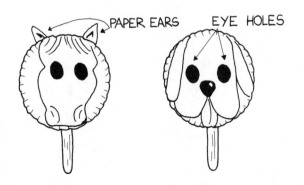

PAPER EARS   EYE HOLES

Once upon a time there was a beautiful hat that lived on the shelf of a small hat shop. Day after day the hat dreamed of the grand adventures it would have someday.

Someday, thought the hat, I will travel to big cities and to faraway places. Someday I will ride in fine parades, and crowds will cheer me. I will attend fancy parties and be the center of attention.

One day the door of the hat shop blew open. A strong wind blew and it blew. *(Everyone blows.)* The hat blew out the door.

"Take me back!" said the hat. "I am not ready for my grand adventures."

But the wind blew and it blew. *(Everyone blows.)* It blew the hat down the road and into the country. Then the wind sat the hat down on the head of a horse. *(Place hat on horse child's head.)*

"Fancy that! Look at my hat!" said the horse. And the horse galloped around the farm country to show off her new hat to all the animals.

"Take me back!" said the hat. "I am not a hat for a horse. I wish to go to faraway places."

So the wind blew and it blew. *(Everyone blows.)* It blew the hat far into the jungle. There the hat landed on the head of a lion. *(Place hat on lion child's head.)*

"Fancy that! Look at my hat!" said the lion.

Now the lion was King of the Jungle. And the jungle was a faraway place. But this was not the kind of faraway place that hat had in mind.

"Take me back!" said the hat. "I am not a hat to wear in the jungle. I wish to go to a big place with bright lights. I want crowds to cheer me."

So the wind blew and it blew. *(Everyone blows.)* So wind picked up the hat and took it to a circus parade. There the hat landed on the head of a clown. *(Place the hat on the clown child's head.)*

"Fancy that! Look at my hat!" said the clown. The clown tossed up the hat and caught it on his head. The crowds cheered and laughed.

"Take me back," said the hat. "I am not a clown hat. I do not wish to be laughed at. I should be the center of attention at a fine party."

So the wind blew and it blew. *(Everyone blows.)* The wind picked up the hat and carried it to the house of a little girl who was having her birthday party. And what a fancy party it was! There were presents and a beautiful, big birthday cake.

Well, the wind blew the hat down, down the chimney of the little girl's house, and the hat landed right in the middle of her birthday cake. The hat was the center of attention. *(Place hat on birthday cake child's head.)*

"Fancy that! Look at my hat!" said the cake.

And that hat looked so good in the middle of the cake that the little girl's dog said, "Fancy that! I'll eat that hat!" And the dog jumped up and ate the whole thing. *(Put hat in dog child's doggie bag.)*

So that was the end of the hat's grand adventures.

Now, I don't know if the hat was really good enough to eat. I'd never eat my hat, would you? Unless, of course, it was made out of sugar and spice and everything nice.

Eat Your Hat

I would never eat my hat
If it were made of straw,
But there are hats so good to eat,
Just tuck these in your jaws.

A hat for ice cream is chocolate sauce,
And icing's the hat for a cake.
For the hamburger hat
Use a fluffy white bun,
And syrup's a hat for pancakes.

A hat for potatoes is gravy.
Put a marshmallow hat on cocoa.
A hat for spaghetti's
A meatball for sure.
Top popcorn with butter to go!

Yankee Doodle had a hat
Called his feather macaroni.
I wonder if he
Ate his hat,
Or if that's just baloney!

Jenny Wren's Best Nest
(A Cut-and-Tell Story)

This story is a good followup to reading *Who Took Farmer's Hat?* (p. 162). Begin by folding an 8-1/2-x-11-inch sheet of paper in half.

It was the spring of the year. Jenny Wren was ready to start her family. But she had no nest. She flew over small foothills and high fields. *(Make first two cuts as shown:)*

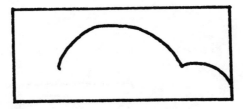

She flew over low valleys. *(Make third cut like this:)*

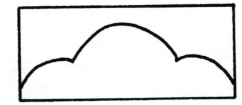

She looked everywhere for bits of this and that to make her nest. Then she looked down at Farmer Nob's orchard. There in the branches of an apple tree was Farmer Nob's straw hat! *(Hold up hat shape.)*

"What a perfect place to raise my family," said Jenny. "This hat will make the best nest."

So Jenny took Farmer Nob's hat *(turn hat shape upside down),* and made a few alterations. *(Cut off ends of hat like this:)*

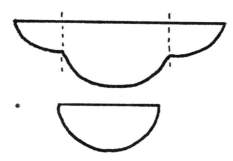

and sat right down to lay her egg. Many weeks later, Jenny heard the egg begin to crack. *(Make first cut like this:)*

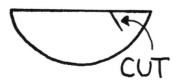

It cracked and it cracked and it cracked. *(Make the next cut like this:)*

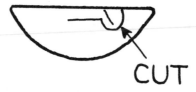

Out of the egg popped a beautiful, big baby bird. *(Unfold the cut shape to show head shape.)* And that baby bird peeped so loud *(push out the beak portion),* that Farmer Nob looked up in the tree.

"So that's what happened to my hat!" he said. But Farmer Nob wasn't angry at all.
He threw back his head and laughed. "That's all right," he said. "I don't mind losing my hat. That's the best nest any wren ever made." And Jenny Wren agreed. After all, it was her best nest.

Sammy Sombrero and Bonnie Blue Bonnet
(A Finger Puppet Story)

Children will be fascinated with this unusual kind of finger puppet. Your index and middle fingers stick through the holes of the figures so your fingers become puppet feet. Prepare two hat finger puppets of Sammy and Bonnie according to the illustration. Draw two light lines on the back of Sammy. You will cut along these lines when Sammy is slashed in the story. Then prepare a horse finger puppet for Sammy and a horse puppet already wearing Bonnie Bonnet.

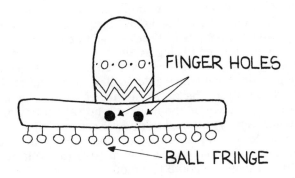

Once there were two hats who lived in a hat shop among many other hats. Sammy Sombrero and Bonnie Blue Bonnet were best friends.

Sammy was a bright red hat with bouncing yellow tassels all around his saucy brim. Bonnie was a soft blue hat with ruffles and a bow.

At the end of the day when the customers left and the shopkeeper locked the door to go home, Sammy and Bonnie shared many good times.

One night Sammy taught Bonnie the "Mexican Hat Dance" and a little song like this:

Oh, it's time now to join in the singing.
Fiesta is now just beginning.
Click your heels, clap your hands both together.
You dance just as light as a feather.

Sammy Sombrero and Bonnie Blue Bonnet danced 'round and 'round until they rolled over for a long siesta.

Another night Bonnie taught Sammy a Viennese waltz and a little song like this:
(to the tune of the "Blue Danube")

I'll show you the waltz, the waltz, the waltz.
It's slow and it's grand, it's grand, it's grand.
Just count out with me, with me, with me.
It goes 1-2-3, 2-3, 2-3
You turn all around, around, around.
Bow down to the ground, the ground, the ground.
You're dancing with me—gracefully.
That's the waltz you dance with me!

And again Sammy Sombrero and Bonnie Blue Bonnet danced 'round and 'round all night long.

The next day a woman came into the hat shop and saw Bonnie on the shelf. Her ruffles and bow were a bit droopy from all the dances she had been dancing, but she was still a beautiful hat.

The woman said, "I want that one!" And she pointed straight at Bonnie.

Sadly Sammy watched the shopkeeper put Bonnie in a big box and hand the box to the woman. The woman took Bonnie out of the shop. Would Sammy ever see her again?

Day after day Sammy just sat. At night he was ever so lonely because he had no one to dance with and no one to sing to him.

One day a tall man came in the shop and bought Sammy. At last Sammy was going out in the big world. Maybe he would go to a fiesta and have some fun!

But the next thing he knew, Sammy was pulled by his brim. Someone slashed his sides and stuffed him down on the head of a horse! Sammy almost cried.

"Hello, Sammy! I thought I'd never see you again."

Sammy looked up, and who do you think he saw? Yes! There on the head of another horse was his old friend Bonnie. Sammy was full to his old brim with joy!

"Do you think we could teach our horses to waltz?" asked Bonnie.

"Certainly!" said Sammy. "Now that we're out in the big world and together again we might even try the fox trot!

Sammy Sombrero and Bonnie Blue Bonnet taught their horses so many fancy steps that they all went on to a circus. There they became big stars. But all the fame never went to their heads. Sammy Sombrero and Bonnie Blue Bonnet were just happy to be dancing together again.

My Thinking Cap

(To the tune of "On Top of Old Smoky")

On top of my shoulders
Sits my old head.
Just so I won't lose it,
It's sewn on with thread.

But the thread might get busted.
My head would roll off.
Then I'd have to chase it
So it wouldn't get lost.

So I made me a nifty
New kind of hat.
It's tied on with ribbons.
It's my thinking cap!

What's under Mat's Hat?

(A Flannel-board Story)

People who keep secrets are often said to be keeping something "under their hats." The sneaky cat in this poem may have a hard time keeping secrets because the objects become so large. In any case, enjoy building the ridiculous exaggeration as you place the objects on a flannel board. Place the objects under the hat so they will make a visible chain of objects from small to big.

This is Matthew,
A sly old cat.
This is Matthew's
Tall black hat.

This is Grandma's
Spool of thread,
That she laid down
On her double bed,
That Matthew hid
Underneath his hat.
Matthew was sneaky,
A sly old cat.

This is Father's
Hammer and drill,
His box of nails,
He dropped and spilled,
That Matthew hid
Underneath his hat.
Matthew was sneaky,
A sly old cat.

This is Mother's
Mop and broom,
She left in the corner
Of the dining room,
That Matthew hid
Underneath his hat.
Matthew was sneaky,
A sly old cat.

This is Sue's bicycle,
With a shiny horn.
She got it last Christmas
Early in the morn,
That Matthew hid
Underneath his hat.
Matthew was sneaky,
What a sly old cat!

This is Grandpa's
Pickup truck.
He parks by the barn
When he does his work,
That Matthew hid
Underneath his hat.
Now Matthew was sneaky, a sly old cat—
But how did he ever, EVER do that?!

Funny Hat

(To the tune of "This Old Man")

After the children understand how the actions and words go together, let them suggest other parts of the body for using the hat.

On my head I wear a hat.
    (Hands on head.)
It is such a funny hat,
    (Shake head.)
That my head will wiggle, wiggle to and fro.
    (Wiggle head.)
Where else can my fun hat go?
    (Hands shoulder high, palms up.)

On my knee I wear a hat.
    (Point to knee, then do actions as
    in last verse.)
It is such a funny hat,
That my knee will wiggle, wiggle to and fro.
Where else can my fun hat go?

(When all the wiggles are out, use this last verse to get settled for the next activity.)

On my hands I wear my hat.
It is such a quiet hat.
My hands don't wiggle, they just go clap,
Then I put them in my lap.

Books about Pass the Hat

Berenstain, Stan, and Jan Berenstain. **Old Hat, New Hat**. Random House, 1970.

An easy-to-read text that reads aloud well, it tells the story of a bear shopping for a new hat. Each new hat is rejected as the old hat ends up suiting its owner, much to the dismay of the shopkeeper.

Blos, Joan. **Martin's Hats**. Illustrated by Marc Simont. Morrow, 1984.

With the aid of a variety of hats, Martin explores caves, acts as a train engineer, becomes chef of a grand repast, delivers mail, puts out a fire, harvests hay, and dons a nightcap to go to bed.

Clymer, Eleanor. **Belinda's New Spring Hat**. Illustrated by Gioia Fiammenghi. Franklin Watts, 1979.

Belinda can't wait for her mother to get her a new spring hat, so she looks for one herself. She tries a lampshade, a wastepaper basket, the cat's basket, a shopping basket, and a flowerpot. Finally her father brings her the long-awaited new spring hat.

Duvoisin, Roger. **Jasmine**. Knopf, 1973.

Jasmine the cow finds a fancy hat and admires the way she looks even though the other barnyard animals call her pretentious. Then the animals find hats, but Jasmine goes hatless. When all the animals get rid of their hats, Jasmine keeps hers. In the end she does not mind being different.

Geringer, Laura. **A Three Hat Day**. Illustrated by Arnold Lobel. Harper & Row, 1985.

R. R. Pottle the Third collects hats, but he is lonely. One day, when he is feeling especially sad, he puts on three hats to go shopping for more. In the biggest hat shop in town, he meets Isabel, who is wearing the perfect hat. Isabel and R. R. marry, but their child, R. R. Pottle the Fourth, does not like hats. She loves shoes!

Hiser, Bernice T. **The Adventure of Charlie and His Wheat-Straw Hat**. Illustrated by Mary Szilagyi. Dodd, Mead, 1986.

Seven-year-old Charlie wants a wheat-straw hat to wear to school, but money is short during the Civil War. Charlie and his grandma make the hat themselves. This "memorat" of a Kentucky school librarian captures the Appalachian flavor of the setting for a pleasing read-aloud book.

Johnson, B. J., and Susan Aiello. **A Hat Like That**. St. Martin's Press, 1986.

Children adventure in a space hat, an undersea helmet, a magician's hat (with a pop-up rabbit), and many more kinds of headgear in this board book with manipulatives. The text is told in simple rhyme.

Keats, Ezra Jack. **Jennie's Hat**. Harper & Row, 1966.

Jennie's aunt sends her such a plain hat that Jennie tries on a variety of objects from a basket to a lampshade. Nothing suits her. On the way home from church, Jennie's plain hat is decorated with flowers, eggs, and valentines by a flock of birds.

Kuskin, Karla. **A Boy Had a Mother Who Bought Him a Hat**. Houghton Mifflin, 1976.

This story in verse tells about a boy whose mother buys him a miscellaneous assortment of items, beginning with a hat "as red as a rose and it kept off the snows." When he loses the hat, the sequence begins again.

Moncure, Jane Belk. **Word Bird's Hats**. Illustrated by Vera Gahman. Child's World, 1982.

Simple, large-print text identifies seven work-associated hats, one for each day of the week.

Roffey, Maureen. **Look, There's My Hat!** Putnam, 1985.

Simple text and die-cut pages explore a child's statements: "Look, there's my hat!" and "Those are my shoes." But as each page is turned, the initial statement takes on a new meaning. The hat on Mommy's head is too big for the child, and the shoes fit Aunt Sally. Size and shape relationships are taught as the young child follows the simple statements in this book.

Seuss, Dr. **The Cat in the Hat Comes Back**. Random House, 1958.

Two children sit inside one wet day and wish for something to do when the Cat in the Hat comes along with lots of tricks under his hat to amuse them.

Slobodkina, Esphyr. **Caps for Sale**. E. M. Hale, 1947.

In this classic tale, a peddler who wears a stack of caps on his head rests under a tree for a nap. When he wakes, they are gone. His caps were stolen by a treeful of monkeys, but he cleverly tricks them into tossing the caps back.

Related Activities about Pass the Hat

Work Hats
(An Action Rhyme)

An astronaut's hat
Is worn out in space.
    (Hands up, walk as if in space.)
A lifeguard's visor
Keeps the sun off her face.
    (Shield eye with hand.)

Quarterbacks wear helmets
To protect their heads.
    (Bend knees, place hands on them.)
Fire fighters wear hats
All bright and red.
    (Mime using fire hose.)

Police wear hats
With a shiny shield.
    (Hand up as if stopping traffic.)
Farmers wear brimmed hats
Out in the field.
    (Mime hoeing field.)

These hats help people
Get their work done.
    (Hands out, palms up.)
But, sometimes, hats
Are just for fun.
    (Clap three times.)

Five Fun Hats

(A Fingerplay)

Hold up one finger for each hat mentioned.

In my box are five fun hats.
The first one is a nurse's cap.
The second one is red for a fire fighter.
The third one, a baker's, is tall and lighter.
Wear the fourth one for baseball—
Take along your bat.
Save the fifth one for your birthday—
It's a party hat!

Pat's Hats

(An Object Story)

This story is a good companion piece to use with *Martin's Hats*. Try to find the same kind of hats mentioned in the story and put them on your head as you tell this story.

Pat loved hats. She loved tall hats and wide hats, soft hats and hard hats. She had boxes and shelves and trunks full of hats. She had fun with hats. But she wanted even more hats.
"What do you want for your birthday?" asked her grandpa.
"I want a hat!" said Pat.
So her grandpa gave her a fishing hat for her birthday. And Pat rowed a row boat down the Mississippi River. She caught a 10-pound fish in her fishing boat.
"What do you want for Christmas?" asked her dad.
"I want a hat!" said Pat.
So her dad gave her a jeweled crown for Christmas. Pat sailed off to a faraway land and became queen for a day in her jeweled crown.
On Valentine's Day Pat's grandma didn't send her a valentine. She knew what Pat wanted—that's right, a hat. So grandma sent Pat a tall baker's hat. Pat put on that hat and got in an airplane and flew to a big city. She marched into a television studio and became the first famous child baker to star in her own cooking show.
When Spring came, Pat's brother gave her a baseball cap. And, of course, Pat joined a major league baseball team that summer. She became a famous baseball player and even got to play in the World Series.
When it was time for school to start in the fall, her mother asked her, "What would you like to wear to school?"
Well, you know what Pat said—"A hat!"
"But what kind of hat?" asked her mother. "You've already had so many adventures."
Pat thought and thought and then she got a bright idea. She got a book and a long string and she tied the book to the top of her head.
"Now that's a hat!" said her dad.
"But what kind of hat?" asked her mother.
"Why, it's my thinking cap, of course!" said Pat.
So Pat went off to school in her very own thinking cap. It was the greatest adventure of her whole life.

The Hatter Makes a Hat

(A Flannel-board Story)

To tell this story, cut out felt shapes: a simple circle with feathers for a face, medium-sized triangles of blue, red, yellow, and green, and a very small green triangle. Place the head on the flannel board to begin the story.

Mr. Hatter made hats. He made big ones and little ones. He made red ones and blue ones, yellow and green ones. All the hats Mr. Hatter made had three corners.

Now one day Mr. Hatter thought, "I have made hats for all kinds of people, but I don't have a hat of my very own. I want a hat for just me. It will have three corners. It will be a green hat, and it will fit just right."

So Mr. Hatter looked around his shop for a green hat that fit just right. The first one he found was this. *(Place blue triangle on head.)* It had three corners. Is it a green hat? *(No.)*

"That," said Mr. Hatter, "is not a hat for a Hatter."

So Mr. Hatter looked around his shop for a green hat that fit just right. The next one he found looked like this. *(Place red triangle on head.)* It had three corners. Is it a green hat? *(No.)*

"That," said Mr. Hatter, "is not a hat for a Hatter."

So Mr. Hatter looked around his shop for a green hat that fit just right. The next one he found looked like this. *(Place yellow triangle on head.)* It had three corners. Is it a green hat? *(No.)*

"That," said Mr. Hatter, "is not a hat for a Hatter."

So Mr. Hatter looked around his shop for a green hat that fit just right. The next one he found looked like this. *(Place the small green triangle on head.)* It had three corners. Is it a green hat? *(Yes!)* But does it fit Mr. Hatter just right? *(No.)*

"That," said Mr. Hatter, "is not a hat for this Hatter."

So Mr. Hatter looked around his shop just one more time for a green hat that fit him just right. This time he found one that looked like this. *(Place medium-sized green triangle on head.)* It had three corners. Is it a green hat? *(Yes.)* And does it fit Mr. Hatter just right? *(Yes!)*

"That," said Mr. Hatter, "IS a hat for a Hatter!"

And so it was.

Fancy Birthday Party Hat
(To the tune of "Twinkle, Twinkle Little Star")

As a followup to this song, make the birthday hats in the craft section of this chapter.

Fancy birthday party hat—
Fit it 'round your head like that.
Add some candles all around.
Now it looks just like a crown.
Birthday hats are so much fun,
'Specially when we all wear one!

Crazy Hat
(A Flannel-board or Object Story)

Tell this story with flannel-board pieces or use a plain felt hat and a hand puppet for the fairy. If you use the real hat, attach small pieces of Velcro® to the hat and to the backs of pictures cut from greeting cards for the decorations. This hat creation can be different each time you tell the story.

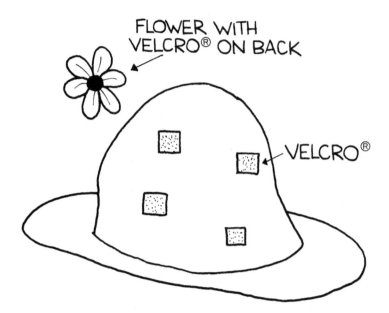

FLOWER WITH VELCRO® ON BACK

VELCRO®

Tabatha had a nice hat. It was a lovely red hat, and it kept her head warm in winter and cool in summer.

One day Tabatha looked at her hat and sighed, "This is a nice red hat. It keeps me warm in winter and cool in summer, but it is so plain. I wish I had a really fancy hat."

Well, before you could say "Sombrero," there was Fairy Hatpin ready to grant Tabatha's wish.

"What would you like on your hat?" asked Fairy Hatpin.

Tabatha had often thought she would like a really fancy hat, but now that Fairy Hatpin was all ready to grant her wish, Tabatha couldn't think of a single thing to put on her hat. She looked around the room, and the first thing that came into her mind was flowers.

"I want a flower on my hat," said Tabatha.

"Good choice," said Fairy Hatpin. And before you could say "Chrysanthemum," there were lovely flowers all over Tabatha's hat.

Now Tabatha had a lovely red hat with flowers on it. It still kept her head warm in winter and cool in summer. But it wasn't fancy enough.

"I wish," said Tabatha, "that I had a really fancy hat."

Well, before you could say "Babouska," there was Fairy Hatpin ready to grant Tabatha's wish.

"What would you like on your hat?" asked the Fairy.

Once again Tabatha wasn't ready. She looked around the room. She looked out the window. She saw a bird sitting on the windowsill. So Tabatha said the first thing that came into her mind.

"I want a pigeon on my hat."

"Good choice," said Fairy Hatpin. And before you could say "Pomegranate seeds," there was a pigeon on Tabatha's hat.

Now Tabatha had a lovely red hat with flowers and a pigeon. It still kept her head warm in winter and cool in summer. But Tabatha looked at her hat and said, "I wish I had a really, *really* fancy hat."

Well, before you could say "Ten-gallon hat," there was Fairy Hatpin ready to grant Tabatha's wish.

"What would you like on your hat?" asked Fairy Hatpin.

Tabatha looked around the room, and she saw a television set, so she said, "I want a TV set on my hat!"

"Good choice," said Fairy Hatpin. And before you could say "Cable hookup," there was a TV set on Tabatha's hat.

So now Tabatha had a lovely red hat with flowers and a pigeon and a TV set on it. It still kept her head warm in winter and cool in summer. But Tabatha looked at her hat and she said, "My hat is lovely, but it still isn't fancy enough. I wish I had a truly fancy hat."

Well, before you could say "Motorcycle helmet," there was Fairy Hatpin ready to grant Tabatha's wish.

"What would you like on your hat this time?" she asked.

Tabatha looked around the room, but she could not think of anything else. Then she looked straight at Fairy Hatpin and she said, "I want Fairy Hatpin on my hat!"

"WHAT?" shrieked Fairy Hatpin. And she disappeared in a puff of smoke.

Fairy Hatpin was never seen again, but Tabatha still had a lovely red hat with flowers and a pigeon and a TV set on it. It kept her head warm in winter and cool in summer. And it was a fancy hat after all.

A Bee in Her Bonnet

(A Participatory Story)

To tell this story, prepare a series of simple animal masks from paper plates: cow, pig, cat, hen, and mouse. Cut eye holes and add distinctive animal features. Attach a craft stick to the bottom of each mask so children can hold them easily, and attach a small piece of Velcro® to the top. Make a fancy paper bonnet with four blue flowers and a red spotted bow, and attach a small piece of Velcro® to the bonnet so it will stick to the masks. Attach a piece of Velcro® to one of the flowers in the bonnet. Make a bumblebee and attach Velcro® to it so it can be attached to the flower in the bonnet. Before you begin the story, invite five children to hold the masks and help you tell the story. Give the cow mask with the bonnet attached to it to the first child as the story begins.

Cow was proud of her new bonnet. It had four blue flowers and a red spotted bow. It kept the sun out of her eyes and the flies out of her ears. It was a fine bonnet!

"Moosey-goosey!" said Cow. "What a fine bonnet!" *(Give the next child the pig mask.)*

But when Pig saw Cow, she saw the fine bonnet. Oh, my, did Pig like Cow's new bonnet! Pig liked that bonnet so much that she took the bonnet right off of Cow's head and put it on her own. *(Move bonnet from Cow to Pig.)*

"Wait," said Cow. "There's a ...." But Pig would not listen. She just said, "Oinkers-boinkers! What a fine bonnet!" And that was that! *(Give the next child the cat mask.)*

When Cat saw Pig, she saw the fine bonnet. Oh, my, did Cat like Pig's new bonnet. Cat liked that bonnet so much that she took the bonnet right off of Pig's head and put it on her own. *(Move bonnet from Pig to Cat.)*

"Wait," said Cow. "There's a ...." But Cat would not listen. She just said, "Meowser-wowser! What a fine bonnet!" And that was that! *(Give the next child the hen mask.)*

When Hen saw Cat, she saw the fine bonnet. Oh, my, did Hen like Cat's new bonnet. Hen liked that bonnet so much that she took the bonnet right off of Cat's head and put it on her own. *(Move bonnet from Cat to Hen.)*

"Wait," said Cow. "There's a ...." But Hen would not listen. She just said, "Cluck-a-diddle-dee! What a fine bonnet!" And that was that! *(Give the next child the mouse mask.)*

Now when Mouse saw Hen, she saw the fine bonnet. Oh, my, did Mouse like Hen's new bonnet. She liked that bonnet so much that she took it right off Hen's head and put it on her own. *(Move bonnet from Hen to Mouse.)*

"Wait!" said Cow. "There's a ...." But Mouse would not listen. She just said, "Squeakers-peekers! What a fine bonnet!"

But that was not quite that. The bonnet began to buzz. All the animals listened. And Cow finally said, "Wait! There's a BEE in that bonnet!"

"Squeakers-peekers! There's a bee in this bonnet!" said Mouse, and she took off the bonnet and gave it back to Hen. *(Put bonnet on Hen.)*

"Cluck-a-diddle-dee! There's a bee in this bonnet!" said Hen, and she took off the bonnet and gave it back to Cat. *(Put bonnet on Cat.)*

"Meowser-wowser! There's a bee in this bonnet!" said Cat. And she gave it back to Pig. *(Put bonnet on Pig.)*

"Oinkers-boinkers! There's a bee in this bonnet!" said Pig, and she took off the bonnet and gave it back to Cow. *(Put bonnet on Cow.)*

"Moosey-goosey!" said Cow. "Yes, there's a bee in this bonnet, and she's my very good friend." So off went Cow in her lovely bonnet with the four blue flowers and the red spotted bow ... and the bee!

Alphabet Cats in a Hat

(A Flannel-board Chant)

This chant is a simple variation of "I Unpacked Grandmother's Trunk." It's the kind of activity that asks children to think of names beginning with each letter of the alphabet. If each child has a felt cat to place on the board, it will give him or her time to think of a name as others place the cats on the board. Prepare twenty-six cats and a large hat from felt for the cats to curl up in.

This activity will also be a good followup to *The Cat in the Hat Comes Back.*

Clap out the rhythm of the beginning rhyme, then let each child place the cats one at a time on the board and give an *A-B-C* name.

A is for Annabelle, my favorite cat.
She likes to curl up in my hat.
How many kittens can you name
In this alphabet-cat-hat game?

(Suggestions to get you started: *A*—Annabelle, *B*—Bethany, *C*—Carrie, *D*—Daniel, *E*—Elizabeth, *F*—Fred, and so on.)

Books about The Hair on My Head

Davis, Gibbs. **Katy's First Haircut.** Illustrated by Linda Shute. Houghton Mifflin, 1985.

Katy had the longest hair in her class, and she loved it. But it begins to be a problem. When she gets it cut and is mistaken for a boy, she regrets her decision. A wise teacher congratulates her on her courage to make the big decision, so Katy feels all right in the end.

Frandsen, Karen G. **Michael's New Haircut.** Children's Press, 1986.

Because Michael is self-conscious about his too-short haircut, he wears his baseball cap all day during school.

Freeman, Don. **Dandelion.** Viking, 1964.

When Dandelion is invited to a party, he gets his hair cut but dislikes his frizzy mane, so he decides to get a stylish set. On the way to the party he also acquires stylish clothes. But when he arrives at the party, he is shut out because the hostess doesn't recognize him. Caught in the wind and rain, Dandelion looks like himself again, and is welcomed to the party after all.

Freeman, Don. **Mop Top.** Viking, 1955.

On the way to the barber shop, a mop-headed boy decides he doesn't need a haircut. But when he is mistaken for a mop, he changes his mind and gets the cut.

Girard, Linda Walvoord. **Jeremy's First Haircut.** Albert Whitman, 1986.

Jeremy is a little scared of getting his first haircut, but it becomes a fun filled adventure with Mom and Dad helping out.

Related Activities about The Hair on My Head

The Hair-Raising Adventure of Sara Susan
(A Flannel-board Story)

To tell this story, make felt pieces of a girl's face, a large head of hair, a neater head of hair, a bee, a mouse, a chick, a pig, a bear, and a red bow. Place the pieces on the flannel board as the characters are mentioned in the story.

Sara Susan never wanted to have her hair cut. Now lots of little girls have long hair. Long hair is pretty when it is combed and clean and curled. But Sara Susan did not want to brush her hair or wash it. It got to be a big, tangled mess.

One day when Sara Susan was out walking in the yard, a bee flew by. And Sara Susan's hair looked so tangled that the bee flew right in.

"Look at me!" said the bee from Sara Susan's hair.

Sure enough, someone did look. That someone was the mouse. He crawled right in with the bee.

"A fine house," said the mouse.

"Look at me!" called the bee from Sara Susan's hair.

Sure enough, someone did look. That someone was the chick. He hopped right in with the bee.

"This is slick," said the chick.

"A fine house," said the mouse.

"Look at me!" said the bee from Sara Susan's hair.

Sure enough, someone did look. That someone was the pig. He waddled right in with the bee.

"What a wig," said the pig.

"This is slick," said the chick.

"A fine house," said the mouse.

"Look at me!" called the bee from Sara Susan's hair.

Well, sure enough, someone did look. And that someone was the bear. He lumbered right in with the bee.

"Is this all hair?" said the bear.

"What a wig," said the pig.

"This is slick," said the chick.

"A fine house," said the mouse.

"Look at me!" called the bee from Sara Susan's hair.

This time, the somebody that looked was Sara Susan. When she saw all those animals, she called, "Mother! I want my hair washed!"

And, when the animals heard that, out lumbered the bear, out waddled the pig, out hopped the chick, out crawled the mouse, and out flew the bee. All came out of Sara Susan's hair.

So Sara Susan's mother washed her hair, and combed it, and curled it. And from then on, the only thing that lived in Sara Susan's hair was a nice red bow!

Knots in My Hair

(To the tune of "Skip to My Lou")

Knots in my hair,
 Now, what'll I do?
Knots in my hair,
 Now, what'll I do?
Knots in my hair,
 Now, what'll I do?
Maybe I should pull them!
 (Spoken:) OUCH!

Should I cut them off instead?
Should I cut them off instead?
Should I cut them off instead?
 (Spoken:) NO!
Mommy might not like that.

Here comes Mommy with a brush.
Here comes Mommy with a brush.
Here comes Mommy with a brush.
Won't you please be careful!

Brush in my hair,
 Now, what'll I do?
Brush in my hair,
 Now, what'll I do?
Brush in my hair,
 Now, what'll I do?
 (Spoken:) Guess I'll have to wear it!

The Hair on My Head
(An Action Rhyme)

Curls and curls
    (Wave fingers next to hair.)
For boys and girls,
Pony tails
    (Hands on back of head.)
And long pig tails.

Hair with bangs.
    (Touch forehead.)
Hair slicked back.
    (Slick back hair.)
Hair that's red,
Blonde, or black.

Crew cut or Afro
    (Touch top of head.)
Piled on top,
    (Raise hand from top of head.)
Hairdo looking
Like a mop.
    (Arms out, hands extended.)

Hair sticks up
    (Touch top of head.)
Like a rooster's head
    (Raise both arms high over head.)
When I get up
From my bed.

Cut it off.
    (Scissors movement.)
This I know:
Hair will always,
Always grow!
    (Hands out, arms extended.)

I Don't Want to Wash My Hair
(To the tune of "Mary Had a Little Lamb")

I don't want to wash my hair,
    wash my hair,
    wash my hair,
I don't want to wash my hair—
Soap gets in my eye! *(Spoken:)* CRY!

Close your eyes so soap stays out,
    soap stays out,
    soap stays out,
Close your eyes so soap stays out—
The water's down my neck! *(Spoken:)* HECK!

Grab a towel and dry me off,
    dry me off,
    dry me off,
Grab a towel and dry me off—
Gee, I'm glad we're done! *(Spoken:)* FUN!

GAMES FOR HATS AND MORE HATS

Pass the Hat

When people want to collect money for a worthy cause, they "pass the hat." Collect good deeds from children with this game. Put slips of paper in a hat. On each slip of paper write down little tasks children can do at school or at home, such as "Help set the table," "Help fold the laundry," or "Pick up your toys." Children receive a small paper crown with a star on it when they complete the task.

Who's Got My Caps?

(To the tune of "Skip to My Lou")

After you've read *Caps for Sale*, do this little hat dance song that will mimic the peddler's and monkeys' antics.

Who's got my grey caps?
Is it you?
    (Point to a child.)
Who's got my brown caps?
Is it you?
    (Point to another child.)
Who's got my blue caps?
Is it you?
    (Point to another child.)
All jump up together!
    (All jump.)

Shake your fist,
    (Do appropriate actions.)
And stamp your foot.
Shake your fist,
And stamp your foot.
Shake your fist,
And stamp your foot.
All jump up together!
    (All jump.)

Throw down my grey caps
    (Do appropriate actions.)
On the floor.
Throw down my grey caps
On the floor.
Throw down my grey caps
On the floor.
All sit down together!
    (All sit.)

Leader: *(Spoken:)* Did anyone see my
    red caps?

Hat Hunt

(To the tune of "Did You Ever See a Lassie?")

Many stories tell about the wind blowing a hat off someone's head as the hat goes on a merry chase. This game will recall such an adventure and teach children to be careful "lookers." It's a calm kind of hunting game because children are instructed to keep quiet and not give away the location of the hidden hat.

Begin by having children sit in a circle and cover their eyes. The leader hides a paper hat somewhere in the room. The hat should be fairly easy to spot. Children uncover their eyes, then sing the following song.

Who has seen my new hat,
My new hat, my new hat?
Who has seen my new hat
The wind just blew off?

The wind came and snatched it.
It reached out and grabbed it.
Oh, who can help me find it?
My head's getting cold!

After children sing the song, they may get up and quietly hunt. As soon as children see the hat, they go back to the circle and sit down. When everyone is seated, the leader lets someone else hide the hat so that everyone can go on another "hat hunt."

Hat Tricks

On slips of paper write out simple tricks. Examples might be "Shake your head 'yes,'" "Shake your head 'no,'" or "Stand on your head." Place these slips in a hat and pass them around the circle. Each child draws out a slip for the leader to read. Then the child does the trick.

Who's Hat Is That?

After you've read some books on work-related hats, such as *Martin's Hats* or *Word Bird's Hats* and used "Work Hats" and "Five Fun Hats," review the children's knowledge of work-related hats with this game.

Prepare a set of pictures from magazines or make large cutouts of hats associated with different occupations. Begin with children sitting down on the floor. Hold up each picture and have children stand when they can identify who wears the hat. Rather than having children call out the appropriate answer, have them mime something that person might do. Examples might be a baker stirring a bowl of batter, a fire fighter hosing down a fire, or a baseball player hitting a ball.

CRAFTS FOR HATS AND MORE HATS

Making and wearing their own hat creations gives young children many hours of enjoyment. Here are just a few ideas to help you exercise your own imagination and use about any scrap materials you have on hand. Some of the projects will be easy enough for young children to make with little adult assistance. Other hats can be made for the children, or you might organize a parent-child hat workshop so the difficult parts can be made without frustration for you or for the children.

Crowns for Kings, Queens, and Birthday Children

This hat is made from a long rectangular strip of paper. For the birthday hat (use this with the "Fancy Birthday Party Hat" song on p. 175), simply cut a rectangle 24 x 8 inches. Write the words "Happy Birthday" and the child's name on the strip. Next, cut out paper birthday candles from construction paper and glue or staple these around the strip. Fit the band around the child's head and staple the ends in place. For a crown, cut one long end of the strip in a zig-zag pattern to make the points of the crown before you fit the crown to the child's head. Decorate the crown with colored foil circles, gummed stars, and lightweight pieces of old jewelry.

Three-Cornered Hat for Patriots or Pirates

The shape for this hat is the same for both kinds of characters, except that the patriot hat is worn with the point in front and the pirate hat is worn with the point in back.

Cut out three shapes (see p. 185) for each hat. The length of each shape is approximately 9 inches and the height is approximately 3 1/2 inches at the curve. Cut the shapes out of black construction paper. Staple at the ends. For the patriot hat, attach four or five strips of curled white paper (each about 1/2 inch wide and 6-8 inches long) to the flat back of the hat for hair. For the pirate hat, glue on designs of a skull and crossbones cut out of white paper.

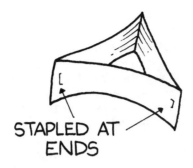

Hats from Anything You Have in the House

Jennie's dissatisfaction with the plain hat in *Jennie's Hat* inspires her to try on a flowerpot and a lampshade. Young children quickly will come up with their own makeshift hats—from pots and pans to goldfish bowls! For this craft, assemble plastic flowerpots, round ice cream cartons, paper bowls, or pie plates. You might ask children to bring these items from home. Provide an assortment of decorations—feathers, small flags, little balloons, artificial flowers, stickers, rickrack, buttons, etc.—to glue or staple on the hats. Have a parade when everyone has finished their creations!

Character Hats Made Easy

Children will be able to make these hats with little assistance so they can become favorite fairytale characters. The shape lends itself to hats for Yankee Doodle, Robin Hood, wood-cutters, or elves.

Give each child a rectangle of paper 9 x 12 inches with the corners rounded off. Cut a slit from one long end about one third up the width of the hat. (See the illustration below.) Overlap the slit ends and staple to fit the child's head. Add paper curls, feathers, paper flowers, or anything else you wish. Paper can be curled with scissors or by rolling it tightly around a pencil. For the Yankee Doodle hat, glue different kinds of macaroni and pasta on the hat and add a stick of candy!

Space Helmet

Ice cream cartons from ice cream stores make wonderful space helmets when they are washed out and dried. Cut an eye piece out (approximately 6 x 2 inches) and tape a piece of heavy acetate (colored acetate report folders will work well) to the inside of the carton. Now let the children decorate their cartons with construction paper, magic markers, and crayons. Pipe cleaners can be attached for antennae if the space helmet is worn by an alien. Paper dials may be attached to helmets with brad fasteners for extra interest.

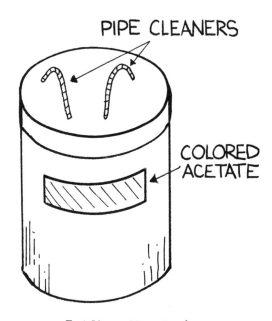

PIPE CLEANERS

COLORED ACETATE

Eat Your Hat Craft

Follow up the story and poem in this chapter about hats that you can eat by making one! A pointed ice cream cone makes a perfect clown hat. Simply add frosting decorations with canned frostings, red hots, and little candies.

Character Hats That Take More Time

Cone-shaped hats and cylindrical hats with brims can be made from construction paper or stiff fabric (such as heavyweight interfacing) if you have enough adults to help. The cone-shaped hat works well for a witch or wizard. The cylindrical hat makes a good magician's hat, a Mad Hatter's hat, a top hat for a fancy occasion, or an Abraham Lincoln hat.

For the cone-shaped hat, begin with one fourth of a circle, approximately 28 inches in diameter. Tape or glue the two straight sides. Fold down the point at the top if you wish a crooked point. To add a brim, cut a circle approximately 10 inches in diameter. Next, cut out the inner circle to fit your head, about 7 or 8 inches in diameter. Now make a slit from the outer circle to the inner circle, and cut 1/2-inch slits all around the inner circle to make tabs. Fold these tabs so you can tape or glue your brim to the inside of the cone section. Overlap the brim piece so the two pieces fit together and fasten the ends of the brim with glue or tape.

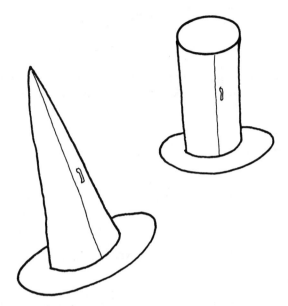

For the cylindrical or top hat, begin with a long rectangle of paper for the crown. A piece 9 x 24 inches will work well. Now cut 1-inch slits along one long edge and fold these to make tabs. This will be the crown. Next, cut an 18-inch circle or oval shape. Then cut out a center circle, about 7 or 8 inches, to fit your head. Now roll up the rectangular piece to make a cylinder (but don't glue the ends yet) and fit it down inside the brim, overlap the sides to fit the circle of the brim. Glue tabs to inside of the brim. Then tape or glue cylinder after you've overlapped it to fit the brim. You can make a top for your hat by using the part you cut out of the center of the brim, or you can make a new piece using this as a pattern. Just glue or tape the top in place.

The Biggest Hat in the World

Draw a simple hat shape in the top half of a pice of posterboard. Give each child a flower, fruit, or bird cut out from greeting cards or magazines. Older children will enjoy placing the figures on the hat in the style of "Pin the Tail on the Donkey" by being blindfolded. Younger children can just take turns taping their decorations on. When the creation is finished, cut a hole in the lower half of the board. Each child can have a turn to "try on the hat" by placing his or her face in the hole. Be sure to have your camera ready! This hat and the pictures will make a wonderful display after the program is over.

DISPLAYS FOR HATS AND MORE HATS

Hat Rack

Borrow a hat rack or hall tree to display a variety of hats: top hats, straw hats, Western hats, berets, hard hats, and so on. Ask people in your community to contribute unusual styles and shapes.

Bobbie Pins and Bows

Collect hair accessories and implements used in creating hairstyles for another display. Hairpins, bobbie pins, hairnets, barrettes, bows, hair combs, rollers, headbands, haircutting scissors, and permanent wave accessories are just a few possibilities.

Create Your Own Hat Participatory Display

Put a simple plain hat on a wig stand and supply objects for children to decorate the hat. Artificial flowers, feathers, junk jewelry, ribbons, and braid trims are good possibilities. Fasten decorations with glue or Velcro®. You might think of this creation as a kind of flannel board that gets decorated again and again. The Velcro® approach will allow children to attach and reattach the decorations.

Hats on the Job

Find pictures of people wearing work hats in magazines and catalogs. Select pictures that clearly distinguish different occupations. Good examples might be fire fighter, policeman, baker, nurse, football player, construction worker, astronaut, and college graduate. You might wish to find pictures (or take them) of people in your own community.

Hats 'Round the World

Find pictures in magazines of hats associated with other lands, such as a turban, a fez, a tam, a beret, a coolie hat, a sombrero, and a British palace guard.

You Must Have Been a Beautiful Baby

Have children bring a hat or bonnet they wore when they were babies. Pin the bonnets to the bulletin board with each child's name next to each hat. Give each child the opportunity to tell something about her or his hat, such as "I wore this hat when I was a year old" or "My uncle gave me this hat. It came from Texas."

Hat Crafts Display

Don't overlook the opportunity to display hats that children make. Those projects described in the crafts section of this chapter will make attractive displays and give children pride in their own accomplishments.

7
Sneakers, Socks, and Happy Feet

INTRODUCTION

Since people first tied animal fur to their feet for foot coverings, shoes have been necessary wearing apparel. Moccasins and sandals have been worn since earliest times for practical reasons. But evening slippers and tennis shoes show us that shoes can be "solely" for fun!

Shoes may be fascinating, but frustrating for young children. Shoes take us on journeys, house our feet, or become a dwelling for "The Old Woman Who Lived in a Shoe." But shoes seem to get lost, worn out, and outgrown so readily that often children prefer to go barefoot or wear only stocking feet.

This chapter covers everyday shoe experiences and fanciful shoe adventures as well as socks and feet themselves. The first subtheme "Shoes for Romping and Running" includes stories and activities about keeping shoes tied, finding lost shoes, and shopping for new ones. "Shoes for Dancing and Dreaming" explores magic shoes or shoes used in unlikely ways. "Sock It to Me" introduces common problems of getting holes in socks, losing them, and discovering new uses for socks. And the last subtheme "Neat Feet" identifies properties of feet or activities feet can do.

Language skills are developed through stories, songs, poems, and games. The game "Foot in the Mouth" graphically illustrates an awkward predicament. The game "Fill My Shoes" provides an opportunity to teach two meanings of this idiom. Explore the rhyme and rhythms of language so natural to young children with the many toe-tapping and shoe-romping poems and songs.

Children will also learn such basic skills as counting and body awareness as well as right/left directional skills from the stories and activities in this chapter. Generations of parents have taught body awareness and counting by reciting "This little piggy went to market, this little piggy stayed home." Preschool teachers and parents have found the "rabbit ears" approach in *When Shoes Eat Socks* encourages youngsters to tie their own shoes. Our activities attempt to turn chores into learning games and help children become more independent.

INITIATING ACTIVITY

Right Shoe, Left Shoe
(A Get-Acquainted Chant)

Have children stand in a circle facing each other so everyone can participate easily in this get-acquainted chant.

189

Leader: Tap your right shoe,
All of you.

Tap your left shoe.
Who are you?
(Leader points to child next to her.)
Child: Amy.
Leader: Let's all say it — Amy.
Group: Amy.

Leader: Tap your right shoe.
Who are you?
(Leader points to next child.)
Child: Joe.
Leader: Let's all say it — Joe.
Group: Joe.

Leader: Tap your left shoe.
Who are you?
(Leader points to next child.)
Child: Michael.
Leader: Let's all say it — Michael.
Group: Michael.
(Leader continues to go around circle until each child has introduced himself or herself. Then the last stanza is repeated.)
Leader: Right shoe,
Left shoe.
Tap, tap, tap!
Hands together,
Clap, clap, clap!

LITERATURE-SHARING EXPERIENCES

Books about Shoes for Romping and Running

Cazet, Denys. **Big Shoe, Little Shoe**. Bradbury, 1984.

Little Rabbit hides his grandpa's shoes so Grandpa won't go out to deliver laundry. Finally they strike a bargain. If Little Rabbit gets the shoes, he can come along. But Grandpa's retort, "I wear the big shoes, and you wear the little shoes," gives Little Rabbit an idea about switching roles.

Corey, Dorothy. **New Shoes**. Illustrated by Dora Leder. Albert Whitman, 1985.

Everybody in the family gets new shoes, including the baby, so a little girl has to wait until she can't wiggle her toes in her old shoes. When she does get to shop for new ones, the decision is difficult, but she chooses red ones and takes them to bed with her.

Hickman, Martha Whitmore. **The Reason I'm Not Quite Finished Tying My Shoes**. Illustrated by Jim Padgett. Abingdon, 1981.

Amanda finds all kinds of reasons for not tying her shoes: she hasn't put her socks on yet; her toes itch; her thumbs might get caught in the loops; her baby brother doesn't know how to tie his shoes. But the real reason she can't tie her shoes is that she can't find her shoes! Any child who has made excuses for not tying shoes will enjoy the humor in this book.

Hughes, Shirley. **Two Shoes, New Shoes**. Walker, 1986.

Jaunty rhyme and typical child-like behavior introduce such clothes as "two shoes, new shoes/bright shiny blue shoes," and "high heeled ladies' shoes for standing tall/button up baby shoes, soft and small."

Klimowicz, Barbara. **When Shoes Eat Socks**. Illustrated by Gloria Kamen. Abingdon, 1971.

Barnaby tries to keep up with the big kids but his shoes keep eating his socks. The trouble is he can't tie his shoes. He learns to make a rabbit's ear with one string, wrap it 'round with the other string, then hunt for the other rabbit's ear and pull it through.

Rice, Eve. **New Blue Shoes**. Macmillan, 1975.

Rebecca and her mother go shoe shopping, and Rebecca decides on blue shoes instead of her usual brown choice. On the way home she begins to have second thoughts, but her mother helps her appreciate her selection.

Sheldon, Aure. **Of Cobblers and Kings**. Illustrated by Don Leake. Parents, 1978.

In the Kingdom of Shodd, Gallo the cobbler solves a carpenter's problem and is made mayor. When he solves the caretaker's problem, he is made governor of the province, and so on, until he is made grand chancellor. But when he discovers children going barefoot because there is no cobbler, Gallo goes back to his old job.

Winthrop, Elizabeth. **Shoes**. Illustrated by William Joyce. Harper & Row, 1986.

A catalog of many kinds of shoes from "shoes to buckle, shoes to tie," to "rubber shoes for muddy squishing," is told in verse with the conclusion that best of all are your own feet!

Related Activities about Shoes for Romping and Running

Lost and Found Shoes
(An Object Story)

Tell the following story with a pair of blue tennis shoes, a pair of red sandals, and a pair of pink ballerina slippers. If you can't find actual shoes, cut out big pictures from colored paper so you can place the shoes around the room as you tell the story.

Once there was a little girl—just about your age—named Sally. She was always losing her shoes.

On Monday she lost her right blue tennis shoe in the sandbox. *(Put blue tennis shoe in one part of the room.)*

On Tuesday she lost her left blue tennis shoe under her bed. *(Put the other blue tennis shoe in another part of the room, preferably under something.)*

On Wednesday she lost her right red sandal under the tomatoes in the garden. *(Put sandal in room next to something red.)*

On Thursday she lost her left red sandal in her toy box. *(Put sandal inside something in the room.)*

On Friday she left both of her new pink ballerina slippers at her friend's house. *(Put slippers in another corner of the room.)*

On Saturday her mother said, "Now Sally, you'll have to find all your shoes today because tomorrow is Sunday. And on Sunday we will be going to church. You'll need to wear your pink ballerina slippers. Then we will be going on a picnic. You'll need to wear your blue tennis shoes to the picnic. And, then, we'll be going to the beach. You'll need to wear your red sandals to the beach.

Sally wondered where her shoes were. Can you help her remember where they all are?

First, the pink slippers were .... *(Let children tell you where to look.)*

And the blue tennis shoes were .... Oh, yes, first the right blue tennis shoe was .... And the left blue tennis shoe was .... And the right red sandal was .... And the left red sandal was ....

Good, you are fine helpers. Now Sally had all three pairs of shoes—the pink ballerina slippers, the blue tennis shoes, and the red sandals. So she went to church, then she went on the picnic, and then she went to the beach. And she had a wonderful day!

Shoe Jumble
(To the tune of "The Farmer in the Dell")

Getting shoes on the wrong feet is a common frustration. Sing this playful song and try a followup activity of drawing around right and left shoes placed correctly and incorrectly so children will see the difference.

I put my right shoe on,
I put my left shoe on.
Now I'm going walking
'Cause I've got my new shoes on.

My feet go inside out,
They wobble all about.
I wonder what's the matter here,
My feet feel kinda weird.

Oh! My right shoe's on the left,
My left shoe's on the right.
I guess I got them jumbled up,
Let's do it all again.

I put my right shoe on,
I put my left shoe on.
Now I got them on O.K.
So I can run and play! Yeah!

Shoe Shopping

Shopping for shoes,
What shall I buy?
Saddle shoes?
Oxfords?
Something with ties?
Penny loafers?
Moccasins?
Slippers with bows?
Shiny patent leather?

I like those!
A pair with buckles?
Or Velcro® straps?
Something that laces?
Something that snaps?
So many shoes—
How to decide?
One thing for certain—
They'd better be my size!

A Little Room to Grow
(An Object Story)

Tell this story with two pairs of shoes, one pair larger than the other. Put the shoes in shoeboxes to take out as you tell the story. At the end, put the boxes on your feet to add to the fun.

Once there was a boy named Greg. Greg had fast-growing feet. So his mother always bought Greg's shoes with a little extra room to grow.

One day when Greg tried to put on his shoes, his feet would not go in. He pushed and he shoved, but the shoes were too small. Or his feet were too big.

"I can't get my shoes on!" shouted Greg.

"That's silly," said his mother, "we just bought those shoes yesterday. Let me try."

She pushed and she shoved, but the shoes would not go on!

Greg and his mother went back to the store. Greg had to hobble with his feet only half way into the shoes.

"Please give this boy shoes with a little extra room to grow!" said Greg's mother.

And the shoe salesman gave Greg an even bigger pair of shoes—with extra room to grow.

The next day Greg tried to put on his new shoes. He pushed and he shoved, but the shoes were too small. Maybe his feet were too big.

"What are we to do?" asked his mother.

"Buy me some new shoes!" said Greg.

So Greg and his mother went back to the store.

"Please give this boy some shoes with a little extra room to grow!" said Greg's mother.

"I'm sorry, Madam," said the shoe man. "I am all out of shoes with a little room to grow."

"What will we do?" asked Greg's mother.

"How about a nice pair of boxes?" asked the shoe man.

Greg thought boxes looked silly on his feet, but, when he tried them on, they didn't pinch his feet.

"We'll take them," said his mother, "and don't wrap them up. He'll wear them home."

The next day Greg got up and put those boxes on his feet. He still thought they looked silly, but he didn't have to push and shove to get them on.

"Hey, Mom!" he shouted, "these new boxes have room to grow!"

So, after that, Greg never wore shoes on his feet again—only very large boxes so there would be a little room to grow.

The Best Shoes

(To the tune of "Mary Had a Little Lamb")

Shiny party shoes go squeak.
(Walk on tiptoe.)
Squeak, squeak, squeak.
Squeak, squeak, squeak.
They are not the best.

Sunny summer sandals flap.
(Walk in place, ankles limp.)
Flap, flap, flap.
Flap, flap, flap.
Sunny summer sandals flap,
They are not the best.

I like sneakers best of all.
Best of all.
Best of all.
I like sneakers best of all.
They run and run and run!
(Run in place.)

Run and run and run and run,
(Continue to run in place.)
Run and run,
Run and run,
Run and run and run and run.
Sneakers are the best—YES!

Where Is Cindy's Shoe?

(A Flannel-board Story)

To tell this story, prepare felt pieces of the following objects: seven dolls, three toy trucks, a bed, a shelf, a closet door or cupboard-style closet, Cindy's red shoes, a dog house, and a dog. Place these objects on the board for the appropriate effects as you tell the story.

Cindy was five years old. She had seven dolls, three toy trucks, and a dog named Fred. And Cindy had a brand new pair of shiny red shoes.

Cindy liked her dolls and trucks and she loved Fred, but the new shoes were so red and so shiny that she thought about them all the time.

One day Cindy's mother called to her, "Cindy, get your new shoes on. We are going to Grandma's."

Cindy scurried around and put on her brand new, shiny red left shoe, but when she went to put on her brand new, shiny red right shoe, it wasn't there.

"Mother," she called. "I can't find my brand new, shiny red shoe."

Mother came up to Cindy's room. "Is it under the bed?" Mother asked. And Fred the dog said, "Roof!" But when Cindy looked under the bed, her brand new, shiny red shoe was not there.

Then Father came in. "Is it on the shelf with your seven dolls?" And Fred the dog said, "Roof!" But when Cindy looked on the shelf, her brand new, shiny red shoe was not there.

Cindy's brother came in. "Did you look in the closet with your three trucks?" he asked. And Fred the dog said, "Roof!" But when Cindy looked in the closet, her brand new, shiny red shoe wasn't there.

Everyone looked behind the sofa, and on top of the refrigerator, and in the laundry hamper, but Cindy's brand new, shiny red shoe wasn't anywhere. And Fred the dog said, "Roof!"

"I guess you'll have to wear your old ones," said Mother. Cindy almost cried, but she put on her old brown shoes and they started to the car.

Cindy's brother went out to put Fred in the dog house while they were gone. Suddenly he shouted, "There's Cindy's shoe!"

They all ran to the backyard, and sure enough, there was Cindy's brand new, shiny red shoe—right on top of Fred's dog house.

"Oh, good," said Cindy's mother, and she got the shoe off the top of the dog house.

"Oh, good," said Cindy's father, and he got the other shoe from inside.

"Oh, good," said Cindy's brother, and he tied up Fred to the dog house.

"Oh, good," said Cindy, and she put on her brand new, shiny red shoes.

All Fred said was "Roof!" Do you suppose he knew all along that the brand new, shiny red shoe was on the roof of his house?

What Does a Puppy Do with a Shoe?
(A Cut-and-Tell Story Poem)

To tell this story, prepare a large cutout of a shoe from construction paper. Hold up the paper shoe as you tell the first part of the story. Hide the shoe behind your back for the second stanza. Then begin tearing pieces off the shoe as the words in the poem direct. Take the last scrap of shoe, cup your hand over it as if it is being eaten, and tuck it in your lap so it appears to be gone.

When Rags was a puppy,
He loved to chew,
So Father gave him
An old brown shoe.

Rags dragged the shoe
Under the couch.
He held it tightly
By the teeth in his mouth.

He chewed up the leather
All 'round the top.
Then he chewed through the heel,
But he still didn't stop.

He chewed and he chewed,
'Til the shoe was a scrap.
Then he gulped down the rest,
And curled up for a nap.

Mommy's High Heel Shoes
(To the tune of "Mary Had a Little Lamb")

Try to make your feet do the appropriate actions and sounds as you sing this song.

Mommy puts her high heels on,
High heels on,
High heels on,
Mommy puts her high heels on.
Her feet go clickety clack.
Clickety,
Clickety,
Clickety clack!
Clickety clack!
Clickety clack!
Clickety,
Clickety,
Clickety clack!
High heels sound like fun!

I try Mommy's high heels on,
High heels on,
High heels on,
I try Mommy's high heels on.
My feet go clompety clomp!
Clompety,
Clompety,
Clompety clomp!
Clompety clomp!
Clompety clomp!
Clompety,
Clompety,
Clompety—FLOP!
I just lost my shoe! *(Spoken:)* PHOO!

Books about Shoes for Dancing and Dreaming

Berson, Harold. **Kassim's Shoes**. Crown, 1977.

Kassim loves his old shoes, but his neighbors declare they are a disgrace, so they buy him a new pair. But Kassim finds the new ones uncomfortable, so he throws them in the river. The shoes are found and Kassim hides them again. Finally a small boy suggests the shoes should remain on Kassim's feet, and everyone agrees.

Ginsburg, Mirra. **Striding Slippers**. Illustrated by Sol Murdocca. Macmillan, 1978.

A shepherd weaves himself a pair of fast-striding slippers to make it easier for him to tend his herd. One hot day he takes them off, tells a stranger about their magic, and they are stolen. The slippers carry the stranger so fast that he's afraid to wear them. In fact, everyone who tries on the slippers can't control them, so the shepherd gets them back in the end.

Heyward, Du Bose. **The Country Bunny and the Little Gold Shoes**. Illustrated by Marjorie Flack. Houghton Mifflin, 1939.

The Country Bunny proves herself to be wise and kind and swift, so she is named the fifth of Grandfather Bunny's Easter Bunnies. Grandfather gives her the most difficult journey of all, but she proves herself brave and is given golden magic shoes to complete her task. This story may be too long for younger preschoolers, but it is magical for those who are ready to listen to a long picture-book story.

Keats, Ezra Jack. **Skates**. Four Winds, 1973.

Two curious dogs find two discarded pairs of roller skates in the trash and a madcap adventure begins.

Lobel, Arnold. "The Journey" from **Mouse Tales**. Harper & Row, 1972.

In order to visit his mother, a mouse drives a car until it falls apart. Next he proceeds on roller skates until the wheels fall off, on boots until they get holes, on sneakers until they wear out. Finally he buys new feet to finish his journey.

Martin, Jacqueline Briggs. **Bizzy Bones and Uncle Ezra**. Illustrated by Stella Ormai. Lothrop, Lee and Shepard, 1984.

Bizzy, a young mouse, and his Uncle Ezra move into a big old work shoe, but the March winds terrify Bizzy. Convinced that they shoe house will blow away, Bizzy persuades Uncle Ezra to tie it down. As the story progresses, the shoe is tied down with a succession of shoelace and string to a number of objects. Finally Uncle Ezra captures the wind in a fanciful fashion for Bizzy.

Rockwell, Anne. **Walking Shoes**. Doubleday, 1980.

A little house is sad because it has no owners, so an elf gives it magic walking shoes to find a family.

Ungerer, Tomi. **One, Two, Where's My Shoe**. Harper & Row, 1964.

A boy asks, "One, two, where's my shoe?" The wordless adventure that follows shows shoes taking an endless variety of escapades—flying with crows, forming the body of an alligator and the chin of an old woman. Children can tell their own stories about how the shoe found its way along this capricious path!

Related Activities about Shoes for Dancing and Dreaming

Where's My Shoe?
(An Action Rhyme)

Many mothers know the cry, "Where's my shoe?" means a search under beds and in the clothes hamper. Have fun with this activity by clapping on each number and doing the actions indicated. Older children may suggest other animals and actions even if they don't always rhyme.

One, two
Where's my shoe?
    (Palms up, shoulder high.)
Three, four
On a kangaroo?
    (Jump!)
Five, six
On a slippery snake?
    (Wiggle body.)

Seven, eight
On a fish in the lake?
    *(Palms together, move hands
    in zig-zag fashion.)*
Nine, ten
Look and see.
    (Circle eyes with fingers.)
Here they are—
Right on me!
    (Point to shoes, then self.)

The Centipede Buys Sneakers
(A Flannel-board Story)

To make the centipede for this story, cut eight to ten circles of green or brown felt. Glue them together, overlapping slightly. On the first circle, draw on eyes and a smile (or use fabric scraps). Cut short pieces of yarn for the other circle sections and glue these on. Next cut out bright-colored felt shoes for the "feet." You may wish to hand these "sneakers" to the children so they can participate in the telling. Begin with the centipede on the flannel board as the story starts.

A centipede lived in the grass under a bush. He was happy there most of the time, but when he climbed up, up, up to the top of the bush, he could see people going to town on the sidewalk.

"I like this bush," sighed the centipede, "but what fun it would be to go to town on the sidewalk. What an adventure!"

So one bright sunny day, the kind that is just right for an adventure on the sidewalk, the centipede climbed out of the bush, walked across the grass, and stepped out on the sidewalk.

It was a big gray sidewalk, and it stretched as far as the centipede could see. What fun it would be to go to town on the sidewalk! What an adventure! So off he set and he sang as he went:

One foot up, two feet down—
I am marching into town!
Three feet up, four feet down—
I am marching into—OUCH!

The centipede stepped on a rock. He rubbed his fifth foot on the left side and started off again.

Five feet up, six feet down—
I am marching into—OUCH!

The centipede stepped into a hole. He rubbed his seventh foot on the right side and started off again.

Seven feet up, eight feet down—
I am marching into—OUCH-

The centipede stepped on a crack. He rubbed his fifth foot on the left and his seventh foot on the right and thought about what he should do. Just then a girl ran by. She was stepping on rocks and holes and cracks, but she didn't say "OUCH!" and the reason was—she was wearing sneakers!

"That's it!" said the centipede. "I'll get sneakers!"

He marched and sang and ouched all the way to the sneaker store. He climbed up on the chair.

"I'd like a pair of red sneakers," he said.

And the saleswoman brought him a pair of red sneakers. *(You may place the sneakers on the first two feet or let children do this. Repeat placing sneakers for the various other feet.)*

"Very good!" said the centipede, "but I have more feet. I like these red sneakers, and I'd like a blue pair, too."

So the saleswoman brought him a pair of blue sneakers.

"Very good!" said the centipede, "but I have more feet. I like these red sneakers, and the blue sneakers, but I'd like a pair of green sneakers, too."

So the saleswoman brought him a pair of green sneakers.

"Very good!" said the centipede, "But I have more feet. I like these red sneakers, and the blue sneakers, and the green sneakers, but I'd like a pair of purple sneakers, too."

So the saleswoman brought him a pair of purple sneakers. *(Continue in this manner until all the feet have shoes.)*

"Very good!" said the centipede. "Very, very good!"

And he set off for home singing:

One foot up, two feet down—
I am marching home from town!

And after that he had many grand adventures on the sidewalk, but never another OUCH!

Hole-y Shoes!
(To the tune of "There's a Hole in the Bottom of the Sea")

You might also enjoy making a flannel board to use as you sing this song. Make the figures and place them on a shoe sole with the hole in the middle of the flannel board. Or place objects in a shoe and pull them out as they are mentioned in the song. Place the objects in order from large to small.

There's a hole in the bottom of my shoe.
There's a hole in the bottom of my shoe.
There's a hole, there's a hole,
There's a hole in the bottom of my shoe.

There's a rock in the hole in the bottom of my shoe.
There's a rock in the hole in the bottom of my shoe.
There's a rock, there's a rock,
There's a rock in the bottom of my shoe.

(Song continues on page 198.)

There's a mouse on the rock in the hole in the bottom of my shoe.
There's a mouse on the rock in the hole in the bottom of my shoe.
There's a mouse, there's a mouse,
There's a mouse in the bottom of my shoe.

There's a gnat on the mouse on the rock in the hole in the bottom of my shoe.
There's a gnat on the mouse on the rock in the hole in the bottom of my shoe.
There's a gnat, there's a gnat,
There's a gnat in the bottom of my shoe.

There's a spot on the gnat on the mouse on the rock in the hole in the bottom of my shoe.
There's a spot on the gnat on the mouse on the rock in the hole in the bottom of my shoe.
There's a spot, there's a spot,
There's a spot in the bottom of my shoe.

There's a speck on the spot on the gnat on the mouse on the rock in the hole in the bottom
    of my shoe.
There's a speck on the spot on the gnat on the mouse on the rock in the hole in the bottom
    of my shoe.
There's a speck, there's a speck,
There's a speck in the bottom of my shoe.

Get them out of the bottom of my shoe.
Get them out of the bottom of my shoe.
Put my foot, put my foot,
Put my foot in the bottom of my shoe.

Cold Feet

(A Participatory Story with Masks)

This story encourages active participation from the children. All children repeat the actions and sounds of the man trying to take his boots on and off. Before the story begins five children are selected to wear masks. These may be grocery bag masks or masks with ties. The children's hands should be free to do the pulling actions. Ask the masked children to stand in the front and place the appropriate masks on the children's heads as each character is mentioned in the story.

Once upon a time there was a man with big feet. His feet were so big he had a hard time finding boots big enough to fit. His old boots had huge holes in the toes, and his feet were getting cold.

So the man got on his horse (clompety-clompety-clompety) and rode to town to buy new boots.

He stopped at the boot shop (Whoa there!), went inside, and asked the bootman for a pair of big boots.

The bootman brought out some big boots. *(Show big size with hands.)*

The man tried to put his big toe in. (Uh, uh, uh!) No! The boot wouldn't go on!

So the bootman brought out a bigger pair of boots. *(Show bigger size with hands.)*

The man tried to put his big toe in. (Uh, uh, uh!) No! That boot wouldn't go on!

So the bootman brought out the biggest boots in the shop. *(Show biggest size with hands.)*

And, once again, the man tried to put his toe in. (Uh, uh, uh! Oof!) The boot went on!

Then he tried the other boot on. (Uh, uh, uh! Uh, uh, uh—this one's going to be harder. Uh, uh, uh! Oof!) And the other boot went on!

The man was so happy he got up and started to dance around. But, uh, oh! The boots pinched his feet. He couldn't wiggle his toes at all.

So he sat down and tried to pull the boots off. (Uh, uh, uh!) No! The boots wouldn't come off.

The man called to the bootman. The bootman took ahold of the man's feet and he pulled and he pulled. (Uh, uh, uh!) No! The boots wouldn't come off.

So the bootman got the man's horse. And the horse took ahold of the bootman's coat. The bootman took ahold of the man's feet. (Uh, uh, uh!) No! The boots wouldn't come off!

So the horse called a big dog to come help. And the dog took ahold of the horse's tail. And the horse took ahold of the bootman's coat. The bootman took ahold of the man's feet. (Uh, uh, uh!) No! The boots wouldn't come off!

So the dog barked at a fat cat to come help. And the fat cat took ahold of the big dog's tail. The big dog took ahold of the horse's tail. The horse took ahold of the bootman's coat. The bootman took ahold of the man's feet. And they pulled and they pulled. (Uh, uh, uh!) No! The boots wouldn't come off!

Then the fat cat found a little mouse. (There wasn't anyone left to help.) The little mouse took ahold of the fat cat's tail. The fat cat took ahold of the big dog's tail. The big dog took ahold of the horse's tail. The horse took ahold of the bootman's coat. The bootman took ahold of the man's feet. And they pulled and they pulled. (Uh, uh, uh! Oof!) And the boots came off!

The man wiggled his toes. (Ooooo!) His feet felt so good. (Ahhhhh!) The man pulled on his old boots. (Oof! Oof!)

He got back on his horse and rode home. (Clompety-clompety-clompety!)

And he never tried on a new pair of boots again. He was afraid that he wouldn't get them off. Now the man can wiggle his toes. (Ooooo!) And he doesn't mind the holes in the toes, even if he does have cold feet!

I Have a Big Shoe Tree

(To the tune of "On Top of Old Smoky")

I have a big shoe tree
That grows in my yard.
It's tall and it's sturdy.
It's strong and it's hard.

It grows white shoelaces,
And blue tennis shoes.
It even grows tube socks,
More than I can use.

So when I get dirty
In mud or in slush,
I don't wipe my shoes off,
I just kick them off.

My mom doesn't scold me
Or do the laundry.
She tells me to go out
And pick more from the tree!

The Magic Shoes

(A Participatory Story)

As the leader tells this story, she asks the children to help by doing the actions and making the sounds. This approach promotes good listening from the start.

Once a man found a pair of beautiful purple shoes under a ginkgo tree. What do you think he did with the shoes? Well, what would YOU do if you found a pair of beautiful purple shoes? That's right. You'd put them on. So let's all put on the shoes. *(Leader mimes putting on shoes and motions for children to do the same action.)*

Now, no sooner were the shoes on the man's feet than he began walking—big steps. *(Everybody does big steps in place.)* The next thing the man knew, the shoes had carried him to a jungle. He didn't know it for sure, but the man guessed the shoes were magic. Well, there in the jungle, the man met a fierce tiger. The tiger roared. (ROAR!) The man was so frightened that he started running. *(Run fast in place.)*

He ran until he was on top of a faraway mountain. The man didn't know it for sure, but he guessed the shoes were magic. There was lots of snow on the mountain, so the man took big jumps. *(Do big jumps in place.)*

Where do you think he landed? Right in the middle of the ocean! Oh no! The man couldn't swim! He started to sink *(everybody sit down)*, but, then, he flipped his feet, and he flipped up—up—up and where do you think he went?

The man went way up into outer space! The man now KNEW the shoes were magic. You know, that man had a wonderful trip in outer space. He swung on the stars *(rock back and forth)*, he swam in the Milky Way *(swimming action)*, and he chased the moon *(run in place)*. He ran and he ran. He ran and he ran. But he couldn't stop.

Finally, he got so tired, he reached down, and took off his shoes. And do you know what happened?

He drifted back down to earth, right beside the ginkgo tree, and there he rested for a long time. *(Everybody sit down.)*

As far as I know, the magic shoes are still in outer space. Maybe they're chasing the moon. If you ever go to the moon yourself, maybe you'll find them and have another magic adventure, too!

This Little Piggy's Piggies

This little piggy wears toe shoes. *(Point to big toe.)*
This little piggy wears slippers. *(Point to next toe.)*
This little piggy wears sandals. *(Point to next toe.)*
This little piggy wears flippers. *(Point to next toe.)*
This little piggy lost his tennies, *(Point to little toe.)*
So his little piggies don't wear any!

The Old Woman Who Lived in a Shoe Retold

Three Presentations

Mother Goose's "Old Woman in a Shoe" has always fascinated children, but the traditional version sounds harsh today. This new version is a happier one.

A variety of presentation methods may be used. The first method uses a flannel board. Prepare a large felt shoe and place small figures of the children on it as each name is mentioned. The second method uses a cardboard "shoe stage."

Simply cut out a large shoe shape from cardboard and make little doors and windows on the shoe. Be sure to leave the doors attached so you can open them to reveal pictures behind. Cut out pictures of children from magazines or catalogs and even include small pictures of children from your community for an extra surprise. The third method uses a shoe bag. It's not necessary to have twenty-six separate pockets, but it's a nice touch. If you have a wall hanging with twenty-six pockets labelled with the letters of the alphabet, this will work nicely. Place pictures of children or little dolls or finger puppets in the separate pockets as each name is mentioned.

Whichever method you use, the presentation will help children practice the alphabet and talk about their names. You may not have an Ursa or Xavier in your class, but you can use this as an opportunity to introduce unusual names and tell what names mean. (*Ursa* means "she-bear" and *Xavier* means "owner of the new house!" Consult your local library for a baby name book. Young children will find this as much fun as prospective parents do!)

More Than a Merry Crew
(A Poem)

There was an old woman
Who lived in a shoe.
She had so many children,
They were more than a merry crew!

There were Amy and Bonnie,
Charles and Darlene,
Ellen and Frederick,
Gary and Helene,
Ida and Janice,
Kate, Liz, and Minnie,
Nathan and Oliver,
Paul and Quinny,
Rob, Sam, and Teddy,
Ursa, Violet, and Wendy,
Xavier, Yancy, Zachary,
And—THAT is the end-y!

There Was an Old Woman Who Lived in a Boot

If you want to add an extra dramatic touch to this story poem, use an old boot with holes in the heel, toe, and sole. Put little finger puppets on all your fingers as the children pop out of the parts of the boot.

There was an old woman who lived in a boot.
She used the tongue for a laundry chute.
She made a clothesline out of a lace.
Where she hung all the stockings neatly in place.

But she had lots of kids so they didn't quite fit
Inside the boot—and it started to split!
Two popped out the heel, two out of the toe,
Three out of the bottom—the poor little souls!

So the old woman put them
Out on the line,
To dry with the socks
Where the sun always shines!

A Really Big Shoe
(A Story Poem with Puppets)

This updated version of the "Old Woman in the Shoe" uses small figures put in pockets of a felt shoe. Cut out a large high top shoe from felt and glue on squares of colorful felt, leaving the top edge open to form pockets. You might like to leave this in the room for children to play with. Collect or make finger puppets or small stuffed figures for the children. The Old Woman could have a house full of small animals instead of children—just substitute animals characters in the poem. Either use a large puppet for the Old Woman or put on a funny hat and play her yourself! The song in the story is sung to the tune of "The Farmer in the Dell." Teach the words to the children so they can enjoy the party, too!

There was an old woman who lived in a shoe,
But her shoe was empty—what is she to do?
Not a child or a pet did the old woman see.
She wanted a party, for she was lonely.
So she put up a sign that said, "Today at two
Come out and visit me at the Big Shoe."
Then she baked and she cleaned
And she cooked and she shined,
And everything was ready
Right on time!
And when the old woman looked out of her shoe,
There was a kitty cat come into view. *(Put cat in pocket.)*
    A party in a shoe,
    A party in a shoe,
    Together we'll have lots of fun!
    A party in a shoe.
Then when the old woman looked out of her shoe
There was a little girl come into view. *(Place girl in pocket.)*

A party in a shoe,
A party in a shoe,
Together we'll have lots of fun!
A party in a shoe.
(Continue in this manner with different figures repeating the song until all the pockets are filled.)
Well this was a party of fun and of song.
It lasted all day and half the night long.
And when it was over she had friends galore.
The Old Woman in the Shoe was lonely no more!

Books about Sock It to Me!

Kent, Jack. **Socks for Supper.** Parents, 1978.

A poor couple exchange a pair of socks for food. The woman proceeds to make more socks from the man's sweater until they are down to only one-half sock. The man receives a new sweater for Christmas and all ends happily.

Selden, George. **Sparrow Socks.** Illustrated by Peter Lippman. Harper & Row, 1965.

Angus McFee and his family own a sock factory with a wonderful machine that makes every kind of sock in the world, but the machine works less and less as people go to the big stores to buy socks. Angus begins making small socks for sparrows, and the people start looking for socks like the ones the sparrows are wearing. The sock machine goes back to clicking and clacking all day long.

Thomas, Patricia. **There Are Rocks in My Socks Said the Ox to the Fox.** Illustrated by Mordicai Gerstein. Lothrop, Lee and Shepard, 1979.

Ox listens to complicated and useless advice from Fox when he needs to remove rocks from his socks. Anyone who has ever avoided the simple solution to taking off shoes and socks in the first place will delight in the absurd results.

Related Activities about Sock It to Me!

Two by Two

The poem will be even more fun if you have a number of the socks mentioned. Pass out the socks and let children hold up the appropriate kinds of socks as you read the poem a second time. Is anyone wearing argyles?

Tube socks,
Knee socks,
Socks with bows.
Bright plaid argyles—
What are those?
Red socks,
Pink socks,

Pom-pom, too.
Dotted, striped socks,
Green and blue.
One thing for sure
Most everywhere—
Socks always, always
Come in pairs!

Stocking Feet
(To the tune of "Turkey in the Straw")

This song may not teach the best habit, but it does address an almost irresistible tendency—throwing your shoes on the floor without untying them!

Take your old shoes off
When you come in through the door.
Don't untie 'em,
Just throw 'em on the floor.

Stretch your feet
And wiggle your toes.
Stocking feet
Feel the best you know!

More Hole Than Sock
(A Tear-and-Tell Story)

Prepare to tell this story by folding a piece of brown paper and tearing as shown to make a pair of socks.

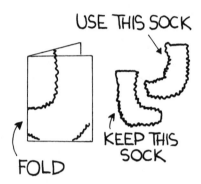

You may also wish to have felt socks in red, blue, and green to put on the flannel board and point to them as Sam counts his socks each day. As you tell the story, tear the sections as indicated to show who was eating the socks. The children will enjoy repeating the words, "And why?"

Every morning Sam counted his socks. "Two blue socks," Sam said on Monday. "And two red socks. Two green socks and two brown socks." *(Show socks.)*
On Monday when Sam counted his socks, he noticed there was a little hole in one brown sock. *(Tear sock as shown.)*

"Who could be eating my sock?" Sam wondered. "And why?"
On Tuesday Sam counted his socks again. "Two blue socks," Sam said. "And two red socks. Two green socks and two brown socks."
On Tuesday Sam noticed that the hole was a little bit bigger. *(Tear sock as shown.)*

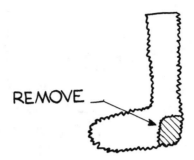

"Who could be eating my sock?" Sam wondered. "And why?"

On Wednesday Sam counted his socks again. "Two blue socks," Sam said. "And two red socks. Two green socks and two brown socks."

On Wednesday Sam noticed that the hole was a little bit bigger. *(Tear sock as shown.)*

"Who could be eating my sock?" Sam wondered. "And why?"

On Thursday Sam counted his socks again. "Two blue socks," Sam said. "And two red socks. Two green socks and two brown socks."

On Thursday Sam noticed that the hole was a little bit bigger. *(Tear sock as shown.)*

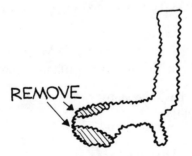

"Who could be eating my sock?" Sam wondered. "And why?"

On Friday Sam counted his socks again. "Two blue socks," Sam said. "And two red socks. Two green socks and two brown socks."

On Friday Sam noticed that the hole was a little bit bigger. *(Tear sock as shown.)*

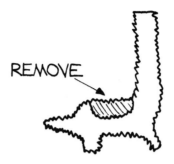

"Who could be eating my sock?" Sam wondered. "And why?"

And on Saturday Sam decided to find out. So he hid in the room where he kept the socks and waited and watched and watched and waited. And before long, this is what he saw. *(Show mouse shape.)*

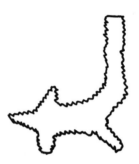

Sam said, "That tells me who is eating my sock, but mice don't really eat socks .... And why?"

So he followed the mouse and found she had taken the sock a bite at a time to make a nest. And, in the nest, toasty warm in Sam's sock, were four new baby mice.

On Sunday Sam counted his socks again. "Two blue socks," Sam said. "And two red socks. Two green socks, and two—no, one brown sock and four new baby mice!"

Sock Monster
(To the tune of "When Johnny Comes Marching Home")

A monster's coming down the steps—
Watch out! Watch out!
A monster's coming down the steps—
Watch out! Watch out!
It nibbles socks and it bites the toes,
And then it leaves a great big hole,
So we'd better get our stockings off the floor!

A monster's coming through the door—
Look out! Look out!
A monster's coming through the door—
Look out! Look out!
It's got my foot and it won't let go.
I'll shake it off and stomp its nose,
Then I'll scoop it up and sweep it out the door!

One Sock Left
(A Fingerplay)

Hold up four fingers to begin this fingerplay, then put one finger down as each sock is lost.

Four dirty socks
Ready for the wash.
Dad picked them up—
Oops! One got lost.

Three dirty socks,
Striped red and blue.
My dog took one—
And this one got chewed.

Two dirty socks—
Well, two makes a pair.
That's all my feet need
For me to wear.

Only one sock
Came out clean.
I think we've got
A sock-eating washing machine!

One sock left—
Should I dump it?
Hey! I know what!
Let's make a puppet!

Christmas Stocking
(An Action Rhyme)

Grandma made me a stocking.
It's much too big to wear. *(Stretch hands out far apart.)*
She only made me one of them, *(Hold one finger up.)*
But I don't really care. *(Shake head.)*
'Cause I'm gonna hang my stocking
By the fireplace tonight. *(Mime hanging stocking.)*
I hope that Santa fills it up, *(Stretch arms up.)*
'Cause I've been extra nice! *(Point to self.)*

Books about Neat Feet

Kroll, Steven. **Dirty Feet**. Illustrated by Toni Hormann. Parents, 1980.

> Penelope wears her favorite sneakers until they become too tight. One day she takes them off and a breeze blows away her hat. In chasing it, she loses her shoes, gets her feet dirty, and has to wash them off at school. The postman returns her shoes, but her mother brings her a new pair.

Le Sieg, Theo. **I Wish That I Had Duck Feet**. Illustrated by B. Tobey. Random House, 1965.

> A young boy announces the advantages of having duck feet—you don't have to keep them dry or wear shoes. Since he can't have duck feet, he imagines horns on his head, a tail, and an elephant nose. In the end he decides to just be himself.

Schertle, Alice. **My Two Feet**. Illustrated by Meredith Dunham. Lothrop, Lee and Shepard, 1985.

> Collage illustrations and text celebrate all the fun things a young girl's feet can do throughout a year's adventures, from running barefoot and making sand prints in the summer, to searching for lost shoes in the fall, and walking through crunchy snow in boots in the winter.

Weiss, Leatie. **Funny Feet!** Illustrated by Ellen Weiss. Franklin Watts, 1978.

Priscilla Penguin has trouble keeping up with her friends because she is pigeon-toed. The doctor advises wearing tie shoes, but Priscilla hates them. Her friends, afraid that she'll spoil their recital, hide her ballet slippers, but Priscilla wears her tie shoes and performs well, much to her parents' pleasure.

Related Activities about Neat Feet

Barefeet Song
(To the tune of "Oh, Where, Oh Where Has My Little Dog Gone?")

Oh where, oh where are the shoes for my feet?
I've looked everywhere that I know.
I looked all around,
But they just can't be found,
I guess I will wear stocking feet.

Oh where, oh where are the socks for my feet?
I've looked everywhere that I know.
I looked all around,
But they just can't be found.
Now I have only barefeet. Neat!

What Should a Bear Wear?
(A Participatory Story with Foot Masks)

For this story, prepare four foot masks. This unusual kind of mask simply is a posterboard pair of shoes with a piece of balsa wood attached to it so the children can hold the foot masks in front of their feet instead of their face. The masks include slippers for Dog, galoshes for Pig, running shoes for Rabbit, and bear feet for Bear. Ask the children to stand in front of the group and pass out the appropriate masks as each animal is mentioned in the story.

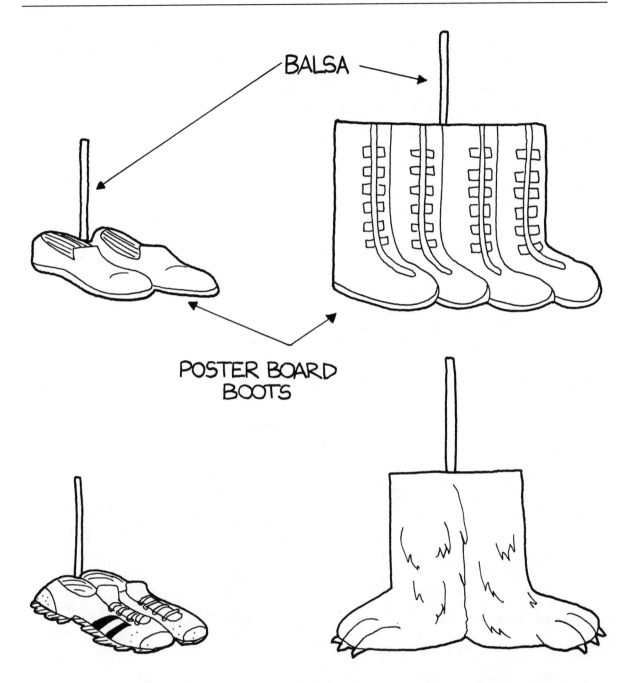

BALSA

POSTER BOARD
BOOTS

Once upon a time there lived a cobbler who made shoes for everyone who came from near and far. He made such good shoes that everyone always went away happy.

One day Dog came to see him.

"What can I do for you?" asked the cobbler.

"How would you like it?" cried Dog. "All day long I have to work for my master. And every night I have to fetch his slippers. I am dog tired."

"I know just what you need," said the cobbler. So he made Dog his own slippers. And Dog went away happy.

Next day Pig came.

"What can I do for you?" asked the cobbler.

"How would you like it?" complained Pig. "All day I slop around in the mud. Everyone says I'm sloppy as a pig. It's a dirty shame."

"I know just what you need," said the cobbler.

So he made Pig two pairs of galoshes to keep his feet clean. And Pig went away happy.

The next day Rabbit came to see the cobbler.

"What can I do for you?" asked the cobbler.

"How would you like to be a rabbit?" he asked. "Everyone expects you to bring their Easter eggs in just one night. I'm running out of time."

"I know just what you need," said the cobbler. So he made Rabbit some running shoes. And Rabbit went away happy.

Then Bear came to see the cobbler.

"Well, what can I do for you?" asked the cobbler.

"Well," said Bear, "you made slippers for Dog, and galoshes for Pig, and running shoes for Rabbit. I just want to know—what kind of shoes should a bear wear?"

The cobbler thought and he thought, then he said, "Why I know what bears should wear!"

"You do?" said Bear.

"I know something you'll never outgrow. Something you'll never wear out. And something that won't cost you anything."

"Where are they?" asked Bear.

"There!" said the cobbler. And he pointed to Bear's own feet. "You're already wearing them."

And, do you know what bears wear? You guessed it—BARE FEET!

So the cobbler didn't make Bear any shoes at all, but Bear went away happy anyway!

Dirty Feet Song

(To the tune of "Mulberry Bush")

I don't want to wear my shoes,
   (Shake head or take off shoes.)
Wear my shoes, wear my shoes,
I don't want to wear my shoes,
So I have dirty feet.

March in puddles, splash and splash,
   (March in place.)
Splash and splash, splash and splash,
March in puddles, splash and splash,
So I have dirty feet.

Run in tall grass, run and run,
   (Run in place.)
Run and run, run and run,
Run in tall grass, run and run,
So I have dirty feet.

Jump in mud holes, jump and jump,
   (Jump.)
Jump and jump, jump and jump,
Jump in mud holes, jump and jump,
So I have dirty feet.

Now I'd better wash them off,
   (Rub feet or put on shoes.)
Wash them off, wash them off,
Now I'd better wash them off,
I don't want dirty feet!

Dancing Feet

(An Action Rhyme)

Make your feet do all the actions in this rollicking rhyme!

Dancing feet!
Prancing feet!
Fancy, Dancey, Prancey feet!

Plopping feet!
Clopping feet!
Sloppy, Ploppy, Cloppy feet!

Wiggily feet!
Piggily feet!
Giggily, Wiggily, Piggily feet!

This Is What My Feet Can Do
(To the tune of "Mulberry Bush")

Do all the actions as you sing this song. Then all sit down to begin the next activity.

This is what my feet can do.
Feet can do, feet can do,
This is what my feet can do—
Can you do it, too?

Let your feet go hop, hop, hop
Hop, hop, hop, hop, hop, hop,
Let your feet go hop, hop, hop,
All around the room.

Make your feet go jump, jump, jump,
Jump, jump, jump, jump, jump, jump,
Make your feet go jump, jump, jump,
All around the room.

Take your feet and skip, skip, skip,
Skip, skip, skip, skip, skip, skip,
Take your feet and skip, skip, skip,
All around the room.

Can your feet go tiptoe-ing,
Tiptoe-ing, tiptoe-ing,
Can your feet go tiptoe-ing,
All around the room?

Now your feet can sit right down,
Sit right down, sit right down,
Now your feet can sit right down,
Quiet, quiet-ly!

GAMES FOR SNEAKERS, SOCKS, AND HAPPY FEET

Shoe Scramble

Children form a circle and take off one shoe. The shoes are placed in the middle of the circle. Music is played, and children walk around the circle. When the music stops, everyone rushes to the middle of the circle and puts on a shoe that does not belong to him or her. The music is played again. Everyone tiptoes around in the strange shoes. When the music stops again, children take off the strange shoes and pass them around the circle. The music is played again. When the music stops, children put on the shoe or shoes they are holding. If someone ends up with more than one shoe, he or she must put them all on—even if they have to wear a shoe on a hand. Play can continue as long as you like until everyone is all scrambled up.

Trick-and-Treat Treasure Tracks

Children love footprints. Cut out large footprints from paper and place these around the room. The first set of tracks should lead to a shoebox filled with slips of paper on which you have written tricks for children to perform. Try to think of tricks children can do with their feet, such as "Jump up ten times," "Skip three skips," or "Take three giant steps forward and three baby steps backward." When all the tricks have been performed, children follow another trail of tracks to another shoebox that contains treats for all.

Sock It to Me Relay

Divide your group into two teams. Give each team a very large sock (one that will fit over children's feet with their shoes on). When the leader says, "Sock it to me," the first child of each team turns around and tries to put the sock on the next child's foot. The child getting the sock pulled on must keep hands behind back until the sock is on. He or she then takes the sock off and puts it on the next child. This continues until the last child in line hops in the stocking foot to the beginning of the line. The team to finish first wins. The leader then pulls out two more socks with treats inside for everyone.

Foot in the Mouth

Play this game like Pin the Tail on the Donkey. Prepare a large open mouth drawing on a posterboard and give each child a little paper cutout shaped foot. Blindfold each child and have them try to place the foot in the mouth. Older preschoolers could play the game with an additional step. Explain that the expression "put your foot in your mouth" means saying something awkward or embarrassing to someone else, something you wish you had not said. After the children place the feet in the mouth, the leader suggests they might solve the "foot in the mouth" problem. She then places a large button or zipper over the mouth.

Shoebox Color Match

Practice color recognition by preparing shoeboxes covered in different colors of paper—red, yellow, blue, green, orange, purple, black, and brown. Put a slit in the tops of the boxes. Then place these boxes in different places around the room. In another shoebox, place paper cutouts of shoes in the same colors. Have each child select a shoe and find the box where that color of shoe would belong. You could let several children select at the same time. After all shoes have been put in the boxes, open up boxes and check to see that the colors have been matched correctly.

One Plus One—Two Plus Two Shoes

Older preschoolers who are starting to learn number facts can practice their skills with this game. Prepare a large shoe cut out from heavy paper. Put two slits in the shoe so that a long strip of paper can be pulled through. On the slip of paper write simple addition facts: $1 + 1 = 2, 2 + 2 = 4, 3 + 3 = 6$, etc. Children can pull the strip through and practice the facts individually or in small groups.

Fill My Shoes

Young children can't resist filling their shoes with sand or dirt, so give them the opportunity to make this into a learning game. Cover the floor with newspaper or a plastic dropcloth. Then give children a baby shoe, a child-sized shoe, and an adult shoe, a large bowl or pan of rice, unpopped popcorn or navy beans, and tablespoons. Let children count the number of spoonfuls of beans, corn, or rice it takes to fill each shoe. This is a good activity for teaching more and less.

CRAFTS FOR SNEAKERS, SOCKS, AND HAPPY FEET

Talky Terry, the Tennis Shoe Puppet

Puppets can be made out of almost anything you have around the house, and most kids have an outgrown or worn-out tennis shoe. Turn tennis shoes into puppets by attaching a shoelace to the tongue. Punch a hole in the tongue and tie the shoelace on. Add fabric eyes to the toe of the shoe, yarn hair, and paper eyes. Slip your hand in to move Terry and manipulate his tongue by pulling the shoelace with your other hand.

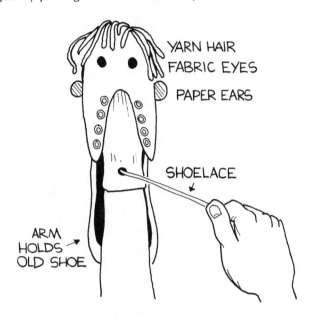

Stinky Sock Monster Puppet

Sock puppets are good old standbys and easy to make with young children. This sock puppet is somewhat different. It is worn on the foot! Give each child an adult-sized sock to pull on the foot. Gather up the extra part of the sock at the toe and stuff with cotton. Wrap a rubberband around to secure. This is the puppet's head. Add big fabric eyes (or moveable eyes purchased from a craft store). Yarn hair and funny ears may also be glued on. Let children practice wiggling and creeping around with Stinky Sock. They will have so much fun with him that they'll probably wear Stinky to bed!

Big Foot, Little Foot Mural

On a large piece of paper (shelf paper with a dull finish or butcher paper), draw around children's feet. You may do this with shoes on and then with shoes off so you can draw around the toes. Write each child's name next to the appropriate feet. Compare sizes of feet; identify right and left feet. Then have children draw on toenails, claws, or decorate feet anyway they wish! (Polka dot? Stripes?) Use this mural as a display in the room as you do the various activities in this chapter.

Sew Your Own Stocking

Practice simple sewing by giving each child two stockings cut from heavy paper. Punch holes around the outline of the stockings. Each child "sews" the two stockings together with bright-colored yarn and ties a knot at the end. Stockings may be decorated as Christmas stockings or with any design. Be sure to print each child's name at the top.

Shoelace Bunny Ears

The book *When Shoes Eat Socks* describes tying bows like bunny ears. Since children often find tying shoes a difficult task, this approach introduces a little fun to the chore. Have the children practice making bows by making a paper plate bunny with shoelace ears. Give each child a thin paper plate with two holes punched at the top. Let the children draw on two eyes, a nose, whiskers, and a mouth. Give the children white shoelaces and instruct them to place the laces through the holes. Then show them how to make the bunny's ears by tying two large, loopy ears when they make the bow.

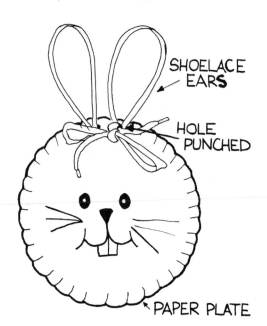

DISPLAYS FOR SNEAKERS, SOCKS, AND HAPPY FEET

String along with Me

Once upon a time, shoe strings only held shoes together, but now they're a fashion accessory. Collect an assortment of different colors and designs of shoelaces to hang on a bulletin board. A more fanciful display might have shoelaces hung from a tree branch. Hang laces like icicles or draped across, or tied in bows.

Interactive Shoe Bag Display

Hang a shoe bag low enough so children will be able to use this display as a learning game. Glue colored dots to the outside of shoe bag pockets. Provide a pile of different-colored shoes for children to match to the colored dots on the shoe bags. If you wish, you could add the letters *R* and *L* to the pockets so children can place right shoes and left shoes in the appropriate pockets.

Match Mates

Fill a laundry basket with socks for children to sort into pairs. Ask them to match socks, then roll them up and put them back into the basket.

Shoebox Scenes

Children find countless uses for old shoeboxes. (We never have enough at our houses!) Cut a large square out of the top of a shoebox and cover with tissue paper so your scene will emit enough light. Make a door or peephole in one short end of the shoebox. Then let children paste magazine pictures inside the boxes, adding small standing figures to the bottom of the box with tabs.

Animal Tracks

Make a mural of footprints different animals make, and let children match the tracks with pictures of the animals.

8
Pockets and Paraphernalia

INTRODUCTION

This chapter takes us beyond the essentials of clothing. Here we have accessory items or parts added to clothing to make them more useful.

"Pockets and Purses" explores the unending fascination and appeal these items have—everything goes into them. Joey the Kangaroo in *Joey* manages to fit all his friends and an odd assortment of items into Mama Kangaroo's pouch. If clothing does not have pockets, we may be resourceful enough to come up with one of our own, such as the portable pocket in *Peter's Pocket*. "Pocket Zoo" and "Pocket Surprise" hold untold treasures. Grandma's purse in "Hold This, Please" will hold nearly everything a child finds.

While pockets may be practical, paraphernalia (patches, bracelets, rings, and suspenders) in "Patches and Paraphernalia" can be "just for fun." Ever since the lady from Banbury Cross appeared in public with "rings on her fingers and bells on her toes," people could not resist the lure of all that glitters. Isadora's frivolous purchase of a boa in *Isadora* and Tan Tan's far-reaching uses of suspenders in *Tan Tan's Suspenders* attest to the desire for the flamboyant. Our stories and activities show how a cow gets carried away in her love of finery in "The Cow's Suspenders" and a wishing ring encourages Harriet's greed in "The Great Bubble Gum Ring."

Also tucked in these pockets are easy ways to teach the skills of association, rhythm and rhyme, creative word play, and stretching the imagination!

INITIATING ACTIVITY

Lots of Pockets

Many storytellers use a special apron with lots of pockets to introduce their stories. To begin this session, put a variety of small items in an apron with many pockets. You may use slogan buttons, rings, bracelets, necklaces, or funny stick-on noses and ears. As children arrive and are seated, allow them to choose one thing to wear during the program. Encourage each child to say his or her name and identify the item he or she is wearing from your pocket.

LITERATURE-SHARING EXPERIENCES
Books about Pockets and Purses

Barrett, Judi. **Peter's Pocket**. Illustrated by Julia Noonan. Atheneum, 1974.

Peter, almost four, collects things—too many things to carry, so he stuffs his pockets. He has lots of pockets in his dungarees, snow jacket, and sweaters, but no pockets in his other clothes. Peter's mother makes him a portable pin-on pocket so he can always have pockets on his clothes. When the pockets wear out, his mother makes new ones, and when they get dirty, she washes them—ready to be filled up again. A pattern for a pocket like Peter's follows the story.

Caple, Kathy. **The Purse**. Houghton Mifflin, 1986.

Katie spends all her money on a purse because her sister tells her that keeping money in a Band-Aid box is for babies. But then Katie has to earn more money to fill her new purse.

Freeman, Don. **A Pocket for Corduroy**. Viking, 1978.

At the laundromat Corduroy overhears Lisa's mother telling her to take everything out of her pockets. Since he doesn't have a pocket, he goes off to find one and gets lost in a laundry bag. A young man mistakes Corduroy for his laundry and puts the bear into the washer. Left overnight, Corduroy plays in soapflake snow and falls asleep in a laundry basket before Lisa finds him the next morning. In the end Lisa makes him a purple pocket and a card with his name on it tucked inside—just what he was looking for!

Kent, Jack. **Joey**. Prentice-Hall, 1984.

Joey the Kangaroo is tucked in his mother's pocket so she can keep track of him. When he wants to go play with his friends, Mother suggests inviting them *in*. So Joey invites Billy the dog, Betty the cat, and Bob the pig. They add a TV, stereo, and assorted musical instruments, until Betty brings her piano. Mother throws them all out and decides Joey can go out to play after all.

Payne, Emmy. **Katy No-Pocket**. Illustrated by H. A. Rey. Houghton Mifflin, 1944.

Katy the Kangaroo is sad because she has no pockets to carry her son, Freddy. She decides to ask other animal mothers how they carry their babies. Mrs. Crocodile carries Catherine on her back. Mrs. Monkey carries Jocko in her arms. Lions follow their mothers. Birds push theirs out of nests. Nothing will work for Katy, so they ask Owl about a pocket. Owl suggests they go to the city, where they sell "that kind of thing." There they see a man with an apron covered with pockets. He gives his apron to Katy who now has room for Freddy—and an assortment of other animals, too. She is happy because she has *more* pockets than any mother kangaroo in the world!

Related Activities about Pockets and Purses

Purses

There are purses that have zippers.
There are purses that have snaps.
Some are made of gold or silver.
Some have tiny little straps.

There are purses with big pockets.
Others look just like a box.
There are ones made of snakeskin,
And some others match your socks!

There are purses that are so big
They have smaller ones inside.
Some have secret hiding places
For a mouse to take a ride.

There are purses with red roses,
Or a tiny bumblebee,
But the best one is my grandma's,
'Cause there's a treat inside for me!

Hold This, Please!
(A Flannel-board Story)

Make a large purse of felt with a big hole in the center. As the items are mentioned in the story, add them to the purse. You will need the shapes of a penny, rock, donut, lady bug, mouse, and elephant.

I like to go for walks with Grandma. She always carries a big, big purse.

One day I saw a shiny penny. "Hold this, please," I said to Grandma.

"Of course," she said. "Just put the shiny penny in my purse."

Then I saw a purple rock. "Hold this, please," I said to Grandma.

"Of course," she said. "Just put the purple rock with the shiny penny in my purse."

Then we ate some chocolate donuts. I only hate half. "Hold this, please," I said to Grandma.

"Of course," she said. "Just put the chocolate donut with the purple rock and the shiny penny in my purse."

Then I saw a tiny lady bug. "Hold this, please," I said to Grandma.

"Of course," she said. "Just put the tiny lady bug with the chocolate donut and the purple rock and the shiny penny in my purse."

Then I saw a fuzzy mouse. "Hold this, please," I said to Grandma.

"Of course," she said. "Just put the fuzzy mouse with the tiny lady bug and the chocolate donut and the purple rock and the shiny penny in my purse."

Then I saw a big gray elephant. "Hold this, please," I said to Grandma.

Grandma smiled. "Let's have ice cream instead."

I like to go for walks with Grandma!

Not Enough Pockets

(A Story with Props or Flannel board)

You may wish to show all the things Freddy mentions in the story as he puts them in his pockets. Or you may place pictures of the object on felt squares that represent Freddy's pockets. Adjust the lists to match what you can find or let the children produce things from their pockets to put in Freddy's.

Freddy liked pockets. He had pockets all year long. In the fall, Freddy had a jacket that had two pockets. In the winter he had a pair of jeans that had three pockets—two in front and one in back. In the spring Freddy had a slicker that had four pockets—three on the outside and one secret one on the inside that no one could see.

In the summer Freddy wore a T-shirt and shorts. In the shorts there was only one pocket. "Not enough pockets," said Freddy to his mother.

His mother said, "All you need in the summer is a pocket for ice cream money. That is enough pockets."

But Freddy liked pockets. So when he found some string he said to his mother, "Not enough pockets. I have a pocket for ice cream money, but I need a pocket for string. I need some summer pockets."

So Mother had an idea. She cut out a square of red material and made Freddy a pocket for his shirt. "Now," she said, "you have a pocket for ice cream money and one for string. That is enough pockets."

But Freddy liked pockets. So when he found some marbles he said to his mother, "Not enough pockets. I have a pocket for ice cream money and one for string, but I need a pocket for marbles. I need some summer pockets."

So Mother cut out a square of blue material and made Freddy a pocket for his shirt. "Now," she said, "you have a pocket for ice cream money, one for string and one for marbles. That is enough pockets."

But Freddy liked pockets. So when he found some paper clips he said to his mother, "Not enough pockets. I have a pocket for ice cream money, one for string, and one for marbles, but I need a pocket for paper clips. I need some summer pockets."

So Mother cut out a square of yellow material and made Freddy a pocket for his shirt. "Now," she said, "you have a pocket for ice cream money, one for string, one for marbles, and one for paper clips. That is enough pockets."

But Freddy liked pockets. So when he found a pink eraser he said to his mother, "Not enough pockets. I have a pocket for ice cream money, one for string, and one for marbles, and one for paper clips, but I need a pocket for a pink eraser. I need some summer pockets."

So Mother cut out a square of purple material and made Freddy a pocket for his shirt. "Now," she said, "you have a pocket for ice cream money, one for string, one for marbles, one for paper clips, and one for a pink eraser. That is enough pockets."

But Freddy liked pockets. So when he found some crayons he said to his mother, "Not enough pockets. I have a pocket for ice cream money, one for string, and one for marbles, one for paper clips, and one for a pink eraser, but I need a pocket for crayons. I need some summer pockets."

Well by now, Freddy's shirt was covered with pockets. So Mother cut out a square of green material and made Freddy a pocket for his shorts. "Now," she said, "you have a pocket for ice cream money, one for string, one for marbles, one for paper clips, one for a pink eraser, and one for crayons. That is enough pockets."

But Freddy liked pockets. So when he found a tennis ball, and some blocks, and some nuts and bolts, and a pencil and some rubberbands, and a frog, he said to his mother, "Not enough pockets. I have a pocket for ice cream money, one for string, and one for marbles, one for paper clips, one for a pink eraser, and a pocket for crayons. But here is a tennis ball, and some blocks, and some nuts and bolts, and a pencil, and some rubberbands, and a frog! I need some summer pockets."

Well, Freddy's mother made a brown pocket for the tennis ball, and a white pocket for the blocks, and a red-and-blue striped pocket for the nuts and bolts, and a green polka-dot pocket for the pencil, and a purple-and-yellow flowered pocket for the rubberbands, and a big red-and-yellow plaid pocket for the frog. By the time she put them on Freddy's shorts and shirt sleeves and baseball hat and even on his socks, Freddy could not move. He could not run or eat or play. And he could not take his ice cream money and walk to the ice cream store. Freddy had too many summer pockets.

"Too many pockets!" cried Freddy. So mother helped him take off all the new pockets. Freddy took a table and chair into the driveway. He made a big sign that said "Garage Sale," and before long people came and bought the string, and the marbles, paper clips, pink eraser, crayons, tennis ball, blocks, nuts and bolts, pencil, and rubberbands. (He decided to keep the frog in a box as a pet.)

Freddy took all the money he made at the garage sale and put it in his one summer pocket in his shorts. Then he and his mother walked together to the ice cream store.

Pocket Zoo
(To the tune of "Old MacDonald Had a Farm")

As you sing this song use the appropriate noises or actions. It would be fun to use puppets to sing each verse and then stuff them all in an oversized pocket.

In my pocket is a zoo.
Ee-i-ee-i-o!
There's a doggie in there, too!
Ee-i-ee-i-o!
With a woof-woof here, and a woof-woof there.
Here a woof, there a woof, everywhere a woof-woof.
In my pocket is a zoo.
Ee-i-ee-i-o!

In my pocket is a zoo.
Ee-i-ee-i-o!
There's a hoot owl in there, too!
Ee-i-ee-i-o!
With a whoo-whoo here, and a whoo-whoo there.
Here a whoo, there a whoo, everywhere a whoo-whoo.
In my pocket is a zoo.
Ee-i-ee-i-o!

In my pocket is a zoo.
Ee-i-ee-i-o!
There's an alligator in there, too!
Ee-i-ee-i-o!
With a chomp-chomp here, and a chomp-chomp there.
Here a chomp, there a chomp, everywhere a chomp-chomp.
In my pocket is a zoo.
Ee-i-ee-i-o!

In my pocket is a zoo.
Ee-i-ee-i-o!
I'll hide it there 'til Mom finds out.
Ee-i-ee-i-o!
Then they'll run away here, and they'll run away there.
Here a run, there a run, everyone will run-run!
In a pocket is a zoo.
Ee-i-ee-i-o!

More Hole Than Pocket
(To the tune of "There's a Hole in the Bucket")

To do this song, make a simple pocket of felt or other material. Cut a large hole in one side. Apply Velcro® around the hole and on the back of a patch-piece of material. When the verse in the song mentions the hole and all the things fall out, rip off the patch and pull out the contents.

As you sing, place the items in the pocket as they are mentioned. Adjust the words to suit the items you have. Older children will enjoy searching their pockets for items for more verses.

What's in my pocket,
My pocket, my pocket?
What's in my pocket?
I bet you can't guess!

There's a ball in my pocket,
My pocket, my pocket.
There's a ball in my pocket.
My pocket has a ball.

There's string in my pocket,
My pocket, my pocket.
There's string in my pocket.
My pocket has string.

There's a frog in my pocket,
My pocket, my pocket.
There's a frog in my pocket.
My pocket has a frog.

AND there's a hole in my pocket,
My pocket, my pocket!
There's a hole in my pocket!
So the rest can fall out.

There's nothing in my pocket,
My pocket, my pocket.
There's nothing in my pocket,
Except for the hole!

Cover Up
(A Flannel-board Story)

To tell this story, prepare a coat with three pockets. Remove the pockets to place the objects behind them as the boy in the story fills his pockets. The coat should be split down the front so the boy can open it up and put more objects down the front of the coat.

Derrick loved his new coat. It had two big outside pockets and one inside pocket for hiding things. It had big, shiny buttons down the front. And it was so big that Derrick could button it all up and there was plenty of room left inside. It was a great cover up.

The first day when Derrick wore his coat, he found a butterfly's wing in the garden. So Derrick put the butterfly's wing in his right outside pocket.

The second day when Derrick wore his coat, he found a robin's egg in his backyard. So Derrick put the robin's egg in his left outside pocket.

The third day when Derrick wore his coat, he found an old snakeskin on a river bank. So Derrick put the snakeskin in his inside pocket.

The next day Derrick wore his coat to school. While he was waiting for the bus, he found a little kitten in a tree. But the pockets of his coat were all full, so he unbuttoned his coat and put the kitten down next to his tummy. Then he buttoned the coat back up again.

The kitten slept all the way to school. Derrick got off the bus. But just as he was going into school, he saw a little puppy dog on the playground. He had always wanted a puppy of his own. There was still room left in the top of his coat. So Derrick unbuttoned the top of his coat and tucked the puppy down the front.

Derrick's teacher told him to hang up his coat on the coat rack, but Derrick didn't want to take it off. He said he was getting a bad cold. His teacher sent him down to the nurse's office.

The nurse felt Derrick's tummy.

"Purrrrr," said the kitten.

"Do you have a tummyache?" asked the nurse.

"No, I don't have a tummyache," said Derrick.

The nurse felt Derrick's chest.

"Ruff! Ruff!" said the puppy.

"Do you have a cold down there?" asked the nurse.

"No, I don't have a cold," said Derrick.

"Well," said the nurse, "what do you have down there?"

"Just stuff," said Derrick.

"Let me see what you're hiding," said the nurse.

So Derrick unbuttoned his coat. And out came the puppy and out came the kitten.

"I see," said the nurse, "that you've got a pet store in there. You'll have to take those animals outside. A coat is not a very good cover up, young man."

So Derrick sadly took the puppy and the kitten outside. But then he remembered he still had the butterfly's wing, the robin's egg, and the snakeskin. His new coat was a pretty good cover up after all.

Body Pockets
(To the tune of "Mulberry Bush")

Perhaps, for this song, older children will think of body pockets of their own.

Body pockets can be fun.
   (Clap hands to beat.)
Lots of fun, lots of fun.
Body pockets are such fun.
Find a body pocket!

Cheeks can be a place for food.
   (Puff out cheeks.)
Place for food, place for food.
Cheeks can be a place for food.
Your cheeks can be a pocket!

Brain has good thoughts tucked inside.
   (Tap head with finger.)
Tucked inside, tucked inside.
Your brain has good thoughts tucked inside.
Your brain's a body pocket!

Hands can hold a little mouse.
   (Cup hands.)
Little mouse, little mouse.
Hands can hold a little mouse.
Your hands are body pockets!

Put your hands down in your lap.
   (Sit with hands folded.)
In your lap, in your lap.
Put your hands down in your lap.
Your lap's a body pocket!

Pocket Plan

One day Zack went to visit Granny. They read stories on the porch swing and drank lemonade. As Zack got ready to set off for home, Granny gave him a big peanut butter chocolate chip cookie. It was big enough for five or six people to have a piece. "Now mind," said Granny. "That is a big cookie, Zack. Make sure you share it."

The last thing that Zack wanted to do with that great big peanut butter chocolate chip cookie was share it. "Granny," said Zack, "I'll share this cookie with anyone who sees it." He carefully tucked it into the pocket of his shirt so he could eat it all by himself. It seemed like a good plan.

Zack walked one block down the street, when he felt hungry. Hungry for a cookie. A great big peanut butter chocolate chip kind of cookie. So he sat down by a tree and took the cookie out of his pocket. Zack was just about to take a big bite when he heard the bell of a bicycle, and he knew his brother was coming. Before you could say "Seems like a good plan," Zack put that cookie back into his pocket. When his brother came by, Zack didn't have to share the cookie because his brother didn't see it. And Zack walked on toward home.

Zack walked a second block down the street, when he felt hungry again. Hungry for a cookie. A great big peanut butter chocolate chip kind of cookie. So he sat down on a bench and took the cookie out of his pocket. Zack was just about to take a big bite when he heard the rumble-click of roller skates, and he knew his sister was coming. Before you could say "Seems like a good plan," Zack put that cookie back into his pocket. When his sister came by, Zack didn't have to share the cookie because his sister didn't see it. And Zack walked on toward home.

Zack walked a third block down the street, when he felt hungry again. He felt hungry for a cookie. A great big peanut butter chocolate chip kind of cookie. So he sat down on the grass and took the cookie out of his pocket. Zack was just about to take a big bite when he heard the click-click-click of toenails on the sidewalk, and he knew his dog Homer was coming. Before you could say "Seems like a good plan," Zack put that cookie back into his pocket. When Homer came by, Zack didn't have to share the cookie because Homer didn't see it. And Zack walked on toward home.

Well, by the time Zack got home he was very, very hungry, but there was his mother and father and baby sister, and he did not want to share the cookie with all of them. So he kept the cookie in his pocket. Zack didn't have to share because his family didn't see it.

The day turned into dusk and the dusk turned into dark, and still Zack did not get a chance to eat his peanut butter chocolate chip cookie. Still, it stayed in his pocket where no one could see it. When Zack got ready for bed the cookie was still there, but Zack's brother and his dog Homer were there, too. So Zack left that cookie in his pocket and didn't have to share it because they didn't see it. Zack hung his shirt over the chair and went to bed.

Now later that night, Zack's father came up to his room and took all the clothes in a big basket downstairs to the laundry room to wash. Zack's shirt with the cookie in the pocket was with them. Into the basket and out of the basket it went and some of the cookie fell out of his pocket. Into the washer and out of the washer it went, and some more of the cookie fell out of his pocket. Into the dryer and out of the dryer it went, and some more of the cookie fell out of his pocket. Shake out the shirt, put it back on the chair, and all of the cookie was gone from the pocket, but for a few crumbs.

Zack got up very, very early the next morning before his brother or his sister or Homer or even the baby was awake. He quietly tiptoed over to the shirt and reached into the pocket to find his peanut butter chocolate chip cookie, but all he found were a few crumbs.

Well, Zack's plan had worked, but not the way he expected. He didn't have to share his peanut butter chocolate chip cookie, but he did not get to eat it, either. Zack realized, as he crawled back into bed, that it would be better to have one part of the cookie than none at all.

"Oh, well," he muttered. "That's the way the cookie crumbles." And the next time he got a peanut butter chocolate chip cookie (or any other kind) from Granny, Zack put it in his pocket and remembered to share it before his father did the wash.

Pocket Surprise

(A Fingerplay)

Right here in my pocket
    (Place hands over shirt pocket.)
Is a surprise for you.
    (Point to children.)
It isn't an umbrella,
    (Touch fingers overhead, bend elbows.)
Or monster who says, "Boo!"
    (Circle eyes with fingers.)
It's not a wiggly spider,
    (Wiggle fingers in air.)
Or a snake that likes to hiss.
    (Wiggle body and hisssss.)
Right here in my pocket
    (Place hands over shirt pocket.)
Is a big two-handed kiss!
    (Hold up both hands in air.)
Mmmmmm-wah!
    (Touch hands to mouth, spread arms wide.)

Books about Patches and Paraphernalia

Brown, Marc. **Arthur's Eyes**. Little, Brown, 1979.

Arthur doesn't want to wear his new glasses because his friends tease him, but he learns to accept them and wear them proudly.

De Paola, Tomie. **Big Anthony and the Magic Ring**. Harcourt Brace Jovanovich, 1979.

Big Anthony borrows Strega Nona's magic ring so he can turn himself into Handsome Big Anthony, but he soon learns that he may be getting more than he bargained for.

Iwamura, Kazuo. **Tan Tan's Suspenders**. Bradbury, 1983.

Tan Tan's suspenders hold up his new pants, but they are so long, they also hang him up to dry, help him swing from trees, take rides, and become a giant slingshot!

Keats, Ezra Jack. **Goggles!** Macmillan, 1969.

When the big boys try to take away the motorcycle goggles that Peter and Archie have found, Willie the dachshund takes them himself and hides.

Lobel, Arnold. "A Lost Button" from **Frog and Toad Are Friends**. Harper & Row, 1970.

Toad loses a button from his jacket when he goes for a walk. Frog helps Toad retrace his steps and along the way they find many more buttons, but not Toad's button. When Toad returns home, he finds the lost button in his own house, but he feels guilty for causing Frog so much trouble. Toad sews all the buttons they found on his jacket and gives the jacket to Frog.

Manushkin, Fran. **Buster Loves Buttons**. Illustrated by Dirk Zimmer. Harper & Row, 1985.

Buster loves buttons so much that he buys all he can. Then he begins stealing them off people's clothes. A high-spirited girl chases him in her plane until buttons spill out all over town. No one is happier than Buster, the button glutton.

Raskin, Ellen. **Spectacles**. Atheneum, 1980.

Iris Fogel sees a fire-breathing dragon coming up the walk, a giant pygmy nuthatch, and a blue elephant until her mother takes her to the eye doctor. Raskin's paired illustrations—one through the eyes of the nearsighted Iris and one brought into clear focus—will fascinate children.

Silver, Jody. **Isadora**. Doubleday, 1981.

Isadora the donkey buys herself a red feather boa, but becomes self-conscious about wearing it in public until she meets a neightbor wearing flashy saddle shoes.

Related Activities about Patches and Paraphernalia

Rings and Things

Rings on fingers.
   (Hold up fingers.)
Rings on toes.
   (Point to toes.)
Pig wears gold rings
In his nose.
   (Point to nose.)

Rings 'round collar
   (Point to neck.)
Of dad's shirt.
Rings on bathtubs
   (Spread arms to indicate a big ring.)
Made of dirt.

"Ring around the
   (Join hands and walk in circle.)
Rosie" dance.
Circus rings where
   (Drop hands, prance in place.)
Horses prance.

Shiny, sparkly,
   (Hold up hands, wiggle fingers.)
Glittery things!
I like every
   (Point to self.)
Kind of ring.

The Great Bubble Gum Ring

(A Participatory Story)

Teach the children to say "poof" with the genie, slap legs like running when you talk about the sneaker, bark for the dog, say "testing, testing," for the microphone, and clap hands loudly for the cymbals. (The words are capitalized in the story when the children should make the sounds.) With older children this story works very well if you have a picture for each figure and let the child holding it make the noises indicated. You may wish to have all the children make the "poof" of the genie.

Harriet's mother gave her a nickel for the bubble gum machine. Harriet liked grape bubble gum best. Clink. Harriet put the nickel in the machine. Cl-cl-cl-cl-click. She pushed the lever over. Tinkly-pinkle. Down the shoot came the prize. To Harriet's disappointment, it was not a ball of grape bubble gum, but a ring.

There were words on the ring that said Magic Ring. Harriet looked at it. Just a cheap plastic ring. Not much magic for five cents.

Suddenly Harriet's nose began to tickle. Then her eyes started to water. "Ah-ah-ah-ah," said Harriet. "Ah-choo!" Harriet sneezed right on the ring. When she opened her eyes, there before her stood a genie. The ring was magic after all!

The genie bowed low. "What do you wish, Mistress?" he asked politely. "What you wish, I can grant."

Harriet could hardly believe her ears! Anything she wanted! So she asked the genie, "Please, Mr. Genie, sir, could I have a pair of Fast Track SNEAKERS?"

So the genie waved his arms, said, "Faster-master-bubble-blaster!" POOF! And quicker than you could say "The shoes with more bounce to the ounce," there for Harriet were the Fast Track Running SNEAKERS. And the genie crawled back into the ring.

Harriet could hardly believe there was so much magic for five cents. She liked the SNEAKERS, but she thought the genie could do more. She sneezed on the ring again. "Ah-ah-ah-ah-choo!" And the genie appeared.

The genie bowed low. "What do you wish, Mistress?" he asked politely. "What you wish, I can grant."

Harriet asked the genie, "This time, Genie, please could I have a Ju-jitzu Pug DOG?"

So the genie waved his arms, said, "Faster-master-bubble-blaster!" POOF! And quicker than you could say "My dog has fleas," there for Harriet was the Ju-jitzu Pug DOG. And the genie crawled back into the ring.

Harriet could hardly believe there was so much magic for five cents. She liked the SNEAKERS and she liked the DOG, but she thought the genie could do more. She sneezed on the ring again. "Ah-ah-ah-ah-choo!" And the genie appeared.

The genie bowed low. "What do you wish, Mistress?" he asked politely. "What you wish, I can grant."

So she told the genie, "This time, Genie, I want a Supersonic Portable MICROPHONE."

So the genie waved his arms, said, "Faster-master-bubble-blaster!" POOF! And quicker than you could say "Let's call it a wrap," there was Harriet's Supersonic Portable MICROPHONE. And the genie crawled back into the ring.

Harriet could hardly believe there was so much magic for five cents. She liked the SNEAKERS, and she liked the DOG, and she liked the MICROPHONE, but she thought the genie could do more. She sneezed on the ring again. "Ah-ah-ah-ah-choo!" And the genie appeared.

The genie bowed low. "What do you wish, Mistress?" he asked politely. "What you wish, I can grant."

So she instructed the genie, "Genie, get me a pair of Musical Marching Band CYMBALS. And hurry up about it."

So the genie waved his arms, said, "Faster-master-bubble-blaster!" POOF! And quicker than you could say "Stars and Stripes Forever," there were Harriet's Musical Marching Band CYMBALS.

As the genie started to crawl back into the ring, Harriet stopped him. "Genie," she said, "I like the SNEAKERS, and the DOG, and the MICROPHONE and the CYMBALS. But look. You are going to give me anything I want anyway, and all this sneezing is just wasting time. Just make me into a genie."

The genie looked at Harriet and his eyes turned jade green. He was thinking, "First she wanted SNEAKERS. I gave her the SNEAKERS and she wanted a DOG. I gave her a DOG and she wanted a MICROPHONE. I gave her a MICROPHONE and she wanted some CYMBALS. Now that she has all that, she wants to be a genie. Enough is enough." And the genie waved his arms, and said, "Faster-master-bubble-blaster!" POOF!

When the smoke cleared, there was Harriet all alone, except for a ball of grape bubble gum. And Harriet decided that really was a lot of magic for five cents.

Pat-a-Patch
(An Action Chant)

Patches, patches
(Clap twice.)
On your knees.
(Tap your knees twice.)
Up,
(Reach up.)
Down,
(Reach down.)
Turn around.
(Turn around.)
I love patches.
(Clap three times.)

Patches, patches
(Clap twice.)
On your knees,
(Tap your knees twice.)
On your elbows.
(Tap your elbows twice.)
Up,
(Reach up.)
Down,
(Reach down.)
Turn around.
(Turn around.)
I love patches.
(Clap three times.)

Patches, patches
(Clap twice.)
On your knees,
(Tap your knees twice.)
On your elbows,
(Tap your elbows twice.)
On your toes.
(Tap toes twice.)
Up,
(Reach up.)
Down,
(Reach down.)
Turn around.
(Turn around.)
I love patches.
(Clap three times.)

Patches, patches
(Clap twice.)
On your knees,
(Tap your knees twice.)
On your elbows,
(Tap your elbows twice.)
On your toes,
(Tap toes twice.)
On your eye.
(Touch eyes twice.)
Up,
(Reach up.)
Down,
(Reach down.)
Turn around.
(Turn around.)
I love patches.
(Clap three times.)

Patches, patches
(Clap twice.)
On your knees,
(Tap your knees twice.)
On your elbows,
(Tap your elbows twice.)
On your toes,
(Tap toes twice.)
On your eye,
(Touch eyes twice.)
On your seat.
(Tap the seat of your pants twice.)
Up,
(Reach up.)
Down,
(Reach down.)
Turn around.
(Turn around.)
I love patches.
(Clap three times.)

The Cow's Suspenders
(A Story with Masks)

To tell this story make masks of paper bags or paper plates. You will use a cow wearing a hat with red flowers on it, a goat, a dog, a duck, and a mouse. You will need a pair of suspenders for the cow. These can be purchased or make suspenders by crossing two wide ribbons and tucking them into the waist of the child who plays the cow. Invite children up front to stand in a line and place masks on them as the story indicates.

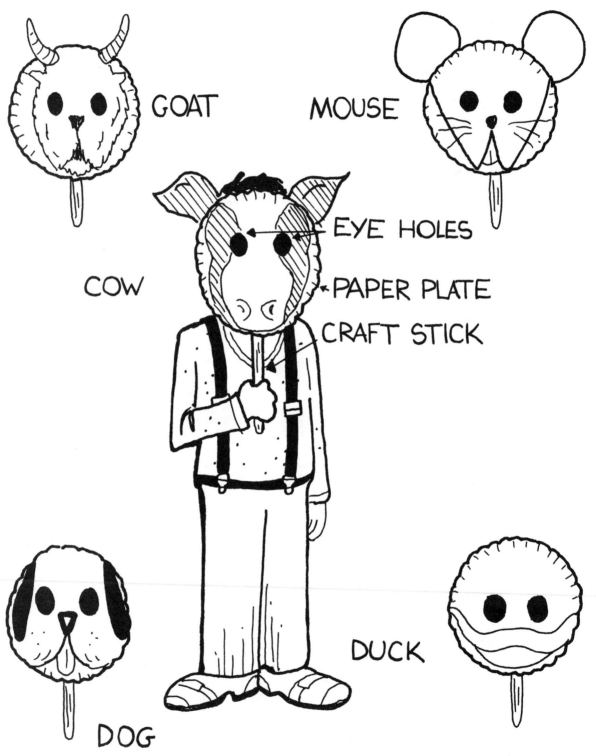

GOAT

MOUSE

COW

EYE HOLES

PAPER PLATE

CRAFT STICK

DOG

DUCK

Cow had been shopping. She got a hat with red roses on it and a wonderful pair of suspenders. *(Put cow mask and suspenders on first child.)* When she looked in the mirror, she thought, "Well, I do look mighty fine. In this hat and suspenders, I can go places!" And the first place she went was to show her new outfit to Goat.

(Put goat mask on second child.) "Goat," called Cow, "don't I look mighty fine? In this hat and suspenders, I can go places."

Well, Goat actually thought the hat was a little silly, but he liked the suspenders, so he agreed with Cow. "No doubt about it, Cow," he said. "You are going places." So they went together to see Dog.

(Put dog mask on third child.) "Dog," called Cow, "don't I look mighty fine? In this hat and suspenders, I can go places."

Well, Dog actually thought the hat was not really flattering, but he liked the suspenders, so he agreed with Cow. "No doubt about it, Cow," he said. "You are going places." And they all went together to see Duck.

(Put duck mask on fourth child.) "Duck," called Cow, "don't I look mighty fine? In this hat and suspenders, I can go places."

Well, Duck thought the roses on the hat would be better to eat than to wear, but she liked the suspenders, so she agreed with Cow. "No doubt about it, Cow," she said. "You are going places." And they all went together to see Mouse.

(Put mouse mask on fifth child.) "Mouse," called Cow, "don't I look mighty fine? In this hat and suspenders, I can go places."

Well, Mouse thought Cow's hat was really quite out of date, but she liked the suspenders, so she agreed with Cow. "No doubt about it, Cow," she said. "You are going places." And all the friends set off on a walk together.

When they came to a puddle, Cow had to stop to admire herself in the puddle. "Don't I look mighty fine? In this hat and suspenders, I can go places."

When they came to a window, Cow had to stop to admire herself in the window. "Don't I look mighty fine? In this hat and suspenders, I can go places."

Well, when she stopped at the pond to admire herself again, the other friends had had enough of her bragging. *(Turn Cow so her back is to the other characters.)*

Goat said, "I'm going to sneak up behind her while she is admiring herself in the pond and pull those suspenders." And all the others agreed.

(Place Goat behind Cow with one hand on her shoulder. The children in the audience may indicate a pulling motion.) So Goat grabbed onto Cow's suspenders and pulled and pulled and pulled, but Cow just kept on admiring herself in the pond.

"Goat needs help," said Dog. *(Place Dog behind Goat with one hand on his shoulder.)* So Dog took hold of Goat, who grabbed onto Cow's suspenders and pulled and pulled and pulled, but Cow just kept on admiring herself in the pond.

"Goat and Dog need help," said Duck. *(Place Duck behind Dog with one hand on his shoulder.)* So Duck took hold of Dog, who took hold of Goat, who grabbed onto Cow's suspenders and pulled and pulled and pulled, but Cow just kept on admiring herself in the pond.

"Goat and Dog and Duck need help," said Mouse. *(Place Mouse behind Duck with one hand on her shoulder.)* So Mouse took hold of Duck, who took hold of Dog, who took hold of Goat, who grabbed onto Cow's suspenders and pulled and pulled and pulled, but Cow just kept admiring herself in the pond.

Well, Goat and Dog and Duck and Mouse decided to try one more time. *(Have all children indicate pulling motion.)* All together they pulled and pulled and pulled and all of a sudden, Mouse's arms gave out and she let go of Duck. *(Remove Mouse's hand from Duck.)* That made Duck let go of Dog. *(Remove Duck's hand from Dog.)* That made Dog let go of Goat. *(Remove Dog's hand from Goat.)* That made Goat let go of the suspenders. *(Remove Goat's hand from Cow.)* SNAP! *(Clap loudly.)* Those suspenders snapped back and sent Cow up over the pond, over the barn, over the town, and out of sight. *(Pick up Cow and set her down a little ways away.)*

Goat and Dog and Duck watched in silence. Then Mouse said, "Cow looked mighty fine. In that hat and suspenders, she is sure going places."

And she did go places. Because after Cow went up over the pond and the barn and the town, the snap of those suspenders made her the first Cow to jump over the moon!

Put It in Your Backpack!

To help children draw associations and learn about rhyming words, use this poem. Begin with the pairs of objects listed, then encourage the children to write more verses with their own rhymes.

Look! Here's a silly *fox.*
He bought his purple *socks.*
Tick-tack, rickrack!
Put it in your backpack.

cat/hat
mouse/house
frog/log
kitten/mitten
crow/bow
kangaroo/shoe
goat/coat
ape/cape

In a Pig's Belt
(A Prop/Participation Story)

Sew the short ends of a pink sheet together. Put a drawstring case in one end and cut armholes in the sides. Use a long strip of fancy material for the belt. Select six children to take the parts of the food. You can take the part of Pig or place a child in the costume. As the food is added in the story, loosen the belt and squeeze another child in. At the end of the story, you will have a very big pig and a belt that won't fit at all.

There was a time when the world was new and corn did not grow quite so high, so that Pig was the most slender and graceful of animals. In fact, of all the animals, Pig had the tiniest waist. Alas, Pig was very vain about her tiny, tiny waist and often pointed out to Cow and Horse and Dog and Sheep how very slender she was.

Now most of the time the animals put up with the vanity of Pig, but the time came when they got tired of it. So Cow called Horse and Dog and Sheep, and they agreed that if Pig would put on some weight, she would be easier to live with. And they watched for an opportunity to make Pig fat.

Their chance came when Pig got a new belt. She thought it was the finest belt, both because it was so lovely to look at and because it showed everyone what a tiny, tiny waist she had. She went to show Cow.

But when she showed it to Cow, Cow said, "It is a lovely belt, but I believe you need to be a bit thinner to look good in it. Have I told you about a diet I know on which you eat nothing but apples? Apples in the morning, apples in the night. Apples, apples, apples." *(Bring out child with apple.)*

So Pig ate apples. Apples in the morning, apples in the night. Apples, apples, apples. *(Take off the belt. Put the child holding the apple under the sheet.)* Then Pig tried on her belt again and went to show Horse. *(Tie the belt on around both children.)*

But when she showed it to Horse, Horse said, "It is a lovely belt, but I believe you need to be a bit thinner to look good in it. Have I told you about a diet I know on which you eat nothing but ice cream? Ice cream in the morning, ice cream in the night. Ice cream, ice cream, ice cream." *(Bring out child with ice cream.)*

So Pig ate ice cream. Ice cream in the morning, ice cream in the night. Ice cream, ice cream, ice cream. *(Take off the belt. Put the child holding the ice cream under the sheet.)* Then Pig tried on her belt again and went to show Dog. *(Tie the belt on around all children.)*

But when she showed it to Dog, Dog said, "It is a lovely belt, but I believe you need to be a bit thinner to look good in it. Have I told you about a diet I know on which you eat nothing but pizza? Pizza in the morning, pizza in the night. Pizza, pizza, pizza." *(Bring out child with pizza.)*

So Pig ate pizza. Pizza in the morning, pizza in the night. Pizza, pizza, pizza. *(Take off the belt. Put the child holding the pizza under the sheet.)* Then Pig tried on her belt again and went to show Sheep. *(Tie the belt on around all children.)*

But when she showed it to Sheep, Sheep said, "It is a lovely belt, but I believe you need to be a bit thinner to look good in it. Have I told you about a diet I know on which you eat nothing but cheesecake? Cheesecake in the morning, cheesecake in the night. Cheesecake, cheesecake, cheesecake." *(Bring out child with cheesecake.)*

So Pig ate cheesecake. Cheesecake in the morning, cheesecake in the night. Cheesecake, cheesecake, cheesecake. *(Take off the belt. Put the child holding the cheesecake under the sheet.)*

But when Pig tried to put on her belt, she was just too fat. And when she walked she was not graceful, but she waddled. And from that day to this, while Pig is no longer the thinnest, most graceful animal, she has become one of the nicest animals. And having good friends is better than having a good figure any day! Even if your belt does not fit.

Ruffles, Fringe, and Beads and Bows

Older children will enjoy repeating the last verse very fast.

Ruffles, fringe, and beads and bows,
Beads and bows, beads and bows.
Ruffles, fringe, and beads and bows.
All of these dress up my clothes.

Ruffles fluff around my neck,
    (Wiggle fingers by face.)
'Round my neck, 'round my neck.
Ruffles, fringe, and beads and bows.
All of these dress up my clothes.

Fringe will wiggle when I walk,
    (Walk in place wiggling hips.)
When I walk, when I walk.
Ruffles, fringe, and beads and bows.
All of these dress up my clothes.

Beads can sparkle and they shine,
    (Wiggle fingers shoulder-high.)
And they shine, and they shine.
Ruffles, fringe, and beads and bows.
All of these dress up my clothes.

Bows can tie in front or back,
    *(Touch thumbs with fingers spread
    first under chin, then behind back.)*
Front or back, front or back.
Ruffles, fringe, and beads and bows.
All of these dress up my clothes.

Ruffles, fringe, and beads and bows,
    *(Do all four actions as items are
    mentioned.)*
Beads and bows, beads and bows.
Ruffles, fringe, and beads and bows.
All of these dress up my clothes.

All That Glitters
(To the tune of "On Top of Old Smoky")

You may wish to teach the refrain first so the children can sing along.

Refrain:
> Spangles and sequins
> And glitter and glow,
> Oh, spangles and sequins
> And glitter and glow.

Out West there's a cowboy,
And Sam is his horse.
He rides all the ranges;
Plays guitar, of course.
> Refrain

One day he rode into
The town of El Blight,
Where lights were a-blazing.
They partied all night.
> Refrain

He partied and danced
'Til the break of the day,
But at the first sunshine
He had this to say:
> Refrain

"I cannot have fun here,
As tired as I am.
I'd rather be riding
My good horse named Sam."
> Refrain

"You keep your bright sequins,
And spangles all night.
Just give me the glitter
And glow of starlight."
> Refrain

Stanley's Glasses

(A Draw-and-Tell Story)

Help Stanley figure out what became of his glasses by following the instructions for the drawings at the end of this story.

When Stanley went to kindergarten he started to wear glasses. Stanley did not mind wearing his glasses when they were on his face, but when he took them off the trouble started.

On Monday as he was getting ready for school, Stanley looked for his glasses, but he could not find them. He called, "I can't find my glasses!"

Mother looked and looked and finally found them under the bed. "How did they get there?" asked Mother.

"I don't know," said Stanley. "Maybe a space creature took them."

On Tuesday, as he was getting ready for his piano lesson, Stanley looked for his glasses, but he could not find them. He called, "I can't find my glasses!"

Mother looked and looked and looked and finally found them inside a flowerpot. "How did they get there?" asked Mother.

"I don't know," said Stanley. "Maybe a space creature took them."

On Wednesday, as he was getting ready to play frisbee, Stanley looked for his glasses, but he could not find them. He called, "I can't find my glasses!"

Mother looked and looked and looked. She finally found them in a box of breakfast cereal. "How did they get there?" asked Mother.

"I don't know," said Stanley. "Maybe a space creature took them."

On Thursday, as he was getting ready for karate class, Stanley looked for his glasses, but he could not find them. He called, "I can't find my glasses!"

Mother looked and looked and looked and finally found them in the microwave oven. "How did they get there?" asked Mother.

"I don't know," said Stanley. "Maybe a space creature took them."

On Friday, as he was getting ready to play with his dog, Stanley looked for his glasses, but he could not find them. He called, "I can't find my glasses!"

(Draw a straight line.) Mother looked in the dog dish *(draw a circle above the line)*, in the clothes dryer *(draw another circle next to it)*, in the sandbox *(draw a square around the two circles)*.

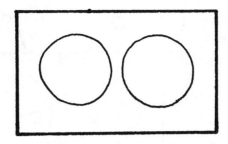

She lifted the lid and looked in the laundry hamper *(draw an inverted v to the right of the circles)*. She lifted the lid and looked inside the piano *(draw an inverted v to the left of the circles)*.

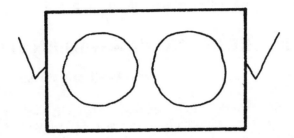

She even looked behind the TV *(draw a pair of antennae on top of the square)*, and under the car *(draw a half circle below the two circles)*.

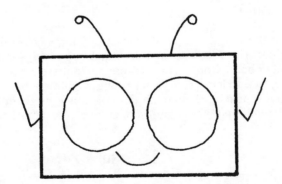

Finally she said, "Stanley, I can't find them. They must be lost for good." So Mother took Stanley to the eye doctor and got him a new pair of glasses. *(Add a nose piece and eyeballs to the space creature wearing glasses.)*

And here is the funny part. Stanley did not have any more problems with lost glasses, but his first pair was never seen again on this planet. Can you figure out where they went?

GAMES FOR POCKETS AND PARAPHERNALIA

My Mother's Purse

Sit in a big circle for this game. You may wish to put a large purse in the middle of the circle. Tell the children that a mother's purse has lots of wonderful things in it—usually everything anyone needs. Then begin to list the things a mother could have in her purse by answering this poem:

Look inside your purse and see
If you have something there for me.
What's in Mother's purse?

You may do this as a variation of the "Grandmother's Trunk" game, keeping track of all the things in order. This will be even more fun if you make a sound or motion about each object to help remember it. You might mention a handkerchief and pretend to blow your nose, for example. Or lick an ice cream cone. Younger children may just want to name things one at a time without repeating them each time or repeating them as a group, so no one is "on the spot." Older children will enjoy the challenge of naming the items in alphabetical order.

Junk Purse

Play this remembering game with a purse and eight to ten assorted objects the children will easily recognize. Place the purse in the center of the circle and take the objects out one at a time to show the children. Then place them all back in the purse and see how many the group can name. Older children will enjoy writing the list on paper and comparing their lists to see how many they remembered.

Where Did I Put My Keys?

Children are all familiar with a mother's hunt for keys in her purse. Have children cover their eyes as you place a set of keys in plain sight. They then hunt for the keys, returning to their places when they see the keys and not giving away the location until all have found them.

Younger children will enjoy a variation where larger cutout paper keys are hidden. As each child finds one, he or she may bring it to the circle and put it in a large purse or keep it.

What's in My Pocket?

Make a simple cloth pocket by sewing or gluing three sides of a square of material. Place various objects that have a distinctive sound or feel in the pocket, and let the children guess what is inside. Suggested objects are a bell, a ball, a stuffed bear, or a rattle. You may wish to attach Velcro® to the fourth side so the pocket can be closed for passing and opened easily to reveal its contents.

Pocket Catch

Choose two children to form a pocket by joining raised hands. As you sing the following words to the tune of "Mulberry Bush," the children will walk under their arms. On the word "pocket" the arms are dropped. The child caught joins raised hands with the others, forming a three-sided pocket. Children follow in and out of the circle and the song continues. On the word "pockets" all arms drop. Children in the center of the circle join the pocket and the game continues until everyone is part of the pocket.

In and out and 'round and 'round,
'Round and 'round, 'round and 'round.
In and out and 'round and 'round.
Someone's in my POCKET!

Buttons and Patches

Give each child a circle sticker for a button or a square sticker for a patch. They may draw designs on the stickers. Hang a picture of a person on the wall. The children can add "buttons and patches" by walking blindfolded to the picture and placing their stickers on the figure.

Anklets and Bracelets

Each child makes an ankle bracelet by touching middle fingers and thumbs together to form an O. Standing in a line or circle, each child, one at a time, encircles one ankle of the child next to him with the "bracelet." Smaller children may prefer to do this sitting down; older ones will have a great time in large circles or long lines seeing if they can all balance until the chain is complete.

CRAFTS FOR POCKETS AND PARAPHERNALIA

What's in Grandma's Purse?

Draw a simple purse outline on thin paper. Help the children place objects such as keys, paper clips, buttons, and coins under the paper and rub with the side of a crayon. The contents of Grandma's purse will magically appear!

Braided Bracelets

Knot three strips of material, each about 6 inches long, together at one end. Help children braid the strips. When the entire length is braided, sew or tie one end to the other to form a bracelet.

Cute as a Button Craft

Provide children with paper plates to make faces and supply various materials, such as yarn for hair, pasta for earrings, construction paper for ears, etc. The dominant feature of the face is, of course, a large button for the nose. If you wish, you may suggest they make pig faces, since buttons are perfect pig noses!

Paper Beads

Cut narrow triangles of paper. Begin with the wide end of each triangle and roll the paper around a pencil. Glue the pointed end of the paper to the newly formed "bead," and slip the paper off the pencil. Coat with a thin layer of glue. Allow to dry before stringing on yarn or string. Use "Safe Needles" found on p. 60.

Paper Towel Beads

Dip strips of paper towel in liquid starch and wring out. Form beads around knitting needles and allow to dry. Slip off when dry and let children string them.

String Along

There is any number of things children can string on thin elastic (the kind used on Halloween masks) to help with learning small motor movement, counting, and colors. Try dry, round cereal or macaroni. Intersperse with colorful paper shapes in which you punch a hole. A piece of tape wrapped around the end of the elastic will help it glide easily through the holes.

Necklaces with No Strings Attached

The children will enjoy joining paper clips, daisies, dandelions, or paper circles together to form necklaces.

DISPLAYS FOR POCKETS AND PARAPHERNALIA

Backpacking It

Hang a variety of backpacks around the room with all the assorted things one can carry in them, such as dolls, bears, toys, snacks, and library books!

Book Pockets

Fill a giant paper pocket on a bulletin board with book jackets and label "A Pocketful of Books." Or fill large purses with paperback books and post a sign reading "Pocket Books for Books and Books for Pocket Books."

Books Can Take You Places

On a bulletin board display a pair of suspenders and a cow jumping over the moon (while she is reading a book, of course!). Add the caption "Books Can Take You Places."

Here's Looking at You

Display an eye chart (borrow from a local optometrist) with the slogan "Be Wise—Check Your Eyes" and perhaps an owl reading a book nearby.

Who's Got the Button?

A display of slogan buttons is an obvious one, but it will create great interest as children and their parents stop to read the messages. (Who can resist reading buttons, T-shirts, and bumper stickers anyway?)

Resource Bibliography

Abisch, Roz. **The Shoe for Your Left Foot Won't Fit on Your Right Foot.** Illustrated by Boche Kaplan. McCall Publishing, 1970.

Left and right directions are taught through simple explanations and the use of the color red for right hand and foot and the color blue for left hand and foot.

Allison, Linda, and Stella Allison. **Rags.** Clarkson N. Potter, 1979.

This resource book for the teacher or older child will inspire you to turn sweaters into hats, gloves into hand puppets, and make jewelry from buttons.

Barkin, Carol, and Elizabeth James. **The Scary Halloween Costume Book.** Illustrated by Katherine Coville. Lothrop, Lee and Shepard, 1983.

Makeup is used instead of masks to turn kids into such scary creatures as a black cat, Dracula, an ogre, and a witch.

Berenstain, Michael. **The Armor Book.** David McKay, 1979.

Armor from the Stone Age and ancient Rome to the Crusades and the Renaissance, up to modern military dress, is described in a short text with black-and-white drawings.

Bruun-Rasmussen, Ole, and Grete Peterson. **Make-Up, Costumes and Masks for the Stage.** Sterling, 1976.

Instant disguises, costumes from ordinary bedsheets, and easy paper masks are included, as well as more elaborate masquerades.

Caney, Steven. **Steven Caney's Invention Book.** Workman, 1985.

Among the "inventions" included that focus on clothes are zippers, Levi's, sneakers, roller skates, and earmuffs. Caney suggests his own fantasy clothes—expandable clothes and stick-on pockets, for example—to inspire children to think of new inventions.

Caney, Steven. **Steven Caney's Kids' America.** Workman, 1978.

This compendium of Americana for kids includes a chapter on American fashion. A brief history of American dress is followed by instructions for making color dyes and for simple hats.

Charlie Brown's Fourth Super Book of Questions and Answers: About Kinds of People and How They Live. Random House, 1979.

Charlie Brown and his gang of friends present facts and information about clothing around the world in the first chapter of this book. Cartoons and photographs show different kinds of uniforms, hats, wigs, and some historical dress.

Clothes. Illustrated by Christine Sharr. Wonder Books, 1972.

A vocabulary-controlled book for young children identifies clothes worn in different climates, for different occupations, and in different historical periods. A simple tie-dyed T-shirt project is included.

Cobb, Vicki. **Sneakers Meet Your Feet**. Illustrated by Theo Cobb. Little, Brown, 1985.

The story of the parts of a sneaker and how sneakers are made and marketed will fascinate older children and provide entertaining information for the teacher of young children.

Cobblestone. V.6, No. 10, October 1985.

This issue, entirely devoted to clothing, includes articles on bloomers, clothing for the disabled, and projects to make.

Cooper, Edmund J. **Let's Look at Costume**. Illustrated by Norma Ost. Albert Whitman, 1976.

This overview of 3,000 years of clothing from ancient Greece and Rome to China, Renaissance England, and modern dress will give older children and adults enough background to appreciate such fascinating fashions as the hoppelande, the doublet, and the bustle.

Cover Ups: Things to Put On Yourself. Puffin, 1978.

Some unusual costumes and decorations are described for kids to make on their own — a pantomime horse, a sari, lumpy skin, and a tail. A minimum of sewing is required.

Cox, Marcia Lynn. **Creature Costumes**. Grosset & Dunlap, 1977.

Step-by-step instructions for eight creepy costumes made from inexpensive materials include a one-eyed thing, a wicked witch, and a papier-mâché monster mask with macaroni teeth!

Do a ZOOMdo. Little, Brown, 1975.

Created by the producers of the television program "Zoom," creative clothing projects include corn-rowing, dashiki shirts, and a hula skirt.

Eisner, Vivienne. **Quick and Easy Holiday Costumes**. Illustrated by Carolyn Bentley. Lothrop, Lee and Shepard, 1977.

Describes "almost instant" costumes to make based on five pieces: the headband, the tunic, the full skirt, the cape, and the sandwich sign. Costumes made from these basic types will outfit the wearer for twenty-three holidays throughout the year.

Fisher, Leonard Everett. **The Hatters**. Franklin Watts, 1965.

One of the Colonial American Craftsmen series, this history of the hat industry provides the teacher with facts about the manufacture of hats during our country's early days.

Fisher, Leonard Everett. **The Shoemakers**. Franklin Watts, 1970.

The history of shoemaking in Colonial America reveals such facts as shoemakers used to pull teeth in addition to their shoe trade. Scratchboard illustrations accompany the text, one of the Colonial American Craftsmen series.

Fisher, Leonard Everett. **The Wigmakers**. Franklin Watts, 1970.

This history of wigs focuses on Colonial American styles and shows the techniques involved in wigmaking. One of the Colonial American Craftsmen series.

Fox, Lilla M. **Costumes and Customs of the British Isles**. Plays, 1974.

Occupational and traditional costumes of England, plus costumes for dances and regional costumes of Scotland, Ireland, and Wales, are described through text and illustrations. Occupational costumes include a fishporter's hat and castermongers' costumes — these colorful people are more commonly called "pearlies" and can be seen in present-day London.

Fox, Lilla M. **Folk Costume of Eastern Europe**. Plays, 1977.

The folk costumes of over twenty separate regions in Eastern Europe, including the Cracow region of Poland and the steppe country of Ukraine, are described through text and illustrations. Some folk clothing is still worn by folk dancers, while others survive in museums.

Fox, Lilla M. **Folk Costume of Southern Europe**. Plays, 1973.

Text and illustrations introduce folk costumes of Italy, Switzerland, the Mediterranian islands, Spain, and Portugal. The introduction makes careful distinctions between regional dress and mixing costumes to result in a "national dress" for each area.

Fox, Lilla M. **Folk Costume of Western Europe**. Plays, 1971.

Illustrations and text introduce folk costumes from Great Britain, France, Belgium, the Netherlands, West Germany, Scandinavia, and Lapland. The introduction explains that people seldom dress in these costumes every day except in remote areas, though they are popular with folk dance groups.

Gates, Frieda. **Easy to Make Monster Masks and Disguises**. Harvey House, 1979.

The introduction to this book discusses the reasons people have worn masks, from religious ceremonies to holiday celebrations, for thousands of years. Step-by-step instructions and patterns are provided for plain paper masks, origami masks, and masks from sculptured paper.

Glovach, Linda. **The Little Witch's Black Magic Book of Disguises**. Prentice-Hall, 1973.

Three categories of costume are included—quick disguises (detective, fortune teller), holiday costumes (Johnny Appleseed, the Easter Rabbit), and storybook costumes (Peter Pan, the Mad Hatter, and the March Hare).

Greenhowe, Jean. **Costumes for Nursery Tale Characters**. Plays, 1976.

Detailed instructions will aid the adult working with children in making costumes for such popular nursery characters as Robin Hood, Cinderella (complete with soft sculpture pumpkin and mice), a hot cross buns salesman (with a tray of buns), Aladdin and his lamp, and the Princess and a bean bag frog.

Hunt, Kari, and Bernice Wells Carlson. **Masks and Mask Makers**. Abingdon, 1961.

Discusses the reasons people wear masks and provides background on masks worn in different cultures. Instructions for making a papier-mâché and plasticene Kari Hunt mask are given.

Katz, Ruth J. **Make It and Wear It**. Illustrated by Sharon Tondreau. Walker, 1981.

Older children who are beginning to sew their own clothes will especially enjoy this book, but many of the accessories (potholder pocketbooks, ribbon spool bracelets, and button necklaces) will be fun for younger children as well.

Kenworthy, Leonard S. **Hats, Caps, and Crowns**. Julian Messner, 1977.

Photographs and informative text introduce all kinds of hats—hats for protection against the weather, hats for safety, hats for special jobs, hats for sports, hats for beauty, and hats for festivities.

Lubell, Cecil, and Winifred Lubell. **Clothes Tell a Story**. Parents, 1971.

A brief history of clothes through the ages is followed by fashions worn on different parts of the body—top: hair and hats; middle: shirts and jackets; bottom: pants and skirts; and toe: shoes. Other chapters cover "underneath" and how cloth is made.

McMillan, Bruce. **Making Sneakers**. Houghton Mifflin, 1980.

Photos and text explain the process of making a pair of sneakers.

McNeill, Earldene, et al. **Cultural Awareness for Young Children.** The Learning Tree, 1981.

Projects include simple clothing from six cultures—Asian (China, Japan); Black (Black American, African); Cowboy (pioneers, early Texan); Eskimo; Mexican (Mexican-American, Mexican); and native American. The ideas are based on experiences at the Learning Tree school in Dallas.

Parish, Peggy. **Costumes to Make**. Illustrated by Lynn Sweat. Macmillan, 1970.

Basic patterns are given for costumes in three categories: other days and other people; holidays; and storybook characters. Many parts are interchangeable, with some sewing required.

Rosenbloom, Jonathan. **Blue Jeans**. Julian Messner, 1976.

Tells the history of blue jeans from their creation by Levi Strauss to their present-day manufacture.

Silberstein-Storfer, Muriel, with Mablen Jones. **Doing Art Together**. Simon and Schuster, 1982.

Based on art projects created in parent-child workshops at the Metropolitan Museum of Art, the chapter "Paper Hats" will give you background on hats and headgear from Japanese helmets to fanciful hats based on a top hat design. Materials and procedures are explained with clear photos accompanying the text. Beginning and advanced projects are included.

Skills List

Self-Awareness Skills
Gross Motor Skills
Color Recognition Skills
Size and Shape Recognition Skills
Rhythm and Rhyming Skills
Counting Skills
Following Directions Skills
Group Cooperation Skills
Musical Skills
Artistic Skills
Role and Dialogue Invention Skills
Sequencing Skills
Classification Skills
Word Recognition Skills
Left-Right Orientation Skills

Breakdown
of Activities
by Skills Area

Refer to Alphabetical Index of Activities for page numbers.

Self-Awareness Skills

All by Myself
Animals Are Lucky!
Barefeet Song
Bend, Stretch, Shake, Wiggle, and Twist
Best Shoes
Big Foot, Little Foot Mural
Biggest Hat in the World
Billy Buttons Up
Bonnie's Rain Boots
Bunny Sleepers
Child-Size Dress Me Doll
Christmas Stocking
Clap for Clothes
Clown Dress
Danny the Dawdler
Desert Clothes and Eskimos
Dirty Feet Song
Do I Have To?
Dress Me Doll or Pet
Dressed in Time
Dressing Teddy Bear
Dressing the Baby
Drizzle, Brrrr, Whoosh, and Shine
Duck Parade
Fancy Birthday Party Hat
Feet 'Round the World
Getting Dressed All Day
Gloves Are Hard to Put On
Hand-Me-Down Game
Hat Clap Chant
Hat Crafts Display
Hold This, Please!
I Don't Want to Wash My Hair
It's Not That Cold Outside
Just a Little Help

Knots in My Hair
Let It All Hang Out!
Let's Go Shopping
Lickety-Split
Lots of Pockets
Magic Hat
Mask-erade
Masquerade
Mommy's High Heel Shoes
My Brand New Snowsuit
My Old T-Shirt
My Very Own Paper Doll
New Sweater
Now You're Getting Dressed
One Sock Left
Overnight Sensation
Pat-a-Patch
Properly Undressed
Purses
Rain Gear
Reasons and Seasons for Clothes
Right Shoe, Left Shoe
Sandy and His Rain Gear
Shoe Jumble
Shoe Scramble
Shopping, Shopping
Stocking Feet
Summertime Clothes
Sunglasses
This Is What My Feet Can Do
This Little Piggy's Piggies
Trick-and-Treat Treasure Tracks
Walk in My Shoes
What Will You Wear?
Where Does It Go?
Where's My Shoe?

Winter Mittens
You Must Have Been a Beautiful Baby

Gross Motor Skills

African Clothing Chant
Alligators All Dressed
Animals Are Lucky!
Anklets and Bracelets
Back to Front
Bee in Her Bonnet
Bend, Stretch, Shake, Wiggle, and Twist
Best Shoes
Body Pockets
BOO!
Bundle Up Game
Bunny Sleepers
Buttons and Patches
Buttons, Zippers, Snaps, and Bows
Christmas Stocking
Clap for Clothes
Clothes Long Ago
Clothes the Year-Round
Clothesline Action Rhyme
Clothesline Fantasy
Cold Feet
Cow's Suspenders
Day the Hippo Unzipped His Zipper
Dirty Feet Song
Dirty Shirt Game
Dress Your Favorite Space Creature
Dressing the Baby
Dress-Up Costume Relay
Drizzle, Brrrr, Whoosh, and Shine
Dryer
Duck Parade
Fan Dancing
Feather Frolic
Five Fun Hats
Fix It
Foot in the Mouth
Frog King
Frog Prince
Funny Hat
Hair on My Head
Halloween Charade
Halloween Dress Up
Hand-Me-Down Game
Hat Clap Chant
Hat Hunt
Hat Tricks
Help!
Hot or Cold
How Many Bubbles in the Laundry Tub?

How to Make a Ghost
How to Marry a Prince
In a Pig's Belt
Is This for Me?
Laundry Relay Race
Lazy Lisa and the Crazy Clothes
Let's Go Shopping
Magic
Magic Hat
Magic Shoes
Magic Up Your Sleeve
Mitten Match Game
Mommy's High Heel Shoes
Mr. and Ms. Snowperson
Mummy Wrap
Needle Needs a Thread
Now You're Getting Dressed
Packing for a Trip—Several Ways
Pass the Hat
Pat-a-Patch
Pick Up the Clothes
Pocket Catch
Pocket Surprise
Pride of the Lion
Properly Undressed
Put It On
Rain Gear
Raindrops
Reasons and Seasons for Clothes
Right Shoe, Left Shoe
Rings and Things
'Round the World
Ruffles, Fringe, and Beads and Bows
Runaway Snowsuit
Scarf
Scarf Dance
Shoe Scramble
Shopping, Shopping
Showcase of Clothes
Sock It to Me Relay
Sock Match
Summer Hats
Sunglasses
Swimming Suits and Trunks Fall Down
Teddy Bears Button Up
Ten Trick-or-Treaters
This Is What My Feet Can Do
This Little Piggy's Piggies
Togas to Turbans
Trick-and-Treat Treasure Tracks
Tub Time
Very Old, Very Greedy Washing Machine
Walk in My Shoes
Washing Machine

What Should a Bear Wear?
What Will They Think of Next?
What Will You Wear?
Where Did I Put My Keys?
Where's My Shoe?
Who's Got My Caps?
Who's Hat Is That?
Witch's Hat
Work Hats
Worn-Out Rags
Yankee Doodle Round
Your Duck Parade
Zip 'Em Up

Color Recognition Skills

Anna, Anna, Second Hander
Baby Llama's Pajamas
Bargain Jacket
Beautiful Bubble Painting
Bee in Her Bonnet
Bonnie's Rain Boots
Centipede Buys Sneakers
Clown Dress
Crazy Hat
Crazy Mixed PJs
Duck Parade
Five Fun Hats
For Rain or for Shine
Frog Fog
Getting Dressed All Day
Grandmother's Kimono
Green Magic
Happiest Animal
Hatter Makes a Hat
Help!
Hot Dog
I Have a Big Shoe Tree
I Have a Red Umbrella
Interactive Shoe Bag Display
Keep Me Warm from the Storm
Lazy Lisa and the Crazy Clothes
Let's Go Shopping
Lickety-Split
Little Red Riding Hood Retold
Lost and Found
Lost and Found Shoes
Lost Mitten Line
Lucky Umbrellas
Magic Umbrella Tales
March Weather
Mitten Match Game
Monkey Business
Monkey's Birthday

Monster Who Didn't Even Wake Up
More Hole Than Sock
New Red Mitten
Not Enough Pockets
Not Yet, Agnes
One Sock Left
Pants That Danced
Party Dress—YES!
Purses
Rabbit's Most Amazing Hat Trick
Runaway Snowsuit
Sammy Sombrero and Bonnie Blue Bonnet
Shoebox Color Match
Sock Match
Something New under the Sun Shirt
Summer Hats
Turn over a New Leaf
Umbrella Flowers
Very Old, Very Greedy Washing Machine
What Does a Puppy Do with a Shoe?
Where Is Cindy's Shoe?
Who's Got My Caps?
Witch's Hat

Size and Shape Recognition Skills

African Animal Masks
Animals Should Definitely Wear Clothing
Beautiful Bubble Painting
Big Foot, Little Foot Mural
Biggest Hat in the World
Buttons and Patches
Cat's Pajamas
Character Hats Made Easy
Character Hats That Take More Time
Christmas Stocking
Cold Feet
Colonial Costumes
Costume Party Masks
Cover Up
Crazy Mixed PJs
Croak, Your Majesty
Crowns for Kings, Queens, and Birthday Children
Day the Hippo Unzipped His Zipper
Dress Your Favorite Space Creature
Duck Parade
Eat Your Hat
Egyptian Mask
Eskimo Spirit Mask
Fair Lady or Fairytale Hat
Feather in My Cap Craft
Fill My Shoes
Grandmother's Kimono
Growing Like a Weed

Hair-Raising Adventure of Sara
    Susan
Handlebar Mustache
Happiest Animal
Hat for a Prince
Hatter Makes a Hat
Help!
Hold This, Please!
Hole-y Shoes!
Hot Dog
In a Pig's Belt
Japanese Bunraku Puppet
Japanese Kimono Crafts
Jenny Wren's Best Nest
Keep Me Warm from the Storm
Knight's Helmet
Life-Sized Halloween
Little Room to Grow
Lost Mitten Line
Make a Jacket for Peter Rabbit
Mommy's High Heel Shoes
Monkey Business
More Hole Than Pocket
More Hole Than Sock
Mr. and Ms. Snowperson
Never Looked Better
New Red Mitten
Not Enough Pockets
One of a Kind Big Wig
Paper Bag Costumes for Pretending
Party Dress—YES!
Pat's Hats
Pocket Plan
Pride of the Lion
Rabbit's Most Amazing Hat Trick
Red Umbrella
Role Play
Runaway Snowsuit Puppet
Scarf
Scrap Bag for Glad Rags
Sew Simple!
Shoe Shopping
Sock Match
Stanley's Glasses
Summer Hats
Sun Visor
Three-Cornered Hat for Patriots or
    Pirates
Too Big for Your Britches!
What Will They Think of Next?
What's in Grandma's Purse?
What's in My Pocket?
What's under Mat's Hat?
Whooo Are Youooo?

Rhythm and Rhyming Skills

African Clothing Chant
All That Glitters
Alligators All Dressed
Alphabet Cats in a Hat
Animals Are Lucky!
Anna, Anna, Second Hander
A-Shopping We Will Go
Baby Llama's Pajamas
Barefeet Song
Bear Suit
Bee in Her Bonnet
Bend, Stretch, Shake, Wiggle, and Twist
Best Shoes
Bobby Socks and Blue Suede Shoes
Body Pockets
BOO!
Boots, Galoshes, Overshoes
Buffalo Clothes
Bunny Sleepers
Buttons, Zippers, Snaps, and Bows
Cape Dance
Catalog Song
Centipede Buys Sneakers
Christmas Stocking
Clap for Clothes
Closets, Trunks, and Chests of Drawers
Clothes Long Ago
Clothes the Year-Round
Clothesline Action Rhyme
Clothesline Fantasy
Clown Dress
Dancing Feet
Desert Clothes and Eskimos
Dirty Feet Song
Do I Have To?
Dress for Dinner
Dressed in Time
Dressing the Baby
Dress-Up Clothes for Play
Drizzle, Brrrr, Whoosh, and Shine
Dryer
Duck Parade
Ducks Should Not Complain
Eat That Hat!
Eat Your Hat
Fan Dancing
Fancy Birthday Party Hat
Feather in His Cap
Feet 'Round the World
Fiesta Finery
Fix It
Flapper
For Rain or for Shine

Frog King
Funny Hat
Garage Sale Shopping
Glad Rags
Gloves Are Hard to Put On
Hair on My Head
Hair-Raising Adventure of Sara Susan
Halloween Dress Up
Hand-Me-Down Game
Hat Clap Chant
Hat Hunt
Hole-y Shoes!
How Many Bubbles in the Laundry Tub?
How to Make a Ghost
How to Marry a Prince
I Don't Want to Wash My Hair
I Have a Big Shoe Tree
I Have a Red Umbrella
Inside Out
It's Not That Cold Outside
J-E-A-N-S
Jeffrey McFarland
Knots in My Hair
Lazy Lisa and the Crazy Clothes
Let It All Hang Out!
Let's Go Shopping
Little Red Riding Hood Retold
Lost and Found
Lost and Found Song
Made in the U.S.A.
Magic
Magic Hat
Magic Things
Magic Up Your Sleeve
Mask-erade
Mommy's High Heel Shoes
More Hole Than Pocket
Mr. Glop
My Brand New Snowsuit
My Mother's Purse
My Old T-Shirt
My Thinking Cap
Needle Needs a Thread
Never Looked Better
New Sweater
Now You're Getting Dressed
Old Blue Jeans
Old Woman Who Lived in a Shoe Retold
One Sock Left
Open Your Umbrella
Overnight Sensation
Pants That Danced
Party Dress—YES!
Pat-a-Patch

Pocket Catch
Pocket Surprise
Pocket Zoo
Pop! On Your Clothes
Pride of the Lion
Properly Undressed
Purses
Put It in Your Backpack!
Raindrops
Really Big Shoe
Reasons and Seasons for Clothes
Right Shoe, Left Shoe
Rings and Things
'Round the World
Ruffles, Fringe, and Beads and Bows
Sammy Sombrero and Bonnie Blue Bonnet
Scarf Dance
Sewing Basket Song
Shoe Jumble
Shoe Shopping
Shopping, Shopping
Shout for Sweaters
Showcase of Clothes
Silly Clothes
Sing a Song of Puddles
Soap and Suds
Sock Monster
Special Dress, Special Days
Stocking Feet
Summer Hats
Summer's Coming!
Summertime Clothes
Sunglasses
Swimming Suits and Trunks Fall Down
Tailor, Tailor Make Me a Coat
Tale of Samuel Strand
Ten Trick-or-Treaters
There Was an Old Woman Who Lived in a Boot
This Is What My Feet Can Do
Togas to Turbans
Treasure Trunk Dress Up
T-Shirt Tops
Tub Time
Two by Two
Umbrella Flowers
Umbrellas Are Fine
Underwear
Walk in My Shoes
Washing Machine
What Does a Puppy Do with a Shoe?
What Will You Wear?
What's under Mat's Hat?
Where Does It Go?
Where's My Shoe?

Who's Got My Caps?
Why a Turtle Doesn't Wear a Turtleneck Sweater
Winter Mittens
Witch's Hat
Work Hats
Worn-Out Rags
Yankee Doodle Retold
Yankee Doodle Round
You Think You Have Problems ...
Your Duck Parade
Zip 'Em Up

Counting Skills

Alligators All Dressed
Bee in Her Bonnet
Centipede Buys Sneakers
Cinderella
Clap for Clothes
Clothes Horse
Clown Face Makeup
Cover Up
Feather Frolic
Fill My Shoes
Five Fun Hats
Frog Fog
Gloves Are Hard to Put On
Great Bubble Gum Ring
Help!
How Many Bubbles in the Laundry Tub?
How to Make a Ghost
Lazy Lisa and the Crazy Clothes
Match Mates
More Hole Than Sock
Not Enough Pockets
One of a Kind Big Wig
One Plus One—Two Plus Two Shoes
One Sock Left
Ready for Bed
Runaway Snowsuit Puppet
Sock Match
Summer Hats
Ten Trick-or-Treaters
There Was an Old Woman Who Lived in a Boot
Trick-and-Treat Treasure Tracks
Two by Two
Where's My Shoe?

Following Directions Skills

African Animal Masks
African Clothing Chant
Alligators All Dressed
Alphabet Cats in a Hat

Animal Tracks
Anklets and Bracelets
A-Shopping We Will Go
Back to Front
Be a Fairy Godmother
Beautiful Bubble Painting
Bee in Her Bonnet
Bend, Stretch, Shake, Wiggle, and Twist
Best Shoes
Big Foot, Little Foot Mural
Biggest Hat in the World
Body Pockets
BOO!
Braided Bracelets
Bundle Up Game
Bunny Sleepers
Buttons and Patches
Buttons, Zippers, Snaps, and Bows
Character Hats Made Easy
Character Hats That Take More Time
Child-Size Dress Me Doll
Christmas Stocking
Clap for Clothes
Clothes Long Ago
Clothes the Year-Round
Clothesline Action Rhyme
Clothesline Fantasy
Clothespin Charlie
Cold Feet
Colonial Costumes
Costume Party Masks
Cow's Suspenders
Croak, Your Majesty
Crowns for Kings, Queens, and Birthday Children
Cute as a Button Craft
Day the Hippo Unzipped His Zipper
Department Store
Dirty Feet Song
Dirty Shirt Game
Dress Your Favorite Space Creature
Dressing Teddy Bear
Dressing the Baby
Dress-Up Costume Relay
Drizzle, Brrrr, Whoosh, and Shine
Dryer
Duck Feet
Duck Parade
Eat That Hat!
Eat Your Hat Craft
Egyptian Mask
Emperor's Real New Clothes
Eskimo Spirit Mask
Fair Lady or Fairytale Hat
Fan Dancing

Fashion Plate Craft
Feather Frolic
Feather in My Cap Craft
Fill My Shoes
Five Fun Hats
Fix It
Foot in the Mouth
Frog King
Frog Prince
Funny Hat
Garbage Bag Coverups
Glove Puppets
Hair on My Head
Halloween Charade
Halloween Dress Up
Handlebar Mustache
Hand-Me-Down Game
Hat Clap Chant
Hat for a Prince
Hat Hunt
Hat Tricks
Hats from Anything You Have in the House
Help!
Hot or Cold
How Many Bubbles in the Laundry Tub?
How to Make a Ghost
How to Marry a Prince
In a Pig's Belt
Interactive Shoe Bag Display
Is This for Me?
Japanese Bunraku Puppet
Japanese Kimono Crafts
J-E-A-N-S
Junk Purse
Keep Me Warm from the Storm
Knight's Helmet
Laundry Relay Race
Lazy Lisa and the Crazy Clothes
Let's Go Shopping
Lost and Found
Lost and Found Shoes
Lots of Pockets
Magic
Magic Hat
Magic Shoes
Magic Up Your Sleeve
Make a Jacket for Peter Rabbit
Match Mates
Mitten Match Game
Mittens for All Seasons
Mix and Match
Mommy's High Heel Shoes
Mr. and Ms. Snowperson
Mummy Wrap

My Mother's Purse
My Very Own Paper Doll
Necklaces with No Strings Attached
Needle Needs a Thread
One Plus One—Two Plus Two Shoes
Overnight Bag
Packing for a Trip—Several Ways
Pants That Danced
Paper Bag Costumes for Pretending
Paper Beads
Paper Towel Beads
Pass the Hat
Pat-a-Patch
Pick Up the Clothes
Pocket Catch
Pocket Surprise
Pride of the Lion
Properly Undressed
Put It On
Rain Gear
Raindrops
Ready for Bed
Reasons and Seasons for Clothes
Red Umbrella
Right Shoe, Left Shoe
Rings and Things
'Round the World
Ruffles, Fringe, and Beads and Bows
Runaway Snowsuit
Runaway Snowsuit Puppet
Safe Needles
Samuel Strand Craft
Scarf
Scarf Dance
Scrap Bag for Glad Rags
Sew Simple!
Sew Your Own Stocking
Shoe Scramble
Shoebox Color Match
Shoebox Scenes
Shoelace Bunny Ears
Shopping, Shopping
Showcase of Clothes
Silly Clothes
Simple Loom
Sock It to Me Relay
Sock Match
Something New under the Sun Shirt
Space Helmet
Spool Sheep
Stinky Sock Monster Puppet
String Along
Summer Hats
Sun Visor

Sunglasses
Swimming Suits and Trunks Fall Down
Talky Terry, the Tennis Shoe Puppet
Teddy Bears Button Up
This Is What My Feet Can Do
This Little Piggy's Piggies
Three-Cornered Hat for Patriots or Pirates
Togas to Turbans
Trick-and-Treat Treasure Tracks
Tub Time
Turn over a New Leaf
Very Old, Very Greedy Washing Machine
Walk in My Shoes
Washing Machine
Weather Match Game
What Should a Bear Wear?
What Will They Think of Next?
What Will You Wear?
What's in Grandma's Purse?
What's in My Pocket?
Where Did I Put My Keys?
Where Does It Go?
Where's My Shoe?
Who's Got My Caps?
Who's Hat Is That?
Witch's Hat
Work Hats
Worn-Out Rags
Yankee Doodle Round
Your Duck Parade
Zip 'Em Up

Group Cooperation Skills

Anklets and Bracelets
Back to Front
Biggest Hat in the World
Cold Feet
Cow's Suspenders
Day the Hippo Unzipped His Zipper
Dirty Shirt Game
Dress-Up Costume Relay
Eat That Hat!
Feather Frolic
Frog Prince
Great Bubble Gum Ring
Hat Clap Chant
Help!
How Many Bubbles in the Laundry Tub?
J-E-A-N-S
Junk Purse
Laundry Relay Race
Let's Go Shopping
Mitten Match Game

Monkey's Birthday
Mummy Wrap
My Mother's Purse
Needle Needs a Thread
Not Yet, Agnes
Pants That Danced
Pick Up the Clothes
Pocket Catch
Put It On
Raindrops
Right Shoe, Left Shoe
Rings and Things
'Round the World
Scarf Dance
Shoe Scramble
Sock It to Me Relay
Sock Match
Trick-and-Treat Treasure Tracks
Walk in My Shoes
What Will They Think of Next?
Where Did I Put My Keys?
Yankee Doodle Round
Your Duck Parade
Zip 'Em Up

Musical Skills

All That Glitters
A-Shopping We Will Go
Barefeet Song
Best Shoes
Body Pockets
Boots, Galoshes, Overshoes
Buttons, Zippers, Snaps, and Bows
Cape Dance
Catalog Song
Closets, Trunks, and Chests of Drawers
Clothes Long Ago
Dirty Feet Song
Dress for Dinner
Dressed in Time
Dressing the Baby
Dress-Up Clothes for Play
Drizzle, Brrrr, Whoosh, and Shine
Dryer
Fan Dancing
Fancy Birthday Party Hat
Fiesta Finery
Fix It
Funny Hat
Glad Rags
Hand-Me-Down Game
Hat Hunt
Hole-y Shoes!

How to Make a Ghost
I Don't Want to Wash My Hair
I Have a Big Shoe Tree
I Have a Red Umbrella
It's Not That Cold Outside
J-E-A-N-S
Knots in My Hair
Lost and Found Song
Made in the U.S.A.
Magic Hat
Magic Things
Magic Up Your Sleeve
Mommy's High Heel Shoes
More Hole Than Pocket
Mr. Glop
My Old T-Shirt
My Thinking Cap
Needle Needs a Thread
Now You're Getting Dressed
Old Blue Jeans
Pants That Danced
Pocket Catch
Pocket Zoo
Pop! On Your Clothes
Properly Undressed
Raindrops
Really Big Shoe
Sammy Sombrero and Bonnie Blue Bonnet
Scarf Dance
Sewing Basket Song
Shoe Jumble
Shoe Scramble
Shopping, Shopping
Showcase of Clothes
Sing a Song of Puddles
Soap and Suds
Sock Monster
Stocking Feet
Swimming Suits and Trunks Fall
        Down
Tailor, Tailor Make Me a Coat
Ten Trick-or-Treaters
This Is What My Feet Can Do
T-Shirt Tops
Tub Time
Underwear
Washing Machine
What Will You Wear?
Who's Got My Caps?
Worn-Out Rags
Yankee Doodle Retold
Yankee Doodle Round
Your Duck Parade
Zip 'Em Up

Artistic Skills

African Animal Masks
Animals Should Definitely Wear Clothing
Be a Fairy Godmother
Beautiful Bubble Painting
Big Foot, Little Foot Mural
Biggest Hat in the World
Braided Bracelets
Buttons and Patches
Character Hats Made Easy
Character Hats That Take More Time
Clothespin Charlie
Clown Face Makeup
Colonial Costumes
Costume Party Masks
Create Your Own Hat Participatory Display
Croak, Your Majesty
Crowns for Kings, Queens, and Birthday Children
Cute as a Button Craft
Duck Feet
Eat Your Hat Craft
Egyptian Mask
Emperor's Real New Clothes
Eskimo Spirit Mask
Fair Lady or Fairytale Hat
Fashion Plate Craft
Feather in My Cap Craft
Garbage Bag Coverups
Glove Puppets
Handlebar Mustache
Hat Crafts Display
Hat for a Prince
Hats from Anything You Have in the House
Interactive Shoe Bag Display
Japanese Bunraku Puppet
Japanese Kimono Crafts
Knight's Helmet
Make a Jacket for Peter Rabbit
Masquerade
Mittens for All Seasons
Mix and Match
My Very Own Paper Doll
Necklaces with No Strings Attached
Overnight Bag
Paper Bag Costumes for Pretending
Paper Beads
Paper Towel Beads
Red Umbrella
Runaway Snowsuit Puppet
Safe Needles
Samuel Strand Craft
Scrap Bag for Glad Rags
Sew Simple!
Sew Your Own Stocking

Shoebox Scenes
Shoelace Bunny Ears
Simple Loom
Something New under the Sun Shirt
Space Helmet
Spool Sheep
Stinky Sock Monster Puppet
String Along
String along with Me
Sun Visor
Talky Terry, the Tennis Shoe Puppet
Three-Cornered Hat for Patriots or Pirates
Turn over a New Leaf
What's in Grandma's Purse?

Role and Dialogue Invention Skills

Baby Llama's Pajamas
Bee in Her Bonnet
BOO!
Bunny Sleepers
Character Hats Made Easy
Character Hats That Take More Time
Cinderella
Clothesline Action Rhyme
Clown Dress
Clown Face Makeup
Cold Feet
Cow's Suspenders
Crowns for Kings, Queens, and Birthday Children
Day the Hippo Unzipped His Zipper
Dryer
Duck Parade
Eat That Hat!
Great Bubble Gum Ring
Halloween Charade
Halloween Dress Up
Help!
Hot Dog
How to Make a Ghost
In a Pig's Belt
Is This for Me?
Keep Me Warm from the Storm
Lazy Lisa and the Crazy Clothes
Life-Sized Halloween
Lost and Found
Magic
Magic Shoes
Mask-erade
Monster Who Didn't Even Wake Up
Old Woman Who Lived in a Shoe Retold
Paper Bag Costumes for Pretending
Pride of the Lion
Prince-less Princess

Puttin' on the Dog
Ready for Bed
Really Big Shoe
Role Play
Runaway Snowsuit
Sammy Sombrero and Bonnie Blue Bonnet
Scarf
Showcase of Clothes
Space Helmet
Stinky Sock Monster Puppet
Summer Hats
Tale of Samuel Strand
Talky Terry, the Tennis Shoe Puppet
Ten Trick-or-Treaters
There Was an Old Woman Who Lived in a Boot
Three-Cornered Hat for Patriots or Pirates
Too Big for Your Britches!
Very Old, Very Greedy Washing Machine
Washing Machine
What Should a Bear Wear?
What Will They Think of Next?
Whooo Are Youooo?
Who's Hat Is That?
Why the Stars Dance in the Sky
Witch's Hat
Work Hats
Your Duck Parade

Sequencing Skills

All by Myself
Anna, Anna, Second Hander
Bargain Jacket
Bend, Stretch, Shake, Wiggle, and Twist
Billy Buttons Up
Blue Jeans Book Bag
Bonnie's Rain Boots
Centipede Buys Sneakers
Child-Size Dress Me Doll
Cinderella
Clothes Horse
Clothes the Year-Round
Cold Feet
Cover Up
Cow's Suspenders
Crazy Hat
Crazy Mixed PJs
Danny the Dawdler
Day the Hippo Unzipped His Zipper
Do I Have To?
Dressed in Time
Dressing Teddy Bear
Drizzle, Brrrr, Whoosh, and Shine
Eat That Hat!

Feather in His Cap
Five Fun Hats
For Rain or for Shine
Frog Fog
From Sheep to Shirt
Getting Dressed All Day
Grandmother's Kimono
Great Bubble Gum Ring
Green Magic
Hair-Raising Adventure of Sara Susan
Help!
Hold This, Please!
Hole-y Shoes!
I Don't Want to Wash My Hair
Jeffrey McFarland
Jenny Wren's Best Nest
Just a Little Help
Keep Me Warm from the Storm
Knots in My Hair
Lickety-Split
Little Red Riding Hood Retold
Little Room to Grow
Lost and Found Shoes
Magic Clothes Hamper
Magic Shoes
March Weather
March Weather — What Next?
Mittens for All Seasons
Monster Who Didn't Even Wake Up
More Hole Than Sock
My Brand New Snowsuit
Never Looked Better
New Red Mitten
Not Enough Pockets
Not Yet, Agnes
Now You're Getting Dressed
Old Blue Jeans
One of a Kind Big Wig
One Sock Left
Overnight Sensation
Packing for a Trip — Several Ways
Pants That Danced
Party Dress — YES!
Pat's Hats
Pocket Plan
Pride of the Lion
Prince-less Princess
Puttin' on the Dog
Rain Gear
Ready for Bed
Really Big Shoe
Reasons and Seasons for Clothes
Recycled Laundry Bags
Scarf

Showcase of Clothes
Simple Loom
Soap and Suds
Something New under the Sun Shirt
Stanley's Glasses
Summer's Coming!
Swimming Suits and Trunks Fall Down
Tailor, Tailor Make Me a Coat
Tale of Samuel Strand
There Was an Old Woman Who Lived in a Boot
Tub Time
Turn over a New Leaf
Very Old, Very Greedy Washing Machine
What Does a Puppy Do with a Shoe?
What Should a Bear Wear?
Where Is Cindy's Shoe?
Why the Stars Dance in the Sky

Classification Skills

All by Myself
All over the World
Animal Tracks
Backpacking It
Best Shoes
Bobbie Pins and Bows
Body Pockets
Boots, Galoshes, Overshoes
Buttons, Zippers, Snaps, and Bows
Closets, Trunks, and Chests of Drawers
Clothes Horse
Cobbler, Cobbler, Mend My Shoe
Dancing Feet
Department Store
Desert Clothes and Eskimos
Dolls the World Around
Dress Me Doll or Pet
Dress-Up Clothes for Play
Eat Your Hat
Fashion Plate Craft
Feet 'Round the World
Fiesta Finery
Good Old Days
Hair on My Head
Hat Rack
Hats on the Job
Hats 'Round the World
Hot or Cold
How We Close Our Clothes Display
Is This for Me?
Lazy Lisa and the Crazy Clothes
Lickety-Split
Lost and Found Shoes
Made in the U.S.A.

Magic Umbrella Tales
March Weather—What Next?
Match Mates
Mitten Match Game
Mix and Match
Monkey Business
Monkey's Birthday
My Mother's Purse
Now and Then
Once upon a Magic Clothes
Overnight Bag
Pat's Hats
Pompadours and Pigtails
Purses
Putting Our Heads Together
Rabbit's Most Amazing Hat Trick
Rings and Things
Ruffles, Fringe, and Beads and Bows
Sandy and His Rain Gear
Scarecrow Clothes
Shoe Shopping
Shout for Sweaters
Summer's Coming!
This Is the Way We Wash Our Clothes
This Is What My Feet Can Do
This Little Piggy's Piggies
Travel to the Orient
Two by Two
Umbrellas Are Fine
Underwear
Weather Match Game
What Should a Bear Wear?
Who's Got the Button?
Who's Hat Is That?
Work Hats

Word Recognition Skills

Alphabet Cats in a Hat
Big Foot, Little Foot Mural
Book Pockets

Books Can Take You Places
Clothes Long Ago
Department Store
Fiesta Finery
Foot in the Mouth
Grandmother's Kimono
Here's Looking at You
J-E-A-N-S
Let's Go Shopping
Lost Mitten Line
Lots of Pockets
Old Woman Who Lived in a Shoe Retold
Put It in Your Backpack!
Rain Gear
Scarecrow Clothes
Sew Your Own Stocking
Showcase of Clothes
Special Dress, Special Days
Togas to Turbans
What Should a Bear Wear?

Left-Right Orientation Skills

Bend, Stretch, Shake, Wiggle, and Twist
Big Foot, Little Foot Mural
Centipede Buys Sneakers
Crazy Mixed PJs
Duck Feet
Interactive Shoe Bag Display
Lazy Lisa and the Crazy Clothes
Lost and Found Shoes
Mitten Match Game
Mittens for All Seasons
Right Shoe, Left Shoe
Shoe Jumble
Shoe Scramble
Shoelace Bunny Ears
Sock It to Me Relay
Sock Match

Alphabetical Index
of Activities Showing
Associated Skills

This index is designed so that it can be used in two ways: All the activities in the book — games, songs, crafts, projects, etc. — are listed alphabetically, each with its page number. Thus we have an activities index. In addition, the skills enriched by the activities in *Glad Rags* are listed across the top of each two-page column, and for each activity Xs mark the associated skills. Accordingly, we have a chart for immediate skill identification.

ACTIVITY

Activity	Left-Right Orientation Skills	Word Recognition Skills	Classification Skills	Sequencing Skills	Role and Dialogue Invention Skills	Artistic Skills	Musical Skills	Group Cooperation Skills	Following Directions Skills	Counting Skills	Rhythm and Rhyming Skills	Size and Shape Recognition Skills	Color Recognition Skills	Gross Motor Skills	Self-Awareness Skills
African Animal Masks (p. 121)						X			X			X			
African Clothing Chant (p. 108)			X	X					X		X			X	
All by Myself (p. 16)			X												X
All over the World (p. 125)															
All That Glitters (p. 231)							X		X		X				
Alligators All Dressed (p. 6)									X	X	X			X	
Alphabet Cats in a Hat (p. 178)		X							X		X				
Animal Tracks (p. 215)			X											X	
Animals Are Lucky! (p. 5)											X				X
Animals Should Definitely Wear Clothing (p. 159)						X						X			
Anklets and Bracelets (p. 235)								X	X					X	
Anna, Anna, Second Hander (p. 39)											X		X		
A-Shopping We Will Go (p. 35)				X			X		X		X				
Baby Llama's Pajamas (p. 26)			X		X						X		X		
Back to Front (p. 28)								X	X					X	
Backpacking It (p. 236)															X
Barefeet Song (p. 208)							X				X				
Bargain Jacket (p. 37)				X									X		
Be a Fairy Godmother (p. 156)						X			X		X				
Bear Suit (p. 91)												X	X		
Beautiful Bubble Painting (p. 62)						X			X						

ACTIVITY	Self-Awareness Skills	Gross Motor Skills	Color Recognition Skills	Size and Shape Recognition Skills	Rhythm and Rhyming Skills	Counting Skills	Following Directions Skills	Group Cooperation Skills	Musical Skills	Artistic Skills	Role and Dialogue Invention Skills	Sequencing Skills	Classification Skills	Word Recognition Skills	Left-Right Orientation Skills
Closets, Trunks, and Chests of Drawers (p. 49)															
Clothes Horse (p. 35)					X	X			X				X		
Clothes Long Ago (p. 98)		X			X		X					X	X		
Clothes the Year-Round (p. 64)		X			X		X		X					X	
Clothesline Action Rhyme (p. 52)		X			X		X					X			
Clothesline Fantasy (p. 142)		X			X		X				X				
Clothespin Charlie (p. 62)							X			X					
Clown Dress (p. 153)	X		X		X						X				
Clown Face Makeup (p. 157)						X				X	X				
Cobbler, Cobbler, Mend My Shoe (p. 125)													X		
Cold Feet (p. 198)		X		X			X	X			X	X			
Colonial Costumes (p. 120)				X			X			X					
Costume Party Masks (p. 157)				X			X			X					
Cover Up (p. 222)				X		X									
Cow's Suspenders (p. 227)		X					X	X			X	X			
Crazy Hat (p. 175)			X									X			
Crazy Mixed PJs (p. 46)			X	X								X			X
Create Your Own Hat Participatory Display (p. 188)							X			X					
Croak, Your Majesty (p. 156)				X						X					

ACTIVITY	Self-Awareness Skills	Gross Motor Skills	Color Recognition Skills	Size and Shape Recognition Skills	Rhythm and Rhyming Skills	Counting Skills	Following Directions Skills	Group Cooperation Skills	Musical Skills	Artistic Skills	Role and Dialogue Invention Skills	Sequencing Skills	Classification Skills	Word Recognition Skills	Left-Right Orientation Skills
How to Make a Ghost (p. 152)		X			X	X	X		X		X				
How to Marry a Prince (p. 130)		X			X	X	X				X				
How We Close Our Clothes Display (p. 31)													X		
I Don't Want to Wash My Hair (p. 182)	X											X			
I Have a Big Shoe Tree (p. 199)			X		X				X						
I Have a Red Umbrella (p. 71)			X		X				X						
In a Pig's Belt (p. 230)		X		X			X				X				
Inside Out (p. 72)			X		X										
Interactive Shoe Bag Display (p. 215)										X					X
Is This for Me? (p. 155)		X					X				X		X		
It's Not That Cold Outside (p. 82)	X				X				X						
Japanese Bunraku Puppet (p. 123)				X			X			X					
Japanese Kimono Crafts (p. 121)				X			X			X					
J-E-A-N-S (p. 36)					X		X	X	X					X	
Jeffrey McFarland (p. 3)			X		X										
Jenny Wren's Best Nest (p. 167)				X								X			
Junk Purse (p. 234)							X	X				X			
Just a Little Help (p. 13)	X										X	X			
Keep Me Warm from the Storm (p. 84)				X			X					X			

New Red Mitten (p. 86)

New Sweater (p. 83)

Not Enough Pockets (p. 219)

Not Yet, Agnes (p. 11)

Now and Then (p. 124)

Now You're Getting Dressed (p. 4)

Old Blue Jeans (p. 46)

Old Woman Who Lived in a Shoe Retold (p. 200)

Once upon a Magic Clothes (p. 158)

One of a Kind Big Wig (p. 99)

One Plus One—Two Plus Two Shoes (p. 212)

One Sock Left (p. 207)

Open Your Umbrella (p. 72)

Overnight Bag (p. 30)

Overnight Sensation (p. 10)

Packing for a Trip—Several Ways (p. 29)

Pants That Danced (p. 141)

Paper Bag Costumes for Pretending (p. 158)

Paper Beads (p. 236)

Paper Towel Beads (p. 236)

Party Dress—YES! (p. 45)

Pass the Hat (p. 182)

Pat-a-Patch (p. 227)

Pat's Hats (p. 174)

Pick Up the Clothes (p. 57)

Pocket Catch (p. 235)

Pocket Plan (p. 223)

Pocket Surprise (p. 224)

Pocket Zoo (p. 220)

Pompadours and Pigtails (p. 125)

Pop! On Your Clothes (p. 9)

ACTIVITY	Left-Right Orientation Skills	Word Recognition Skills	Classification Skills	Sequencing Skills	Role and Dialogue Invention Skills	Artistic Skills	Musical Skills	Group Cooperation Skills	Following Directions Skills	Counting Skills	Rhythm and Rhyming Skills	Size and Shape Recognition Skills	Color Recognition Skills	Gross Motor Skills	Self-Awareness Skills
Space Helmet (p. 186)					X	X			X						
Special Dress, Special Days (p. 108)		X									X				
Spool Sheep (p. 61)						X			X						
Stanley's Glasses (p. 232)												X			
Stinky Sock Monster Puppet (p. 213)				X	X	X			X						
Stocking Feet (p. 203)											X				X
String Along (p. 236)						X	X								
String along with Me (p. 215)						X			X						
Summer Hats (p. 75)				X	X				X	X	X	X	X	X	
Summer's Coming! (p. 74)			X								X				
Summertime Clothes (p. 77)											X				X
Sun Visor (p. 94)						X			X			X			
Sunglasses (p. 79)									X					X	X
Swimming Suits and Trunks Fall Down (p. 80)				X			X		X		X			X	
Tailor, Tailor Make Me a Coat (p. 46)					X						X				
Tale of Samuel Strand (p. 79)				X			X				X				
Talky Terry, the Tennis Shoe Puppet (p. 213)				X	X	X			X						
Teddy Bears Button Up (p. 28)									X		X			X	
Ten Trick-or-Treaters (p. 151)					X		X			X				X	

ACTIVITY

Activity	Self-Awareness Skills	Gross Motor Skills	Color Recognition Skills	Size and Shape Recognition Skills	Rhythm and Rhyming Skills	Counting Skills	Following Directions Skills	Group Cooperation Skills	Musical Skills	Artistic Skills	Role and Dialogue Invention Skills	Sequencing Skills	Classification Skills	Word Recognition Skills	Left-Right Orientation Skills
What's under Mat's Hat? (p. 171)				X	X										
Where Did I Put My Keys? (p. 234)		X					X	X							
Where Does It Go? (p. 28)	X				X		X								
Where Is Cindy's Shoe? (p. 193)	X	X	X									X			
Where's My Shoe? (p. 196)					X	X	X								
Whooo Are Youooo? (p. 152)				X							X				
Who's Got My Caps? (p. 183)		X	X		X		X		X						
Who's Got the Button? (p. 237)													X		
Who's Hat Is That? (p. 184)		X					X				X		X		
Why a Turtle Doesn't Wear a Turtleneck Sweater (p. 140)					X										
Why the Stars Dance in the Sky (p. 143)											X	X			
Winter Mittens (p. 86)	X														
Witch's Hat (p. 164)		X	X		X		X				X				
Work Hats (p. 173)		X			X		X				X				
Worn-Out Rags (p. 44)		X			X		X		X				X		
Yankee Doodle Retold (p. 99)					X				X						
Yankee Doodle Round (p. 118)		X			X		X	X	X						
You Must Have Been a Beautiful Baby (p. 188)	X														
You Think You Have Problems … (p. 3)					X										
Your Duck Parade (p. 92)		X			X		X	X	X		X				
Zip 'Em Up (p. 15)		X			X		X	X	X						

Literature Index